I Love Lucy™

CELEBRATING **50** YEARS OF LOVE AND LAUGHTER

THE **OFFICIAL** EPISODE GUIDE

revised edition

by ELISABETH EDWARDS

AUTHORIZED BY CBS BROADCASTING INC. AND THE ESTATES OF LUCILLE BALL AND DESI ARNAZ

RUNNING PRESS

PHILADELPHIA · LONDON

9 8 7 6 5 4 3 2 1
Digit on the right indicates the number of this printing

Library of Congress Control Number 2001087567

ISBN 978-0-7624-3983-6

Picture research by Elisabeth Edwards
Designed by Debbie Berne Design
Edited by Nancy Armstrong and Cindy De La Hoz
Typography: Interstate and Spectrum

Running Press Book Publishers
2300 Chestnut Street
Philadelphia, Pennsylvania 19103-4371

Visit us on the web!
www.runningpress.com

ACKNOWLEDGMENTS

It takes many people to write a book. The author never works alone, but always in conjunction with the rest of his or her world. In light of this fact, there are many people I need to thank.

To Lucie Arnaz and Laurence Luckinbill, and Desi and Amy Arnaz. Not only have you been my friends for almost two decades, but you have given me complete trust. Thank you for your love and friendship.

To my husband, John Moscone, and our son, Andrew. Thanks for putting up with late nights, grumpy moods, and cold dinners. I hope you think it was worth it. I know I could not have gotten through it without you.

To the irreplaceable Kieth Dodge, who I miss every day.

To the folks at CBS Worldwide Inc., especially Marty Garcia who has always been a friend and an advocate.

To Bruce Bronn for his love and support. To Debbie Bronn for her heavenly guidance.

To Shara Bronn, just because.

To Alissa Bronn, Brian Eich, and Mark Shachtman for their endless help.

To the wonderful people at Running Press, especially my brilliant editors, Nancy Armstrong and Cindy De La Hoz, and my talented designer, Debbie Berne.

To Gregg Oppenheimer, for the material on his father.

To writers Madelyn Pugh-Davis, Bob Carroll Jr., Bob Schiller, and Bob Weiskopf for their generosity and kindness.

To "Little Ricky" actor Keith Thibodeaux for his time and assistance.

To my mother, Penny Edwards, and my sister, Susan Edwards, who have always been in my corner. To my father, Don Edwards, for teaching me to love history.

To my other sister, Susan Consentino, for all the years. And to her parents, Big Bear and Mrs. C, for the introduction.

To Wooster School, its values and its teachers, for the inspiration and the knowledge.

To all the wonderful licensees who keep *I Love Lucy* alive with their terrific products, and who make my job so much fun.

To all the celebrities and fans who contributed letters, photos, and thoughts for this book.

To George, Bob, Jeff, Ann, and the others at Ridgefield Photo for their hard work.

To Wanda Clark, Tom Watson, Bart Andrews, Tom Gilbert, Steve Sanders, Ric Wyman, Geoffrey Fidelman, Michael Stern, and all the others who adore Lucy and Desi.

To all the fans, young and old, who continue to find joy and laugh along with the Ricardos and the Mertzes.

Finally to Lucille Ball, Desi Arnaz, Vivian Vance, Bill Frawley, Keith Thibodeaux, Jess Oppenheimer, Madelyn Pugh-Davis, Bob Carroll, Jr., Bob Schiller, Bob Weiskopf, Marc Daniels, William Asher, James Kern, Jerry Thorpe, Bert Granet, Argie Nelson, Al Simon, Herb Brower, Karl Freund, and all the others, for the magic that is *I Love Lucy*.

CONTENTS

A MAGICAL MIX

FROM THE BEGINNING, critics and fans alike have used glowing accolades to describe *I Love Lucy*. It is the show that has been seen in almost every country in the world; the show that has been dubbed into dozens of languages; the show about two married couples who are also friends, who live their lives together and adore each other. After fifty years of laughter and love, TV's legendary classic can be summed up as a simple story about family, friendship, and fun.

When asked to explain the wild and long-lived success of *I Love Lucy*, Desi Arnaz gave the nod to Lucille Ball. Most *I Love Lucy* fans would probably agree. Clearly Lucille was the star of the show; the sitcom was built around her in the fashion of her successful CBS radio show, *My Favorite Husband*. Even though Lucille Ball played the same wacky and childlike redheaded character throughout her forty years on radio and TV (Liz Cugat/Cooper, Lucy Carmichael, Lucy Carter, Lucy Barker), she is most well known and loved for the role of Lucy Ricardo on *I Love Lucy*. There is something about *I Love Lucy* that makes it stand out from the rest of television. We cheer for the Ricardos. We rejoice when they kiss and make up. We shed tears when Lucy tells Ricky he is going to be a father. The Ricardos and Mertzes are part of our collective heritage.

We think of them as family.

The reason *I Love Lucy* is arguably the world's most beloved situation comedy may lie in its origins. When Lucille Ball was asked to take the character of *My Favorite Husband*'s Liz Cooper to television, she agreed, but only if her real-life husband, Desi Arnaz, was hired to play her TV husband. She and Desi had been separated by divergent careers for ten years, and they both desperately wanted to solidify their marriage and begin their family. Lucille thought that working together at something they both loved was the answer. Desi could act, run the business and production ends of things, and live at home with his wife. A perfect solution.

The impossible-to-miss chemistry was another factor in the success of *I Love Lucy*. Lucille Ball and Desi Arnaz were married and in love (and, for a few months, expecting their real-life son). Lucille and Vivian developed a lifelong, sister-like relationship. Desi and William Frawley were real-life friends, and had a huge amount of respect for each other's talent. The writers were partners, and friends. The crew worked wonderfully together. First and foremost, *I Love Lucy* was all about family, off screen as well as on.

Lucille and Desi adored and nurtured the community-type atmosphere that existed behind the scenes of *I Love Lucy*. They hosted parties and dinners for the cast, directors, and writers. They held summer picnics for all Desilu employees and their families. Each year employees were given personal Christmas gifts from Lucille and Desi. Desi once paid for surgery for the child of one of his employees. Desilu Productions was started by a family, and became a family on its own.

Although built around the comedy of Lucille Ball, *I Love Lucy* was a story about two couples and their friendship. After all, as funny as Lucy Ricardo was, would the show have been the same without Ricky there to say "no" every time Lucy wanted to get into the act? What would the Ricardos have done if they didn't have the Mertzes to fight with; scheme with; celebrate with; and work with? The success of *I Love Lucy* cannot be summed up in one word, or in one person. Lucille Ball was clearly the star, but she did not work alone. A small team of talented writers wrote the funny lines she spoke, and the comic routines she performed. A small group of unforgettable actors played on stage with her every week. Teams of directors and producers, of cameramen and editors, all played a part in the wonder of *I Love Lucy*. Even the audience members, and the fans, young and old, played a role in making *I Love Lucy* a fifty-year-old phenomenon.

The world of *I Love Lucy* is a place people constantly want to come home to. The cast members are people you would like to have as friends, or neighbors, or even landlords. In the end, it's all about love and fun and adventure and family. Nothing remarkable, each on his or her own, but together—magic!

THE ENSEMBLE

DESIDERIO ALBERTO ARNAZ III
1917-1986

DESI ARNAZ WAS BORN ON MARCH 2, 1917, in Santiago de Cuba, the son of the mayor of Santiago and his wife, Dolores Acha y de Socias. She was one of the most prominent and beautiful women in Latin America, whose father was one of the three original founders of the Bacardi Rum Company. The family owned three ranches, a palatial home in the city, and a vacation home on a private island in Santiago Bay.

In 1932, Desi's father was elected to the Cuban Congress. On August 12, 1933, when the Batista revolution exploded in Cuba, the Congress was dissolved and most of its members, including Dr. Arnaz, were imprisoned. In a matter of twenty-four hours, the Arnaz properties were confiscated, and their homes were burned to the ground.

DESI ARNAZ HAS THE UNIQUE DISTINCTION OF HAVING HAD A REVOLUTION DICTATE HIS START IN SHOW BUSINESS.

After escaping to Havana with his mother, sixteen-year-old Desi successfully arranged his father's release from prison. In June of 1934, Desi and his father received permission to emigrate to Florida, where his mother would join them some years later.

For Desi, life in his newly adopted country was both difficult and exciting. Realizing that he needed to learn English in order to get along in the U.S., Desi enrolled in St. Patrick's High School, and received his diploma in 1937. He worked at whatever jobs he could find, including driving taxis and cleaning bird cages at a local pet store in the mornings before school.

At about this same time, he discovered he could combine his love of music with his need for money. He bought a five-dollar guitar at a pawn shop and joined a rumba band called the Siboney Septet, which worked at the Roney Plaza Hotel in Miami. It was there that he first heard Xavier Cugat. Soon after auditioning for him, young Desi was on his way to New York with Cugat's orchestra.

Several months later, after leaving Cugat in New York in order to form his own band, Desi introduced the Conga at Mother Kelly's in Miami Beach. The conga soon became a dance craze all over the United States.

In 1939, while appearing at New York's La Conga, he was cast in the Rogers and Hart musical *Too Many Girls*. Soon after, RKO bought the film rights to Broadway hit, and signed Desi to play his stage role in the film.

It was in Hollywood in 1940, on the set of *Too Many Girls*, that Desi met actress Lucille Ball. While both in New York fulfilling work commitments during their tempestuous five-month courtship, they eloped to Greenwich, Connecticut. They were wed in a private, hastily arranged ceremony at the Byram River Beagle Club on November 30, 1940. Back in California in 1941, the couple bought a home in the Chatsworth area of the San Fernando Valley, which they christened the Desilu Ranch.

Desi tried to break into movies in Hollywood, but directors were wary of casting anyone who had an accent. During the early World War II years he made three movies for RKO, including the patriotic 1943 film, *The Navy Comes Through*. His best break came in 1943, when he had a major role in the movie *Bataan*, for which he received a Photoplay Award. This, however, was to be his last major Hollywood film for a decade.

After receiving his citizenship papers in 1943, Staff Sergeant Arnaz served in the U.S. Army Medical Corps at Birmingham Hospital. Although he had wanted to be a bombardier in the Air Force, an accident in which he tore cartilage in his knee prevented him from fulfilling that dream. After the war ended in 1945, he formed the Desi Arnaz Orchestra and toured the country. All the touring kept him from Lucille for months at a time, and they began a desperate search for a project they could work on together.

In 1950, CBS asked Lucille Ball to take her popular radio program, *My Favorite Husband*, to the new medium of television. Her answer was yes, if Desi could play her husband. CBS did not like the idea of the all-American Lucille being married to a Latin band leader on television, so Lucy and Desi decided to take their act on the road, to see if the American public would accept them as a couple. Their vaudeville act attracted crowds and delighted fans across the country. They went back to CBS and pitched their idea again. This time it worked. Lucille Ball and Desi Arnaz entered into negotiations to star in a new CBS comedy entitled *I Love Lucy*.

Meanwhile, CBS hired Desi to host a weekly musical radio program called *Your Tropical Trip*. This allowed Desi to keep his band together, perform the music he loved, and still be near Lucille as they awaited the start of production of *I Love Lucy*.

After they filmed the pilot for *I Love Lucy* and got a sponsor for the show, the problem of where to shoot the show arose. Lucille and Desi wanted to stay in California, but CBS wanted them to move to New York, where all the TV shows were then filmed. Desi said they would stay in California, shoot the show in front of a live audience and put it on film, to be sent to New York.

Everyone at CBS was shocked—but Desi knew that Lucille worked best before a live audience, so he further developed the idea for the three-camera technique so the show could be shot on film in front of the audience. At the time, almost all TV shows were being filmed on kinescope, which produced only a very grainy image for audiences. By using multiple cameras and 35mm film, the *I Love Lucy* cameramen were able to get clear shots at different angles on film which was easily preserved. If it were not for this ingenuity, *I Love Lucy*, and many other shows of the period, would be forever lost.

In 1957, after six seasons as a top-rated show, *I Love Lucy* became *The Lucille Ball-Desi Arnaz Show*, airing once a month. Desi and Lucille had purchased RKO Studios and Desi was now running a major television production business. He was acting, directing, producing, and running a business at the same time.

Sadly, the stresses of business, personal, and family life grew too difficult for the Arnaz marriage, and in 1960, one of the world's most beloved couples was divorced. Although they were no longer married, Desi continued to run Desilu Productions and work with Lucille until 1962. At that time, he sold his interests in the company to his former wife.

Desi was married to Edith Mack Hirsch from 1963 until her death in 1985. During the early 1970s he produced and directed his own show, *The Mothers-In-Law*, starring Eve Arden and Kaye Ballard. He also owned, bred, and raced horses from his Corona Breeding Farm. In 1976, Desi published his autobiography entitled *A Book*, which was well received.

Desi Arnaz died of lung cancer on December 2, 1986, at his home in Del Mar, California. His ashes were scattered into the sea that he loved throughout his life. He is survived by his two children, Lucie and Desi IV, and his grandchildren.

Although Desi Arnaz will always be remembered as the sidekick to the world's zaniest redhead, he was so much more. It was his business savvy and forward-thinking ways that helped lead to the creation of the three-camera technique, which allowed shows to be filmed before a live audience. Having it all done on film also allowed for the reruns we enjoy to this day. We can thank Desi Arnaz for the fact that *I Love Lucy* still exists—decades years after its debut—for future generations to treasure and enjoy.

LUCILLE DESIRÉE BALL
1911-1989

FROM THE OBSCURITY OF A DOUBTFUL CAREER as a New York model to stardom in motion pictures, radio, television, and the theater, Lucille Ball made an indelible mark on the entertainment industry. Not only did Lucille—or Lucy, as she is known the world over—realize all of her early ambitions as a performer, but she also became one of television's most influential leaders.

Born in Jamestown, New York, on August 6, 1911, Lucille Desirée Ball, the daughter of a pianist and a telephone lineman, quickly discovered her love of performing. At age fifteen, she was off to New York City to try her luck at a dramatic school. When that failed, she supported herself working as a waitress and dress model, while trying to land chorus jobs on Broadway. Through dress-modeling, she became a poster girl for Chesterfield cigarettes, a lucky break which allowed her to join the cast of the Samuel Goldwyn film *Roman Scandals* as a chorus girl. In 1933, at the age of twenty-two, Lucy was off to California.

In Hollywood, Lucille quickly became the "Queen of the Bs," acting in over forty movies in six short years, many of them low-budget affairs that allowed her to gain valuable experience. Among her best early films was *Stage Door*, a 1937 comedy-drama starring Katharine Hepburn and Ginger Rogers. In 1940, while filming the movie version of the Broadway hit *Too Many Girls*, Lucy met and fell in love with Desi Arnaz, a Cuban-born bandleader also starring in the movie. They married five months later, on November 30, 1940, in Greenwich, Connecticut.

Lucy starred in twenty-eight more films between 1940 and 1951, sharing the screen with such stars as Bob Hope, Judy Garland, Ann Sothern, Victor Mature, William Holden, Esther Williams, Henry Fonda, and Red Skelton. She added live theater to her resume when she performed the lead female role in a national tour of the play *Dream Girl* beginning in June, 1947. In July 1948, she began starring opposite Richard Denning on the CBS radio hit *My Favorite Husband*. After two years, she was approached with the idea of transferring the show to a new medium—television.

Lucy was interested in a television show, but since she and Desi had been separated for so many years by World War II and by divergent careers, she would consider the show only if Desi could play her husband on television. At first CBS balked at the idea, but after Lucy and Desi put together a vaudeville act, took it on the road, and delighted audiences all over the country, CBS decided to give them a try. The result was *I Love Lucy*, one of the most beloved shows of all time.

Before filming for *I Love Lucy* began, Lucille Ball gave birth to her first child, Lucie Desirée Arnaz. In 1953, Lucille became pregnant again, with son Desi Arnaz, IV. Her pregnancy was written into the plot of the series, and she became the first visibly-pregnant woman on television. During the *I Love Lucy* years, Lucy and Desi also starred in two movies together—*The Long, Long Trailer* (1954) and *Forever, Darling* (1956).

The rigors of creating *I Love Lucy* week after week, coupled with raising two children, led Lucy and Desi to change the format of the show in 1958. The new show aired once a month for an hour, and was renamed *The Lucille Ball-Desi Arnaz Show*. It ran from 1957 until 1960, at which time the Arnazes decided to call an end to their failing marriage, and television's most popular couple divorced.

In October 1960, Lucy hit the Broadway stage starring in *Wildcat*, a musical by N. Richard Nash, Cy Coleman, and Carolyn Leigh. Although the show was not critically acclaimed, it sold out every performance due to the popularity of its star, Lucille Ball. On November 19, 1961, Lucille married comedian Gary Morton.

In 1962, Lucy came back to television in *The Lucy Show*, another Desilu production. This time she starred as Lucille Carmichael, a widow raising two children. Her co-star from the *I Love Lucy* days, Vivian Vance, also starred on this series as Lucy's best friend, Vivian Bagley, a divorcée with a son. This show featured the two single women sharing a house and raising their children together. Gale Gordon, a co-star from her *My Favorite Husband* days, was featured as Mr. Mooney, the bank president in charge of the widow's trust fund. This series ran until 1968 and produced 156 episodes.

When Desi retired as president of Desilu Studios, also in 1962, his entire holdings were purchased by his ex-wife. Lucille Ball became the first female president of a major Hollywood film-producing company.

In 1967, Lucy sold Desilu Studios to Gulf and Western and formed her own company, Lucille Ball Productions. She also began filming her third television series, *Here's Lucy*, which ran for six seasons. Throughout its run the show never fell out of the top ten in ratings. This series, filmed in color, stared Lucy as Lucille Carter. Her real children, Lucie Arnaz and Desi Arnaz, Jr., played her television children, Kim and Craig. Gale Gordon also co-starred in this series as Lucy's brother-in-law and boss, Harrison Carter, who ran the Unique Employment Agency.

The *Here's Lucy* writers took advantage of Lucille Ball's popularity with many Hollywood celebrities by inviting such guest stars as Eva Gabor, Jack Benny, Wayne Newton, Carol Burnett, Tennessee Ernie Ford, Liberace, Elizabeth Taylor, Richard Burton, Vincent Price, Johnny Carson, Ginger Rogers, Helen Hayes, Joe Namath, and Ann-Margret, among a galaxy of other stars, to appear on the show with Lucy.

LUCILLE BALL IS TRULY ONE OF THE MOST REMARKABLE WOMEN IN THE HISTORY OF SHOW BUSINESS.

Between the years 1960 and 1974, Lucy continued to star in major films including the film version of the hit Broadway musical *Mame*, in which she was cast in the title role. In 1985, she returned to the dramatic form in the made-for-television movie *Stone Pillow*, in which she played a wily homeless woman on the streets of New York City.

Life with Lucy, an Aaron Spelling Productions show, was Lucy's last series, filmed in 1986. In it she played a feisty grandmother, not unlike the Lucy Ricardo of the 1950s.

Over the years Lucille Ball collected a multitude of honors and awards including four Emmy Awards, five Motion Picture Daily Awards, a Television Academy Hall of Fame Award, the Friars Club Lifetime Achievement Award, a Kennedy Center for the Performing Arts Lifetime Achievement Citation, and the 1989 Presidential Medal of Freedom.

Lucille Ball died on April 26, 1989, in Los Angeles, California, of complications due to heart surgery. Her ashes were interred at Forest Lawn Memorial Park in Hollywood, next to her beloved mother, DeDe. Lucille Ball's legacy remains undiminished to this day. The fact that her television shows and movies are still seen daily by millions of viewers worldwide is a tribute to her undeniable talent. However, Lucille Ball's greatest legacy is the laughter, which her memory continues to generate in her fans, both young and old, throughout the world.

WILLIAM CLEMENT FRAWLEY
1887-1966

OF IRISH DESCENT, his tenor voice and his love of performing made an acting career the obvious choice. The actor who racked up the most credits among the four major *I Love Lucy* cast members, Frawley had more than 110 movies and over a dozen major plays on his resume.

Born on February 27, 1887, to Mike and Mary Ellen Frawley of Burlington, Iowa, William (called Bill) was the second of four children. He lived a middle-class life as a child, attended school and church regularly, and loved baseball, football, and boxing. He was industrious, with big blond curls and bright blue eyes. As a young man he was a newspaper boy and took on after-school work with the railroad.

Bill was still working for the railroad at the age of twenty, when he was "discovered" singing in a pub in Chicago. After being given an opportunity to become a member of the chorus in the play *The Flirting Princess*, Frawley was hooked. But a few weeks into rehearsals, his older brother arrived with a note from their mother claiming she would rather see him dead than to see him make his living as an actor. Filled with guilt, Frawley soon returned home to his old job at the railroad. Although his mother tried her best to steer him away from a life in the theater, he was back on stage for good less than a year later.

WILLIAM CLEMENT FRAWLEY WAS BORN TO BE ON STAGE.

After a few months on the road performing a vaudeville act with his brother Paul (who would later become a Broadway star himself), Bill wrote a script called *Fun in a Vaudeville Agency*. He earned over $500 for his efforts; after this he began to tour the nation with a vaudeville group. It was during this time that Frawley began to hone his craft and develop the comedic talent and timing that would help him to land his most famous part—Fred Mertz.

In 1914, Bill Frawley married fellow vaudevillian Edna Louise Broedt of San Francisco. They developed an act that they performed all across the country on the prestigious Orpheum circuit—playing the famed Palace Theatre in New York and the Majestic Theatre in Chicago—until they separated in 1921. They were legally divorced in 1927. Frawley's first major hit was in the musical comedy *Merry, Merry*, in 1925. He continued to act on and off Broadway until 1933.

Frawley's movie career lasted over fifty years, during which he made a total of 111 films, the vast majority between 1933 and 1951. In 1916, he made his motion picture debut in the silent film *Lord Loveland Discovers America*. In 1933, he signed a seven-year contract with Paramount Pictures.

During the length of his contract, Frawley appeared in many different genres of film, including comedy, drama, musical, western, and romance. Although he played mostly supporting character roles, he acted in some very important movies, among them *Ziegfeld Follies* (1946, with Lucille Ball), *Miracle on 34th Street* (1947) and *The Lemon Drop Kid* (1934 and 1951). Frawley was often praised for his acting abilities, but he never could land the big role which would catapult him to stardom.

Bill Frawley was nobody's first choice for the role of Fred Mertz. Indeed, when the show was first written, there was no Fred Mertz character. The Mertzes were developed sometime after, as foils for the Ricardo characters, replacing an original regular character named Jerry, Ricky's manager, who was dropped to recurring status. *I Love Lucy* writer Jess Oppenheimer remembers that the Mertzes were developed in order to provide plot material for the show. It could be couple against couple or women against men. The Mertzes would be older, and less affluent, than the Ricardos. Gale Gordon, who played the male friend role on *My Favorite Husband*, was originally considered for Fred Mertz, but his exclusive contract with the show *Our Miss Brooks* put him out of the running. Another character actor, James Gleason, was also considered, but his high salary demand made it impossible for Desilu to hire him.

Legend has it that Frawley called Lucille and Desi and asked them to consider him for the role. Although they were eager to hire him, CBS and sponsor Philip Morris were less sure because of the actor's reputation as a heavy drinker. Desi Arnaz remembers that he met Frawley at Nickodell's restaurant and made him an offer—if he missed three days of work for any non-legitimate reason, he would be fired. The almost-broke Frawley took the deal, and $350 a week to start, and was never absent for any reason having to do with alcohol.

As Fred Mertz, Bill Frawley was often called upon to display his musical and dancing talents, which he had honed for years in vaudeville and on the Broadway stage. He enjoyed the episodes in which he had to sing or dance, as it brought back fond memories of his days on the vaudeville circuit. His other great passion, sports, was often incorporated into the *I Love Lucy* scripts. Whether it was baseball, football, fishing, golf, horse racing, or "the fights," Fred Mertz loved it all.

In 1957, *I Love Lucy* became *The Lucille Ball-Desi Arnaz Show* and Fred Mertz went along with it. When it ended in 1960, he chose to keep working even though he was in his seventies. On September 28, 1960, only months after the last original

Lucille Ball-Desi Arnaz Show was broadcast, Frawley debuted as Bub O'Casey in *My Three Sons*, along with Fred MacMurray. The two men had made two Paramount movies together in the 1930s, and MacMurray had been a Lucy guest star. Bill loved his years on *My Three Sons*, and enjoyed playing the Irish cook who was the father-in-law of MacMurray's character.

Eventually, Frawley became too ill to continue his role on *My Three Sons*, and in 1965 he left the show. He was to have one more TV role, however, as a horse trainer on *The Lucy Show* episode "Lucy and the Countess Have a Horse Guest," which aired on October 25, 1965. A few months later, on March 3, 1966, Bill Frawley was struck with a heart attack and died at the Roosevelt Hotel in Hollywood. Desi Arnaz was a pallbearer at the funeral. Frawley was laid to rest at the San Fernando Mission Cemetery in Mission Hills, California.

Although William Frawley graced the arenas of vaudeville, Broadway, television, and film, he will always be best loved for his role as Fred Mertz on *I Love Lucy*.

VIVIAN ROBERTA JONES
1909-1979

ALTHOUGH HER FIRST LOVE WAS THE STAGE, her role as Ethel Mertz forever endears her to television fans around the world.

Vivian Jones, second daughter of Robert and Euphemia Ragan Jones, was born on July 26, 1909, in Cherryvale, Kansas. Her parents were strict and religious, and often critical of young Vivian for her fun-loving, outgoing nature. From an early age, Vivian enjoyed performing and relished being the center of attention. Her parents disapproved of their daughter's love of the stage, and tried to discourage her dreams of becoming an actress.

Vivian became involved in drama at Independence High School in Independence, Kansas. She was a natural from the start, and was considered to be a talented and versatile actress. She enjoyed being a cheerleader too, and was also involved in beauty contests. After she graduated from high school, Vivian changed her last name to Vance, after Vance Randolph, a member of her Independence theater clique.

Vivian was married for the first time to Joe Danneck on October 6, 1928, at the age of nineteen. This marriage lasted only a few months, and after her divorce, she lived in Albuquerque, New Mexico, near her parents. At that time a group of displaced New York actors were forming the Albuquerque Little Theatre. Vivian was cast in their very first production, *This Thing Called Love*, and was instantly recognized as a great talent. She was soon off to New York to further develop her skills as an actress.

In September 1932, twenty-three-year-old Vivian arrived in New York. Her first job there was as a member of the cast of *Music in the Air*, a musical performed at the Alvin Theatre for which she was paid $35 a week. On January 6, 1933, Vivian married again, this time to George Koch, a violinist.

In 1934, Vivian was cast in the Broadway hit *Anything Goes*, as a chorus girl and understudy to the show's star, Ethel Merman. Several years later she won her first major Broadway role, opposite comedian Ed Wynn, in the production of *Hooray for What!*, which opened at the Winter Garden Theatre on December 1, 1937.

Vivian met fellow actor Philip Ober in 1939, while they were both in the cast of *Kiss the Boys Goodbye*. A year later she divorced George Koch and began a love affair with Ober, who was married and the father of a daughter. Phil Ober's marriage ended in a scandalous divorce, after which Vivian and Phil married, on August 12, 1941, in Marblehead, Massachusetts.

Between her third marriage and her debut as Ethel Mertz on *I Love Lucy*, Vivian Vance acted in a few plays and one movie (*The Secret Fury*, 1950). During this time she began to suffer terribly from mental illness. She first experienced mental distress in the thirties; it was a depression that she could not control. In 1946, she had a full mental breakdown and was forced to leave the play she was appearing in, *The Voice of the Turtle*. During the next few years, she spent a great deal of time in analysis, discovering the causes of her emotional problems and working on coping with them.

In the summer of 1951, Vivian received a phone call from actor/director Mel Ferrer who was putting together a new production of *The Voice of the Turtle*. At first Vivian had no interest in reprising her role in this play, but she was finally convinced to take the part that would transform her life.

On July 28, 1951, *I Love Lucy* director Marc Daniels took Desi Arnaz and writer Jess Oppenheimer to see *The Voice of the Turtle* at the La Jolla Playhouse in La Jolla, California. Daniels knew Vivian personally and thought she would be perfect for the role of landlady and best friend Ethel Mertz. First choice for this role had been Bea Benaderet, who had played Iris Atterbury, Lucy's sidekick on *My Favorite Husband*, but she was already committed to a role on *The Burns and Allen Show*. By the end of the first act of *The Voice of the Turtle*, Arnaz and Oppenheimer agreed that they had found their Ethel.

At first, Vivian had no interest in the TV show. She could not imagine that the new medium of television was going to amount to anything. After Marc Daniels convinced her that it would be foolish to turn down the role, she finally agreed to give it a try, and signed a contract for $350 a week. The salary for her part would eventually peak at $2,000 a week.

Vivian was never completely happy with the role of Ethel Mertz. Although she loved performing and the accolades she received (including Best Series Supporting Actress Emmy in 1953), she was distressed that her character was perceived as older, overweight, and frumpy, and she hated the fact that she was "married" to much-older William Frawley.

After *I Love Lucy* ended in 1960, Vivian took a break. She had divorced Ober in 1959 and was temporarily unemployed, so she spent her time acting in theatrical productions. On January 16, 1961, she was married for the fourth and final time, to publisher John Dodds, a man twelve years her junior, and the two moved to Connecticut. In 1962, she was convinced to return to television to play Lucille Ball's sidekick once again in *The Lucy Show*. This time, however, she demanded that she have equal star billing, a much better wardrobe, a huge pay increase, and that her character be called by her own first name; thus, divorcée and mother Vivian Bagley was born.

Vivian stayed with *The Lucy Show* for three seasons, after which she returned to the quiet life she craved—on her farm with her husband. She would appear in commercials and as a guest star on *The Lucy Show, Here's Lucy*, and in several other TV shows and specials, in addition to returning to the theater.

In 1973, Vivian found a cancerous tumor in her breast, and a stroke in 1977 left her partially paralyzed. Despite these physical setbacks, Vivian bravely appeared in her second-to-last TV appearance with old chums Lucille Ball and Gale Gordon in a Lucille Ball special, "Lucy Calls the President" (1977).

Unfortunately, the cancer that was thought to be gone had spread throughout Vivian's body, and she died of bone cancer on August 17, 1979, at the age of seventy. Her remains were cremated, and her ashes scattered in San Francisco Bay.

Vivian Vance is remembered by TV viewers as second-banana to Lucille Ball, but in the hearts of her fans worldwide, she will always be the beloved and unforgettable Ethel Louise Roberta Mae Potter Mertz.

VIVIAN VANCE IS PROBABLY THE SINGLE MOST RECOGNIZABLE FEMALE SIDEKICK IN THE HISTORY OF TELEVISION.

THE ROAD TO LUCY

MY FAVORITE HUSBAND
1948-1951

ON JULY 5, 1948, a Sunday night fill-in show called *My Favorite Husband* debuted on CBS Radio in place of the unexpectedly delayed premiere of radio comedy *Our Miss Brooks*, starring Eve Arden. The thirty-minute episode was based on the Isabel Scott Rorick book *Mr. and Mrs. Cugat: The Record of a Happy Marriage*, about a typical American couple; George, a serious banker, and Liz, his daffy wife, were married for ten years and living in Sheridan Falls, a small town in the Midwest. The Cugats were introduced to the audience as "two people who live together and like it."

The show was an immediate although unexpected hit, and CBS vice-president Harry Ackerman quickly made plans for it to be a weekly show. Actor Lee Bowman played George in the premiere episode, but due to other commitments, he was replaced by actor Richard Denning, who would play the role throughout the series. Ruth Perrott, who would later be a regular extra on *I Love Lucy*, played Katy, the maid. Original writers Frank Fox and Bill Davenport returned to their regular jobs at the *Ozzie and Harriet* radio show after the first ten episodes. They were replaced by talented, young CBS staff writers Madelyn Pugh and Bob Carroll, Jr., who at the time were writing for Steve Allen's radio comedy, *It's a Great Life*. Jess Oppenheimer, an experienced comedy writer, was brought in as head writer as well as the show's producer.

The show did not immediately have a sponsor, but CBS believed so strongly in the cast and writers that they agreed to cover the costs until one was found, which happened in December 1948 (General Foods). The last show of 1948 aired on December 26. On January 7, 1949 the series returned, but this time the characters' names had changed to Liz and George Cooper. Lucille and her writers quickly became a very tight team. She loved the way they wrote for her, and they admired her talent for comedy, mimicry, and performing in front of a live audience. On March 11, 1949, George Cooper's boss Rudolph Atterbury—played by comedic actor and Lucille Ball's life-long pal Gale Gordon—was written into the script for the first time. Two weeks later, on March 25, Atterbury's wife, Iris (Bea Benaderet), entered the picture. The addition of the older, more affluent couple launched the relationship that Oppenheimer, Pugh, and Carroll would later employ so brilliantly with the Ricardos and the Mertzes.

In 1950, Harry Ackerman approached Lucille Ball with the idea of taking the popular radio show to television. Lucille was excited at the prospect, and more importantly, at the idea that if Desi could play her husband, they could finally work together and begin their much-anticipated family. At first CBS balked at the idea, as did General Foods, which refused to sponsor the show without the Ball-Denning team. They felt that the public would not accept pale, strawberry-blond American Lucille married to dark, sexy Cuban musician Desi. In order to prove them wrong, Lucille and Desi, with the help of Oppenheimer, Pugh, Carroll, actor Buster Keaton, and friend Pepito Perez, developed a short vaudeville act which they took on the road, opening June 2, 1950, at the famed Chicago Theatre. They were an immediate hit and played to audiences across the country. In June the couple ecstatically announced the news of their impending parenthood. Sadly, a month later they suffered a miscarriage, after which they retreated to their California home to recover from their loss.

Jess Oppenheimer, Lucille Ball, and Richard Denning

The third season of *My Favorite Husband* began on September 2, 1950, after the summer hiatus. By December Lucille and Desi had finally firmed up a deal with CBS to shoot the "test" episode of their new television show in early 1951. The last broadcast of the 124 episodes of *My Favorite Husband* aired on March 31, 1951. By that time the *I Love Lucy* kinescope test had already been made, and radio hit *My Favorite Husband* was on its way to becoming television phenomenon *I Love Lucy*.

THE LUCILLE BALL-DESI ARNAZ TV SHOW TEST FRIDAY, MARCH 2, 1951

IN THE EARLY DAYS OF TELEVISION, what we now call "pilot" episodes were not broadcast on TV. They were shot on kinescope (a process in which images are recorded on film from a TV monitor), and used by television networks to find corporate sponsors for the shows in order to put them on the air.

The original script for the pilot episode of the Lucille Ball-Desi Arnaz TV show featured Lucy and Larry Lopez. He was a wealthy, successful bandleader and she was his successful actress wife. But before the show was shot, the writers decided to change the format and make the characters more down-to-earth, so that the average American viewer could relate. Larry became Ricky

```
LUCILLE BALL - DESI ARNAZ TV SHOW ( AUDITION )  (REV)
                    SECOND REVISION
MUSIC:  THEME
SIMULTANEOUS WITH CARD WHICH
READS
                                    ANNCR
                          Lucille Ball and Desi Arnaz.
WE DISSOLVE TO A PANORAMIC STILL
PICTURE OF A LARGE CITY.
                                    ANNCR
                          In this city live Lucy and Ricky
                          Ricardo.  Of course, you know Ricky
                          is the famous Latin-American
                          orchestra leader and singer and
                          Lucy is the famous - uh, well, she's
                          the uh - her hair is very red and
                          she's married to Ricky.
CAMERA MOVES FORWARD TOWARD
PICTURE..AND WE DISSOLVE TO A
CLOSER SHOT.  ONE APARTMENT HOUSE
STANDS OUT FAIRLY WELL.
                                    ANNCR
                          (AS NEW PICTURE APPEARS)  In this
                          district close to theatres and night
                          clubs, where Ricky works, they have
                          a little apartment, where they
                          laugh love and thoroughly enjoy
                          life.
CAMERA MOVES IN ON PICTURE AND
DISSOLVES TO SCALE MODEL OF
APARTMENT HOUSE
```

A page from the Lucille Ball-Desi Arnaz TV Show audition script.

Ricardo, a moderately successful orchestra leader who was constantly challenged by his wacky, show biz wanna-be wife, Lucy Ricardo. They lived in a modest apartment, they had a budget (which Lucy constantly and conveniently forgot), he worked, and she tried to get into the act. Ricky's agent, Jerry, was to be a regular cast member. Best friends and landlords Fred and Ethel Mertz did not yet exist.

On March 2, 1951, Jess Oppenheimer registered the idea for the new series with the Screen Actors Guild. He paid the $1 fee, and provided the following information: "He is a Latin-American orchestra leader and singer. She is his wife. They are happily married and very much in love. The only bone of contention between them is her desire to get into show business and his equally strong desire to keep her out if it. As show business is the only way he knows to make a living, and he makes a very good one, the closest he can get to his dream is having a wife who's out of show business and devotes herself to keeping as nearly a normal life as possible for him."

Because of time constraints, the writers based the pilot on a *My Favorite Husband* script, and included the Arnazes' vaudeville routine. Pepito the Spanish Clown, who had helped develop the routine, played himself. The show was shot on March 2, 1951 (Desi Arnaz's thirty-fourth birthday) at Studio A in Columbia Square, which was then the headquarters for CBS West Coast Radio and TV. CBS paid all production costs—totaling $19,000. The stage consisted of two sets, the seventh-floor New York apartment of the Ricardos, and Ricky's nightclub. The show was shot before a live audience, as all future *I Love Lucy* episodes would be. Lucy's wardrobe consisted of pajamas and a robe, and a baggy tuxedo outfit, which hid her pregnancy. Finally, all the couple had dreamed of for ten years was coming true—they were living and working together, and expecting their first child.

Hollywood Reporter columnist Dan Jenkins—whose name would often be used in *I Love Lucy* episodes—said of the pilot, "We saw the audition kine of CBS' *I Love Lucy* yesterday and are happy to predict the immediate ascendancy of Lucille Ball and Desi Arnaz to TV stardom come airing of the first filmed show in the fall. And by stardom, we mean in the top five of everybody's rating system in every area. Keep your eyes peeled for this one—it's a honey."

Unfortunately, CBS was not able to sell the show very quickly. Its asking price of $26,500 an episode was steep. Agents were still wary of television, and more wary of the show's possibilities. Finally, on April 23, 1951, powerful ad-executive Milton H. Biow, whose Biow Agency represented Philip Morris, decided to take a gamble. Philip Morris Cigarettes, it was announced, would sponsor the show. They bought the show that would change the face of television. The show that would be shot on film in front of a live audience. The show that would feature the first pregnancy on television. The show that would introduce the rerun. The show that would make household names out of Lucille Ball, Desi Arnaz, Vivian Vance, and William Frawley.

LET THE LAUGHTER BEGIN
JUNE-SEPTEMBER 1951

THERE WERE STILL MANY WRINKLES TO BE IRONED OUT before *I Love Lucy* was ready to go on the air. Lucille Ball retired to her home to spend the last weeks of her pregnancy in peace while Desi Arnaz worked out the production problems.

Television was a relatively new medium and shows were normally shot in New York, but the Arnazes insisted on staying in California to raise their family. At first CBS and Philip Morris objected, saying the shows would have to be filmed in New York. With the deal on the line, Desi made the bold decision to take a pay cut in order to finance the extra expense of filming in Hollywood. He also added the provision that he and Lucille would own one-hundred percent of the rights to the show. CBS agreed.

After weeks of searching, production manager Al Simon found Stage 2 at General Service Studios at 1040 North Las Palmas Avenue in Hollywood. There was room for several permanent sets; plenty of space for the audience of 300, which would attend every taping; and the $1,000-a-week price tag was tough to beat. At the time, the contract between CBS/Desilu Productions and General Service Studios to produce fifty-two half-hour episodes on the lot was the largest studio rental deal ever signed.

After that, the problem of the actual filming was tackled. Certain shows which were shot in New York, such as *Amos n' Andy*, were being filmed with one camera shot at several different angles. Desi and his team decided that would not work for *I Love Lucy*. There was also the problem of how to film the show using 35mm cameras without blocking the view of the live audience. To help solve this problem, Lucy suggested hiring world-renowned cinematographer and Academy Award-winner Karl Freund. She had first worked with Freund in 1942 on the MGM Technicolor film, *DuBarry Was a Lady*. Freund was not interested when first approached. He did not think highly of television, and the problem placed before him—how to film with multiple cameras on

dollys, without retakes, using different angles, and all before a live audience—seemed outrageous. But after a meeting with Lucille and Desi, he was convinced to try. With the help of others, Freund developed a sophisticated camera and lighting technique that is still employed fifty years later.

Another problem that was solved during those short summer months was the casting of the Ricardos' friends and landlords, Fred and Ethel Mertz. The couple was named after Indiana neighbors of writer Madelyn Pugh. It was decided they would be older and slightly less affluent than the Ricardos. The addition of the Mertzes would allow many plot devices, such as women versus men and couple versus couple.

Desi Arnaz gives the audience a warm-up speech prior to filming "The Bullfight."

Lucille Ball remembers that she received a phone call from veteran movie actor William Frawley asking whether or not there was a role for him in her new show. CBS was concerned because of the actor's reputation for drinking, but Desi met with him and the two made a deal that Bill would never miss work because he had been drinking. Convinced that Bill was right for the role of Fred Mertz, Desi gave his okay.

Finding Ethel was a little tougher. The role had been offered to *My Favorite Husband* actress Bea Benaderet, but she was committed to other projects and could not oblige. Late in July, director Marc Daniels had a brainstorm. He remembered working with an actress named Vivian Vance who had both stage and movie credits to her name. He convinced Desi and producer Jess Oppenheimer to go see the actress in her play, *The Voice of the Turtle*. After the first act, Desi and Jess agreed that Ethel Mertz had been found. Convincing Vivian was a bit harder, but eventually she agreed to move to Hollywood and give it a thirteen-week trial.

On September 3, 1951, the cast and crew assembled for the first time. Lucille Ball—who was still recovering from childbirth and caesarean surgery—met Vivian Vance for the first time as they all sat through the first reading of the first script. Everyone was nervous, particularly the writers who were concerned with pleasing Lucille and Desi. The first few weeks on the set were not all smooth sailing, as glitches involving filming, editing, and lighting were ironed out. Within a very short time, however, the cast and crew had become a well-oiled machine, with Desi at the helm handling business and technical problems, and Jess Oppenheimer and the writers managing the heavy load of weekly scripts. The strong work they had already done on *My Favorite Husband* helped the writers; many of the first season's plot lines of the TV show were based entirely upon episodes of the radio show. Rehearsals were taken very seriously and each show was meticulously run through until it was perfect. Each show was shot in less than an hour, and, unfortunately for fans, there are no existing outtakes or gag reels.

Fifty years ago, four actors and a crew of writers, producers, and directors set out to make a television show. Lucille Ball and Desi Arnaz thought they might make a few funny "home movies" that they could show to their children one day. When they began, no one had any idea how to accomplish their goals, or even if the show would find an audience. They were on their own. There were so many things they didn't know when they began—the main one being that they were about to make history.

Behind the scenes with Lucille Ball and Vivian Vance.

I LOVE LUCY:
THE EPISODES

THE PREMIERE SEASON

1951-1952

LUCY THINKS RICKY IS TRYING TO MURDER HER

LET THE TRIVIA BEGIN:

[1]
How long have Ricky and his orchestra been held over?
(a) six months
(b) indefinitely
(c) four weeks
(d) one year

[2]
What are the names of the dogs in the new act Ricky has hired?

[3]
Where does Ricky get a charley horse and why?

Ricky (on the phone): I'll probably miss her some, but in a couple of weeks I'll get another one, and she'll be just as good. Maybe even better!

Lucy is reading *The Mockingbird Murder Mystery* when she hears Ricky discussing hiring a new act for the club. She thinks Ricky is trying to do away with her and replace her with a new wife! She and Ethel devise a scheme to thwart him; they end up at the Tropicana where Lucy notices the dog act hired to replace the club's singer.

In the opening scene, Lucy is seen sitting at her vanity reading *The Mockingbird Murder Mystery* eating crackers and cheese. There is a jar of cold cream next to the cheese—of course Lucy chooses the wrong jar. This is the first recorded *I Love Lucy* laugh.

This episode was the first one filmed—on September 8, 1951, less than two months after Lucille Ball gave birth to daughter Lucie Desirée on July 17.

THE GIRLS WANT TO GO TO A NIGHTCLUB

For the Mertz's eighteenth wedding anniversary, the boys want to go to the fights; the girls want to go dancing. After an argument, the ladies decide to get dates and go dancing. After Lucy discovers the boys have dates too, she and Ethel dress up as hillbillies and pose as the dates. In the end they go to the fights after all.

In order to make the boys jealous Lucy whispers the names of two men she and Ethel can get to take them out to a nightclub. Who are they? Little Boy Blue and Peter Cottontail!

While trying to ditch the dates when they arrive, Ricky says he and Fred are named Sam and Elmer. Lucy calls herself Euncie.

Ricky discovers the girls are Lucy and Ethel when his "date" knows exactly where the Ricardos keep their cigarettes.

[4]
Ethel wanted to go to the _____ to dance, and Fred wanted to go to Charlie's _____ and then to the fights.

[5]
What did Ricky do with his little black book?
a) threw it in the ocean
b) burned it
c) lost it
d) gave it away

BONUS: Why?

[6]
Ricky calls _____ to get dates for Fred and himself.

Lucy (to Ethel):
We must know two men who are single and attractive.

Two men who are single? Two men?

A boy and a dog?

35

BE A PAL

Lucy is afraid the honeymoon is over, and tries to make Ricky happier by surrounding him with things that remind him of his youth. She creates "Cuba" in her living room, complete with a live mule and a flock of chickens. Lucy dresses as Carmen Miranda and lip-syncs "Mama Yo Quiero." Ricky falls in love with her all over again.

[7]
What is the most important rule of the "Be a Pal" system?

[8]
True or False: Lucy pours water on Ricky's paper to get his attention.

[9]
What or who does Ricky kiss goodbye instead of Lucy?
a) the dog
b) Ethel
c) the air
d) a grapefruit

Lucy (to Ethel):
As a dancer I got two left feet, and as a singer I sound like a bull moose pulling his foot out of the mud.

Legend has it that Lucille Ball asked Brazilian-born actress and singer Carmen Miranda (1909–1955) for permission to portray her in this episode.

Lucy used DUZ brand soap flakes.

Ricky claims to have five brothers.

Lucy and Ricky have been married for almost eleven years.

THE DIET

Lucy learns that a job is opening at the Tropicana, but she needs to lose twelve pounds in four days to fit into the size-twelve dress! She and Ethel develop a diet-and-exercise program that leaves her famished and weak, but determined. She is able to perform "Cuban Pete/Sally Sweet" with Ricky before she collapses from hunger.

Fred and Ethel's dog, Butch, made his first and last appearance in this episode.

In the first three days, Lucy loses less than two pounds.

Ricky, Ethel, and Fred dine on steak, potatoes, biscuits, and string beans while Lucy is handed a stalk of celery on a plate.

Lucy claimed to have weighed 110 pounds on her wedding day.

Lucy locked her rival in the club's closet.

[10]
Who is quitting Ricky's act?
a) Joanne
b) Rosemary
c) Marco
d) Pepito
BONUS: Why?

[11]
True or False: Fred ate sixteen oysters at dinner.

[12]
Lucy tells Ethel, "I'm as strong as . . . a very weak _____."

ETHEL:

ON BEHALF OF OUR TUBBY TRIO, I WELCOME YOU TO OUR FLABBY FOURSOME.

37

THE QUIZ SHOW

Lucy's spending is out of control and Ricky cuts off her credit. Lucy appears on a radio program called *Females are Fabulous* hoping to win the first prize cash bundle. Her stunt is to pretend to Ricky that she has a long-lost first husband. After almost ruining her marriage she wins the prize, but when her debts are paid she is left with only fifty cents.

[13]
What is first prize on the radio show *Females are Fabulous*?
a) $250
b) $500
c) $750
d) $1,000

[14]
What are the names of the two men who show up at the Ricardo apartment?

[15]
According to her account books, Lucy spent _____ cents on toothpaste.

Lucy: I've been going around stalling our creditors. I jollied them out of it.

Ricky: Oh, you did?

Lucy: Yeah. Except that this month I'm afraid they're going to want more money and less jolly.

This is Frank Nelson's first appearance as Freddy Fillmore, the game show host. He would appear several times on *I Love Lucy* as Freddy, the host of different programs (*The Mr. and Mrs. Quiz Show*, Episode 32, and *Be a Good Neighbor*, Episode 88). He also had a recurring role as Ralph Ramsey, the Ricardos' Westport, Connecticut, neighbor.

John Emery, who played Harold the tramp, was a very distinguished stage, film, and television star. He appeared again in *I Love Lucy* Episode 165.

The original name the writers had for the radio program was *Women are Wonderful*.

THE AUDITION

Lucy learns a talent scout will be at the Tropicana and you know she has to be there! When Buffo the clown gets injured he offers to let her take his place. Dressed as "The Professor," Lucy plays the cello and acts like a trained seal in order to get discovered. She is offered a contract, but turns it down so she can stay home with her beloved.

Pepito Perez, a friend of the Arnazes, played Pepito the clown in the pilot and later in Episode 52. He was not available for Episode 6, so Pat Moran filled in and they renamed the character Buffo.

Lucy comes on stage looking for "Risky Riskerdo."

This episode is almost exactly like the pilot episode, which no one but the sponsors had yet seen.

Vivian Vance did not appear in this episode.

[16]
What happened to Buffo's bike that caused him to crash?

[17]
True or False: After Lucy is a hit at the club, a depressed Ricky stays out until 2AM.

[18]
What is Fred's solution to get rid of Lucy for the day?
a) send her on a wild goose chase
b) lock her in the bathroom
c) send her shopping with Ethel
d) send her downtown to the lawyer

Lucy: You know, I've been thinking about shows like *Burns and Allen.* George Burns uses his wife on the show. Why don't you?

Ricky: I'd love to. Do you think she would leave George?

THE SÉANCE

Lucy has recently gotten into numerology and horoscopes, so when a producer calls to hire Ricky for a job, Lucy says no (it is a "say no to everything" day for Ricky). The producer is a horoscope nut too, so to try to get Ricky's job back, Lucy and Ethel hold a séance which the producer attends. He is so thrilled by the memorable evening that he re-offers Ricky the job. Whew!

[19]
According to Lucy's book on numerology, everyone has a number. Match the correct number to the person:

Lucy   1
Ricky   7
Ethel   3
Mr. Merriweather   5

[20]
Ricky and Lucy make a bet. How much does Ricky owe Lucy when he loses?

BONUS: What was the bet?

[21]
Ricky's barber is named _____.

Lucy: Mr. Merriweather, I'd like to present Madame Ethel Mertzola. She's going to be our medium tonight. She's psychopathic.

Lucy is a Taurus, Ethel is a Leo, Ricky is a Gemini, and Mr. Merriweather is a Scorpio.

Ricky says if his deal goes through he will buy Lucy the biggest diamond ring in town; a full-length mink coat; and the longest, shiniest Cadillac in the whole world.

Mr. Merriweather's Cocker Spaniel was named Tillie, and his wife was Adelaide.

Mr. Merriweather's original script name was Mr. Simpson.

According to numerology, Ricky's "perfect" name is Genevieve.

MEN ARE MESSY

Ricky is a slob, so Lucy divides the apartment in half—his and hers. When a photographer shows up at the apartment for a photo shoot with Ricky, he is aghast at what he sees—it looks like a broken-down barn, complete with chickens and bales of hay! Lucy isn't laughing when she learns he is from *Look* magazine.

Ricky reads a musical magazine titled *The Halfbeat*. Bandleader Tommy Dorsey is featured.

Ricky dances with Maggie the club maid while he's rehearsing.

Lucy's picture, in all her hayseed glory, shows up on the next cover of *Look* magazine.

[22]
When Ricky comes home and messes up a tidy apartment, what does
Lucy call him?
a) Ricky Ricardo, Chief Mess Cat
b) Pig Pen Ricardo
c) Ricardo the First, King of the Slobs
d) Ricky Ricardo, Duke of Disorder

[23]
What is the name of Ricky's press agent?

BONUS: What actor plays that character in this episode?

[24]
Ricky cracks walnuts with his _____.

Lucy (angry at the sloppy Ricky): Look honey, there's a new invention you'll just love. It's a hole in the wall, it has a long pole in it, little metal things hanging on it, and it's called a coat closet.

DRAFTED

[25]
Lucy and Ricky got a postcard from the Bishers who were vacationing in _____.

BONUS: According to the postmark, what time was the postcard mailed?

[26]
True or False: Ricky and Fred brought their wives glasses of water.

[27]
What does Lucy do to keep her mind off Ricky being "drafted"?
a) buy a hat
b) talk to Ethel
c) cry all day
d) take a walk in the park

Ricky: You've been married for a long while, haven't you?

Fred: Now why bring that up when we're having such a good time?

Ricky: Well, maybe you know women better than I do. Lucy's been acting strange lately.

Fred: Strange? How can you tell?

Ricky gets a letter from the War Department telling him to report to Fort Dix. Fred is going with him. Have the boys been drafted? The girls can't stop crying and knitting socks, leading Ricky and Fred to think their wives must be pregnant! Each pair plans a party for the other (hiding guests in a closet) before they learn the truth.

Ricky and Fred are going off to perform for the troops at Fort Dix in New Jersey. When this episode was shot, the US was involved in the Korean War.

The Sedgwicks, Orsattis, and Buzzells were real-life friends of Lucille and Desi. Ed Sedgwick, who tutored Lucille in comic technique when she first arrived in Hollywood, gave the bride away at the Arnazes' 1949 church wedding.

There were six people shoved into the closet.

Ricky had the rank of "general," while Fred was only a "colonel."

The "Four Santas" skit first appeared at the end of this episode, which originally aired on Christmas Eve. It appeared again in 1952 and 1953, and was be expanded to a full half-hour program in 1956.

THE FUR COAT

Ricky rents a mink for a club act, but Lucy thinks it is for her. She refuses to take it off, so he comes up with a plan to have it "stolen" by a "burglar" (Fred). When the plan goes awry and Lucy learns the truth, she gets even by buying a cheap fur and cutting it up in front of Ricky so she can have a mink t-shirt. Who's crying now?

[28]
What gifts does Ricky buy to make up for not giving Lucy the fur coat?

[29]
What was the price tag on the mink coat Ricky brought home?
a) $1,000
b) $5,000
c) $2,500
d) $3,500

[30]
Fred is seen fixing the _____ in the Ricardo kitchen.

BONUS: When did the Ricardos first tell him it needed fixing?

Ethel (to Ricky): Oh, a mink coat! Oh Ricky, Lucy'll just go out of her mind!

Fred (to Ricky): I oughtta slug you. What are you trying to do, make a bum outta me?

Ethel (to Fred): Don't blame that on him. You were a bum before he was born.

The first time Ricky comes in and says, "Lucy, I'm home!" occurs in this episode. He uttered these famous words many more times during the series (Episodes 16, 40, 57, 61). In the later years, this was changed to "Honey, I'm home!" (Episodes 67, 69, 71, 76, 117, 122, 137).

Fred thinks that Ricky should tell Lucy the mink is contaminated and she will get "mink pox."

Lucy claims she was living in "a mink's paradise."

LUCY IS JEALOUS OF GIRL SINGER

Lucy: Oh Ethel, it's just a publicity story. Ricky is trustworthy, fine, honest, and loyal.

Ethel: Well, if he was brave, clean, and thrifty he'd be a Boy Scout.

A notice in the gossip column of a local paper indicates that Ricky might have a girlfriend. Lucy later finds a piece of black lace that Ricky brought home! To keep her eye on him she grabs a spot in the chorus line at the Tropicana and upstages the star, Rosemary, but does not impress Ricky or the audience with her dancing abilities.

Lucy and Ricky read *The Daily Mirror* and *The New York Times*.

Ricky lies and says he was so upset he went to the park all day and fed the pigeons.

Lucy makes Ricky's favorite meal for him, *arroz con pollo* (chicken and rice), which, coincidentally, was also one of Desi Arnaz's favorite meals.

THE ADAGIO

Lucy wants a spot in Ricky's new French apache dance number. Fred offers to teach her, but Ethel finds a real Frenchman to do the job. The dance teacher has *amour* on his mind and when Ricky finds him hiding in the bedroom closet, there is some 'splainin' to do! The two men agree to a duel, but fake it to teach Lucy a lesson.

During the first season of *I Love Lucy*, they showed previews of the next week's episode to get people to tune in. The first time they did this was at the end of Episode 12. This method is still used today, in everything from soap operas to comedies to reality shows.

Ricky mentions moving to the country, either Long Island, Westchester, or New Jersey. The Ricardos don't actually move until the 1956–57 season.

[34]
Ethel finds a dance partner for Lucy. Who does Lucy first imagine it is?
a) Jean Valjean Raymond
b) Gene Kelly
c) Fred Astaire
d) Fred Mertz

[35]
When Jean first meets Lucy he immediately _____.

[36]
How many children does Jean have?

Ricky (watching Fred): What's that for?

Fred (crosses fingers): Well, I'm always hoping that this time'll be the charm.

Ricky: What do you mean?

Fred: Ethel keeps going out to put on a new face, but she always comes back with the old one.

[37]
Lucy reads a book to help her learn to sing. What is it called?

BONUS: What is the name of the author?

[38]
Ethel and Fred win _____ cents from Lucy and Ricky in the card game.

[39]
What snack do Ricky and Fred munch on after the card game?
a) chicken legs
b) popcorn
c) sandwiches
d) peanuts

BONUS: What else is on the door?

Lucy: So you can't get Ricky, you still have me. After all, what's Ricky got that I haven't got except a band, a reputation . . .

Ethel: . . . and talent.

THE BENEFIT

Ethel's club is staging a benefit and she wants Ricky to perform. Lucy says no, unless she can have a spot in the show. Ricky picks a duet routine in which he will have all the funny lines and Lucy will be the straight man. Unable to stand playing second banana, Lucy switches their lines and she manages to get all the laughs.

Ethel's women's club is called the Middle East 68th Street Women's Club in this episode. In later episodes she and Lucy are members of the Wednesday Afternoon Fine Arts League. Fred and Ricky sometimes call it the Wednesday Afternoon Fang and Claw Society, among other names.

Ethel and Fred won a total of 14,625 points in the card game—Lucy and Ricky got 73.

THE AMATEUR HOUR

Lucy has to get a job, but what skills does she have? She finds an ad for a babysitter at $5 an hour! But the "baby" is a set of rotten twins who make her miserable. When mom can't make it back to perform with the twins, Lucy steps in. When a frog is dropped down her back she does a great dance and wins first prize—$100!

This is the first episode in which the Ricardo address is mentioned. They live at 623 East 68th Street, which, according to most maps, is somewhere in the East River.

The sponsor of the contest is the Blue Bird Club.

Lucy's dress cost $59.95 and she needs to shorten it by 2½ inches.

Lucy finds the ad for the babysitter job in *The New York Times*.

Ricky takes sugar in his coffee.

Lucy is kicked in the shins three times by the twins.

[40]
Lucy bought a great dress on sale. Ethel bought a
_____.

[41]
What is the name of Jimmy's pet frog?
a) Homer
b) Marvin
c) Theodore
d) Elmer

[42]
True or False: Mrs. Hudson brought the twins over at 2PM.

LUCY:
WHAT KIND OF NITWIT DO YOU THINK I AM?

JIMMY:
I DON'T KNOW. WHAT KIND ARE YOU?

LUCY PLAYS CUPID

[43]
What does Lucy serve Mr. Ritter when he comes over for their "date"?
a) roast turkey
b) dessert and coffee
c) steak
d) pot roast

[44]
How many children does Lucy pretend to have?

BONUS: How many are missing?

[45]
True or False: Miss Lewis can't get her hope chest open because she lost the key.

Ricky (to Lucy):
I think marriage is wonderful. Why I think marriage is the greatest thing there is in the whole world. It's the only way to live. But if the guy has been clever enough to 'scape it this long, why louse him up now?.

The Ricardos' spinster neighbor, Miss Lewis, has a crush on the local grocer, so Lucy arranges a date for them. But when Mr. Ritter falls for Lucy instead, she has to do some fast thinking! She dresses up to look like an old hag and pretends to have a house full of children. In the end, Miss Lewis and Mr. Ritter fall for each other.

Lucy Ricardo makes fresh orange juice using her own juicer.

Mr. Ritter comes to the Ricardos' apartment at 7:30 in the evening, and brings Lucy a bag of gumdrops as a gift.

Miss Lewis was played by Bea Benaderet. Miss Benaderet played Iris Atterbury on *My Favorite Husband*, and was Lucille Ball's first choice for the role of Ethel Mertz.

Miss Lewis has been carrying around her diner invitation for Mr. Ritter for five years.

LUCY FAKES ILLNESS

Ethel tells Ricky if he doesn't hire Lucy for his show she might develop a complex. After she pretends to be a famous actress, develops amnesia, and acts like a pre-schooler, Ricky takes pity on her. Fred tells Ricky that Lucy is faking, so Ricky asks a friend to pretend to be a doctor who diagnoses Lucy as having "the fatal gobloots"!

The teddy bear that appeared in this episode was seen in many later episodes. In Episode 136, almost four years later, a similar teddy had a featured role when Mommy Lucy goes to see Little Ricky in the hospital.

At first, Ricky calls Dr. Stevenson to come help Lucy. Ricky asks her, "Could it be possible that you're suffering from magnesia?"

[46]
According to the "doctor," Lucy needs an operation called a _____.

[47]
Ricky places an ad in *Daily Variety*. What kind of talent is he looking for?

[48]
What children's game does "Little Lucy" want to play with Ricky?
a) May I?
b) Tag
c) Jacks
d) Hide and Seek

Lucy: I got this book at the library and it says anybody who is constantly frustrated may do all sorts of things.

Ethel: So?

Lucy: So look.

Ethel (reads book): Abnormal Psychology.

Lucy: Yeah, I'm learning to act abnormal.

Ethel: For this you need a book?

LUCY WRITES A PLAY

Lucy enters a contest for the best new play, but when Ricky won't play the male lead she switches the scene from Cuba to Britain so Fred can take the part. After Ricky learns that a Hollywood producer will be the contest judge, he has to be in the play. But he doesn't know about the switch, so Havana meets London in a huge mix-up.

[49]
How long is Lucy's play, *A Tree Grows in Havana*?
a) 100 pages
b) 75 pages
c) 200 pages
d) 125 pages

[50]
Ricky eats _____ while waiting for his cue.

[45]
True or False: Mrs. Glazingham wrote a play called *Knit One, Pearl Two*.

Ethel (reading from Lucy's script): You look very pretty Lucita. Your hair is shining, your eyes are bright, and your nose is continued on the next page.

The contest judge is Darryl B. Mayer. In real life, Louis B. Mayer was a Hollywood producer and head of Metro-Goldwyn-Mayer (MGM). Lucille worked for Mayer while she was under contract at MGM, and the Ball-Arnaz movies *The Long, Long Trailer* (1954) and *Forever Darling* (1956) were made at MGM.

BREAKING THE LEASE

After a lovely evening together, the Ricardos and Mertzes fight, and the Ricardos threaten to move out. When the Mertzes demand the lease be paid off, the Ricardos decide to break it by getting thrown out! Ricky invites his band over to rehearse and the noise knocks plaster from the ceiling! By moving day, of course, all is forgiven.

Lucy and Ricky wear matching pajamas.

The Harwood Manufacturing Corporation actually produced *I Love Lucy* pajamas in the 1950s—they sold for $6.95 a pair and came in men's and women's sizes.

The Ricardos and Mertzes go on trips together; they have pictures of them taken together in Atlantic City.

Lucy likes to sleep with the window wide open but Ricky likes it closed tight.

Lucy insults Ethel by saying her diamond rings came from a box of Cracker Jack.

This is the first time we hear "Nertz to Mertz," and the first time the two couples fight (but not the last!).

[52]
How many times does Lucy brush her hair every night?
a) 100
b) 50
c) none
d) 500

[53]
Lucy says she wants to live in the Mertzes' apartment building for how long?

[54]
The foursome sing the song _____ and dedicate it to their wonderful friendship. (And Lucy can actually carry a tune this time!)

Ethel (to Lucy): You're the nicest tenant I ever had.

Lucy (to Ethel): And you're certainly the nicest landlady I've ever had.

Fred (to both): And this is the most sickening conversation I've ever heard.

THE BALLET

Madame Lemond: Madame Ricardo, I am afraid you have not quite had the experience I had hoped for.

Lucy: Well, I guess I am a little rusty.

Madame Lemond: I think we should go to the barre.

Lucy: Oh good 'cause I'm awful thirsty.

Ricky needs a ballet dancer and a burlesque comic for his new club act. Lucy wants the ballet job so she enrolls in a school run by Madame Lemond. She is a total failure, so she hires a comic to teach her the burlesque number. When she is called to the club to replace a sick performer, she does the wrong act, and a star is not born.

Lucy Ricardo took four years of ballet lessons as a teenager.

Veteran actress Mary Wickes, who played Madame Lemond, was a long-time friend of Lucille Ball and appeared in her later television series.

Fred first mentions his vaudeville partner, Ted Kurtz, although we do not meet him until Episode 102 ("Mertz and Kurtz"), and by then his name has changed to Barney.

THE YOUNG FANS

When teenaged Peggy falls for Ricky, and her boyfriend Arthur develops a crush on Lucy, the Ricardos have to put a stop to it! They dress up like octogenarians, complete with glasses, wigs, and wheel chairs. The "kids" are convinced that older is not better, and they flee the scene together, leaving the Ricardos in hysterics.

Actor Richard Crenna, born November 30, 1926, was a World War II veteran when he played high schooler Arthur Morton. He had already acted on radio, and in 1952 first appeared on TV in the Desilu production of *Our Miss Brooks*. He went on to act in many television series and movies.

Peggy says boys her age are "icky," but she thinks Arthur looks like Gregory Peck. Peggy thinks Ricky is "pushing 23."

Ethel and Fred did not appear in this episode.

[58]
What does Ricky call Peggy Dawson?

[59]
Peggy pays Lucy a compliment by calling her
a) neat-o
b) swell
c) the greatest
d) keen

[60]
Arthur has the letter _____ sewn on his letter sweater.

Peggy: I can't believe this whole thing. Why I just saw you at rehearsal yesterday, dancing around and beating your conga drum.

Ricky: Oh yes, well, I'm glad you saw that. That was my farewell performance.

Lucy: Yeah, he's ba-ba'd his last lu.

53

NEW NEIGHBORS

[61]
What household item was broken by the moving men?
a) a chair
b) a vase
c) a lamp
d) a picture

[62]
Match up the characters with the rooms they were guarding:

Lucy   bedroom
Ricky   kitchen
Ethel   hallway
Fred   living room

[63]
Lucy calls the local police station and speaks to _____.

BONUS: At which precinct does he work?

RICKY:

YOU SEEN LUCY?

ETHEL:

LUCY WHO?

RICKY:

LUCY RICARDO, MY WIFE.

ETHEL:

OH, THAT LUCY.

New tenants are moving into the building and Lucy and Ethel can't help snooping. Hiding in their closet, Lucy hears the new couple rehearsing a play and jumps to the conclusion that they are foreign spies! She calls the police and the foursome wait with guns ready. After almost shooting an officer they all wind up in jail, and the couple moves out!

Mr. O'Brien's first name is Tom. We never hear Mrs. O'Brien's first name.

Ethel keeps Ricky busy playing gin while Lucy is hiding in the O'Briens' closet.

Ricky has a rifle and Fred has two shotguns.

The next day's newspaper headline reads, "Orchestra Leader Jailed in Shooting Spree."

3/10/52

EPISODE

22

FRED AND ETHEL FIGHT

The Ricardos scheme to get the Mertzes to make up, but then the Ricardos fight and Ricky moves to the Tropicana! To get him back, Lucy pretends she was hit by a bus, while Ricky pretends the building is on fire so he can save Lucy. The heroic Ricky rescues the mummified Lucy, but then Ethel moves home to her mother. Ai yi yi!

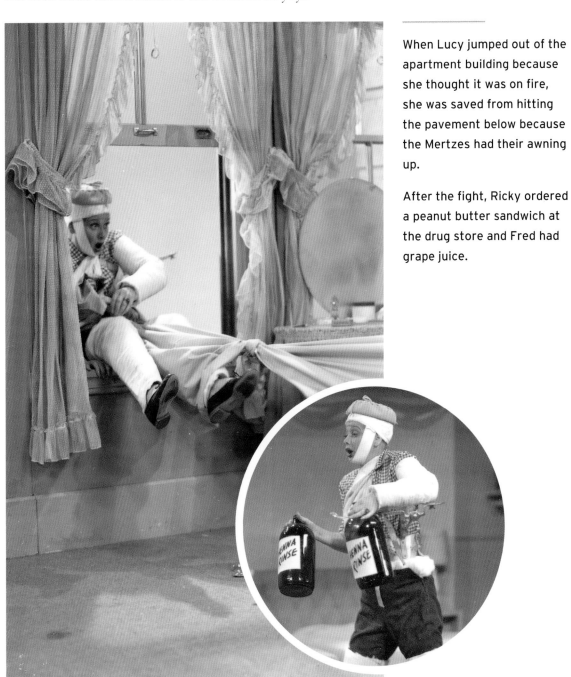

When Lucy jumped out of the apartment building because she thought it was on fire, she was saved from hitting the pavement below because the Mertzes had their awning up.

After the fight, Ricky ordered a peanut butter sandwich at the drug store and Fred had grape juice.

[64]
Lucy served what meal to Fred and Ethel when they came over for dinner?

BONUS: On what did Fred and Ethel sit to eat dinner?

[65]
What did Lucy save from the "fire" in the apartment?
a) her shoes
b) her picture of Ricky
c) her henna rinse
d) her wedding gown

[66]
Ethel said Fred's mother looked like a _____.

Ethel (indicating Fred): Lucy, is that my date? (Lucy nods yes) He's not a dream, he's a nightmare.

Fred (indicating Ethel): Is that your idea of a cute, young chick? (Lucy nods yes) You'll never shop for my poultry!

Ricky (discussing Bulldog Cement Remover #3): They don't make it anymore.

Lucy: You mean, you mean I'll have to keep this on forever?

Ricky: Well, honey I guess it'll wear off eventually.

Lucy: Well, what happens in the meantime?

Ricky: Well, honey, I really should let you suffer, but I don't have the heart to do it. There's one simple solution. And I'll do it for you.

Lucy: What?

Ricky: I'll get you a job as the bearded lady in the circus.

THE MOUSTACHE

Ricky grows a moustache for a movie role but Lucy hates it, and glues on a fake beard, which she won't take off until he shaves. Ricky gives in, but Lucy used rubber cement to attach the beard! When the movie producer comes by she hides her face behind a harem veil but scares him half to death when he sees the "real" Lucy!

Ethel used to be known as the Queen of the Nile because she could do a Middle Eastern dance.

Fred played vaudeville in Peoria in 1925.

Ethel thinks Lucy looks like a billy goat with her fake beard.

Ricky Ricardo shows one of Desi Arnaz's real scrapbooks to Mr. Murdock, the talent scout who comes to see Ricky about the movie. The scrapbooks were huge (3 feet x 2 feet) and Lucille and Desi collected well over one hundred of them during their lives.

THE GOSSIP

Ricky is fed up with Lucy's gossiping ways. They make a bet to see who can keep from blabbing the longest—the girls or the boys. Ricky tells a juicy tale in his "sleep" in hopes that Lucy will tell Ethel. The girls are caught in the act, but devise a plan to make it look like the story was true. Since Ricky "gossiped" first, the girls win!

[70]
True or False: Ricky and Fred order grapefruit juice, three eggs, bacon, and coffee for their breakfast in bed.

BONUS: What did Lucy and Ethel order?

[71]
Lucy concludes, "Wait a minute, if they weren't asleep, they were _____!"

[72]
Lucy gossips to Marge about what couple?
a) Betty and Jack
b) Sally and Dave
c) Carolyn and Charlie
d) Pauline and Steve

Ricky thinks gossip is vicious and petty.

This is the first time we hear of neighbor Grace Foster. She later appeared in Episode 36.

Since they won the bet, the wives will get breakfast in bed for a month.

In this episode, the Fosters live in apartment 3B; later they live in apartment 2A.

Fred (through the furnace pipe): Ethel Merrrrrtz. You ought to be ashamed of yourself.

Ethel: Who's that?

Fred: This is your conscience. You have been gossiping.

Lucy: Ethel, you've got the loudest conscience I ever heard.

Ricky (through the furnace pipe): Luuuuucy Ricardo. This is your conscience. You've been gossping too.

Lucy: Oh fine, my conscience has an accent.

[73]
How many dishes has Lucy Ricardo washed since she got married?
a) 211,000
b) 314,000
c) 219,000
d) 113,000

[74]
Wanna bet? Match the name to the amount the character wanted to bet.

Lucy	$30
Ricky	$10
Ethel	$50
Fred	$20

[75]
Ethel made a plate of butter that only cost her $_____.

Ricky: Listen, your grandmothers didn't have any of these modern electrical conveniences, and they not only washed the dishes but they swept the floor, they churned the butter, they baked the bread, they did the laundry, and they made their own clothes!

Lucy: Sure, where are those women today? Dead.

PIONEER WOMEN

An argument over housework leads to a bet about which gender has it harder. Life in "1900" is hard—old-fashioned clothes, riding a horse to work, bathing in an old tin tub. And cooking! Lucy and Ethel churn butter and bake bread. But thirteen cakes of yeast instead of three leads to the longest loaf of bread anyone has ever seen!

When pretending to live in the year 1900, Lucy Ricardo dropped an egg (shell included) into the coffee pot. Her explanation? Her grandmother was Swedish. In truth, Lucille Ball's step-grandmother, Sophia Peterson, with whom she lived for a time in her youth, was Swedish and spoke little English.

Lucy and Ethel played canasta while waiting for the bread to bake.

That morning Lucy offered Ricky a breakfast choice of "toast, coffee, a transfusion?" when he came to the table after shaving with a sharp-edged razor in cold water. Ouch!

The eight-foot-long rye bread was baked by the Union Made Bakery company. After the taping, the loaf was cut and divided for everyone to take home.

THE MARRIAGE LICENSE

Convinced their marriage is invalid because Ricky's name is incorrect on their marriage certificate, Lucy demands that Ricky marry her all over again, so they drive to the exact same spot and Ricky proposes. They end up at a run-down motel where the justice of the peace performs the ceremony. You may kiss the bride.

Ricky's last name on the Ricardos' license is spelled Bicardi (sic). In real-life, Desi Arnaz's maternal grandfather, Alberto Acha, was one of the founders of Bacardi Rum.

Fred was disappointed that his name was spelled correctly on his marriage license.

The cost of things certainly has gone up! In 1952 when this episode was filmed, a tank of gas cost $3.25 and a hotel room was $4 a night! (At the Eagle Hotel, anyway.)

[76]
Lucy claimed she wouldn't marry Ricky again if he were _____.

BONUS: Where were they when she said this?

[77]
What position was not held by Mr. Willoughby?
a) fire chief
b) bell boy
c) gas station attendant
d) mayor

[78]
True or False: In her despair over being "revoked," Lucy walked all the way to East Orange, New Jersey

Ricky (confused): What happened honey?

Lucy (weepy): I was cleaning out the desk and I found this.

Ricky: It's our marriage license.

Lucy: Yeah.

Ricky: Well, what's the matter? Don't tell me it's expired?

THE KLEPTOMANIAC

[79]
What are the three names Ricky gives his breakfast pancakes?

[80]
Acting like crooks for Ricky and Fred, Lucy and Ethel call themselves Lucy the _____ and _____ Ethel.

[81]
What valuable floor plan do the girls have a copy of?
a) The Chase National Bank
b) The Empire State Building
c) The Museum of Natural History
d) The United Nations

Ethel (pretending, holding gun): Did you get any of 'em?

Lucy (also pretending): Yeah, I got two. A flat foot and a private eye. I got the eye in the foot and the foot in the eye.

Lucy is collecting for a charity event, but when Ricky finds $200 in cash and a closet full of silver and valuables, he thinks she is stealing. He hires a psychiatrist to "help" his wife, but she is on to his plan and pretends to actually be a kleptomaniac. In the end she brings in a baby elephant she has "stolen" from the circus!

Fred has a beloved cuckoo clock that he won at Coney Island, but Ethel hates it and wants to auction it off at the women's club bazaar without him finding out.

Lucy "stole" a baby elephant from the Clyde Beatty Circus.

Lucy claims to be able to do the bird calls for the South African Yellow Bellied Sapsucker, the hummingbird, the cuckoo, and the English Sparrow.

CUBAN PALS

Ricky's Cuban friends are in town and Lucy is feeling left out. When she sees beautiful Renita, a dancer at the club, she plots to keep an eye on her husband. She arranges to fill in for Renita in the dance number. What she doesn't know is that Renita's partner wears a voodoo mask in the act and Lucy is scared out of her wits when he takes the stage.

After Ricky and his Cuban friends toast each other in Spanish, the multi-cultural Lucy toasts them all with "L'Chaim."

Renita and her partner Ramon do a number called "The African Wedding Dance."

When Ramon tries to dance with Lucy, she hits him in the head with a violin.

[82]
Lucy and Ethel dress as _____ to get into Ricky's club.

[83]
What are the names of Ricky's Cuban friends?
a) Maria and Carlos Perez
b) Maria and Carlos Ortega
c) Maria and Carlos Martinez
d) Maria and Carlos Franco

[84]
True or False: Ricky brings Dr. Scott Simpson home to see Lucy.

Lucy (speaks to Cuban friends of Ricky): Ricky told me about your dancing group and what a success it was in Cuba. Where do you think you'll go from here?

(Carlos and Maria give perplexed look)

Lucy: Do you know where you'll go from here?

Carlos (consults translation book): Wee doh knot.

Lucy: Wee doh knot? Sounds like someplace in Arkansas.

Carlos (wife points in book): Oh! Wee doh knot speak English!

THE FREEZER

[85]
Lucy doesn't serve bacon because it costs _____ cents a pound.

[86]
What do Lucy and Ethel do because they think they will be saving so much money on meat?
a) go to the beauty parlor and get "the works"
b) shop for new furniture
c) go to lunch and a movie
d) buy new dresses and hats

[87]
What is the name of the company that delivers the meat?

BONUS: How many pounds of meat do they deliver?

Lucy (to customer in butcher shop): Come 'ere. Are you tired of paying high prices? Are you interested in a little high-class beef? Do you want a bargain? Tell you what I'm gonna do. Step up a little closer, I don't wanna block the traffic. Now you look like a smart dame, what'll it be? I got sirloin, tenderloin, T-bone, rump, pot roast, chuck roast, ox-tail stump . . .

Without their husbands' permission, Lucy and Ethel buy a huge freezer so they can buy meat in bulk. They order two sides of beef for a total cost of $483! They try to sell some at a local butcher shop with no luck. When Ricky wants to see the freezer Lucy runs down to hide the meat, and gets locked in the freezer in the process!

Ricky says his eggs look "absolutely naked" without bacon on the plate.

When the Ricardo-Mertz meat order arrives, Lucy says it looks like "a side of elephant."

Ethel has an Aunt Emmy and an Uncle Oscar. They call her "Little Ethel."

LUCY DOES A TELEVISION COMMERCIAL

Ricky is hosting a big TV show and Lucy wants to be part of it. She schemes her way into the part of the Vitameatavegamin Girl. Rehearsing over and over with the 23 percent-alcohol tonic, Lucy begins to feel a bit woozy. By the time the live show begins she is totally drunk and ruins Ricky's big number. Classic television comedy.

Lucy: Well, I'm your veeda-vida-vigee-vat girl. Are you tired, rundown, listless? Do you pop out at parties? Are you unpoopular? Well are you? The answer to all your problem is in this little old bottle. Vitameatavegamin. (looks at bottle) That's it. Vitameatavegamin contains vitamins and meat and megetables and vinerals. (hiccup) So why don't you join the thousands of happy, peppy people and get a great big bottle of uh, vita-veedee-vidi-meanie-minie-moe-amin. I'll tell you what you have to do—you have to take a whole tablespoon after every meal. (She can't spoon it out so she drinks from bottle.) It's so tasty too. Just like candy. So, everybody get a bottle of . . . this stuff.

Vivian Vance does not appear in this episode; Ethel was visiting her mother. It doesn't say where her mother lives, but in Episode 113 ("Ethel's Home Town"), her father is living in Albuquerque, New Mexico.

This was the first episode for which Desi Arnaz received a producer's credit.

It takes less than ten tablespoons of Vitameatavegamin to make Lucy tipsy.

This episode is one of the three most often noted by fans as their favorite.

The Vitameatavegamin syrup was made from apple pectin.

[88]
Which of these instructions did Ricky *not* want Fred to give to the actress doing the commercial?
a) be there at 1 pm
b) report to director Ross Elliot
c) go to Studio Ten
d) address is Television Center

[89]
What is the name of the TV special Ricky is hosting?

[90]
Lucy waves hello to _____ while Ricky is singing on camera.

THE PUBLICITY AGENT

Lucy: I'm not a Maharincess—I'm a *Henna*rincess!

Poor Ricky. He can't seem to get his name in the paper, so Lucy devises a scheme to make the public think he is an idol. She becomes the Maharincess of Franistan and arrives at the Tropicana where she is "introduced" to Ricky Ricardo. She swoons when Ricky sings "I Get Ideas," but later the truth unravels in dramatic fashion.

Lucy inventories all her jewelry and appraises its value as $43. Perhaps she should have waited to do it until she got her string of pearls in Episode 36 ("The Anniversary Present").

Ricky decides that the country of Franistan is "tucked right in between Switzerland and Persia."

Ethel's aunt was once Queen for a Day.

LUCY GETS RICKY ON THE RADIO

After Ricky gives all the right answers for a radio quiz, Lucy is convinced he is a genius and signs them up to appear on the *Mr. and Mrs. Quiz Show*. The problem? Ricky only knew the answers because he was in the studio at the time of the taping. He saves the day with a brilliant bonus answer and Lucy is off the hook.

[94]
What is the *Mr. and Mrs. Quiz Show* jackpot prize?
a) a trip to Europe
b) $500
c) new kitchen appliances
d) a new bedroom set

[95]
Lucy and Ricky were the only husband and wife team on the Mr. and Mrs. Quiz Show to do what?

[96]
Freddy Fillmore won the _____ Award for Best _____.

Ricky might want to brush up on a little trivia. The only thing he knows about American history is that, "Columbus discovered Ohio in 1776." In real life Desi Arnaz became an American citizen in 1943 and knew much more about his adopted country than Ricky did!

Freddy Fillmore (from the radio): Who was the youngest man to be inaugurated president of the United States?

Ricky (answering): Theodore Roosevelt.

Lucy: Theodore Roosevelt? Oh no. It was one of the earlier ones. Adams or McKinley. Wasn't it Ethel?

Ethel: Ask Fred. He was probably there.

LUCY'S SCHEDULE

Lucy's perpetual lateness manages to mess up Ricky's promotion so he decides to set her straight. He makes up a schedule for her entire day—including bathing, eating, and shopping. Lucy begins to like the structure until she hears that Ricky has been telling his boss that Lucy is a trained seal. Pretty soon the food starts flying.

[97]
Name the three items Mrs. Littlefield made for the dinner the Ricardos missed.

BONUS: How much weight does Mr. Littlefield say he gained after dinner?

[98]
The Littlefields expected the Ricardos to arrive at what time?

[99]
Lucy tells Ricky that _____ are not on the schedule.

Ricky: I'll make out a schedule so you can budget your time.

Lucy: Budget my time? You mean like I budget my money?

Ricky: Heaven forbid.

Fourth time's a charm? Lucy says no to all the dresses Ricky picks for her to wear to the movies. Ethel has seen the first too much, everyone has seen the second one too much, and the third one is too tight.

Lucy, Ethel, and Mrs. Littlefield "served" the following dinner—split pea soup, salad, steak, frozen peas, and hot biscuits. Too bad Lucy couldn't fit chewing into the schedule.

The Littlefields' first names are Alvin and Phoebe.

Character actor Gale Gordon played Rudolph Atterbury on the radio show *My Favorite Husband*. He was Lucille's first choice to play Fred Mertz and would later co-star with her in her TV series *The Lucy Show*, *Here's Lucy*, and *Life with Lucy*.

RICKY THINKS HE'S GETTING BALD

Ricky is afraid he is losing his hair so Lucy tries to convince him otherwise. She hosts a "bald men" party to show him he is not bald, but to no avail. Desperate, she gets a contraption that fits over Ricky's head and is supposed to massage his scalp. To that she adds oil, eggs, and a stocking cap. Amazingly enough, he likes it!

[100]
When Ricky wears a hat to the table, Lucy puts one on too. What classic feat does she demonstrate with hers?

[101]
What food item does Lucy not put on Ricky's scalp?
a) beer
b) vinegar
c) eggs
d) oil

[102]
True or False: Mr. Thurlow from the hair product store is not bald.

Lucy tells Ethel she wants her apartment to look like "a sea of honeydew melons" when the bald men show up. She has to pay them each $10 and cook them dinner, and Ricky never even shows up!

In real life, Jess Oppenheimer, *I Love Lucy* creator and writer, was bald at an early age.

At Mr. Thurlow's store Lucy asks for the products that "smell the worst and hurt the most."

LUCY:
IF YOUR HAIRLINE WAS ANY LOWER, THEY'D HAVE TO BILL YOU AS RICKY RICARDO, BOY SHEEPDOG.

RICKY ASKS FOR A RAISE

[103]
Mrs. Littlefield wants Lucy's recipe for _____.

[104]
Who does not get a reservation at the Tropicana?
a) Harry and Bess Truman
b) Mrs. Thompson
c) Scarlett Culpepper
d) Mr. and Mrs. Ackerman

BONUS: What was Mrs. Ackerman's first name?

[105]
What entertainer replaced Ricky at the Tropicana?

LUCY (DRESSED AS TROPICANA CUSTOMER):

RICKY RICARDO AIN'T HERE NO MORE? WELL, I'M GETTING OUT OF THIS CRUMMY DUMP.

Lucy convinces Ricky that he needs to ask for a raise. When he does he gets fired! In order to save his job Lucy and Ethel reserve all the tables in the Tropicana (under pseudonyms) and then arrange to "arrive" as the guests. When they hear the news that "Ricky Ricardo isn't here anymore," they walk out! Ricky's job is saved.

When Mr. Littlefield says no to Ricky's raise, Lucy tells the boss Ricky has twelve other offers for jobs! Later, Ricky quits—sort of. He tells Mr. Littlefield, "Well then I quit! K-W-I-T!"

This was the last show of the first season. At the end of the original broadcast Lucy and Desi are seen packing a trunk. They say they will be taking "a little vacation" but that they will be back soon.

The 1951-52 broadcast season ended with Episode 35, but the busy cast and crew filmed Episodes 36 through 40 in May and June.

By this time, Lucille and Desi already knew they were expecting their second child. They returned to the studio in August, ahead of schedule, so they could tape the next fifteen episodes before Thanksgiving, when Lucille went on maternity leave. They resumed filming in mid-March 1953, only two months after Lucille gave birth by caesarean section. During the almost-four month leave, the taped episodes aired, including the "pregnancy" series.

Being on the edge of your couch, chair, or whatever you happen to be resting your rear end on, waiting for those glorious moments of unpredictability from a great actor or actress is definitely an experience I live for. I live for it as a viewer, and most certainly I live for it as an actress as well. It is this ability that audience members unknowingly put aside all of their prime-time household chores for; it is for this ability that family members don't talk during dinner while they tune in; and it is this ability that has kept me excited and inspired to continue creating and enjoying and laughing throughout my own work. I thank Lucy, Ricky, Fred, and Ethel, who shared with us their ability to keep us always waiting for that next great, unknown hilarity.

JENNA ELFMAN
ACTRESS, *DHARMA AND GREG*

THE SECOND SEASON

1952-1953

THE ANNIVERSARY PRESENT

[106]
At what jewelry store does
Grace Foster work?

[107]
When Grace calls Ricky at
home, Ricky tells Lucy it's
_____ on the line.

[108]
What trick did Lucy not try
to jog Ricky's memory so he
would remember their an-
niversary?
a) circle it on the calendar
b) persuade Ethel to remind
   him
c) leave her wedding ring on
   the table
d) cook rice for breakfast

Lucy (crying over Ricky): I still can't believe that he chose her over me. After all, don't eleven years of faithful service count for anything?

Ethel: Oh, you poor little thing.

Lucy: You'd think that if he was going to let me go like this, he'd at least give me a gold watch. Or a letter of recommendation.

Ricky arranges to buy a string of pearls through Grace Foster, a neighbor, but Lucy thinks the two are engaged in a love affair. She and Ethel listen through the furnace pipe and then go out on the ledge dressed as painters so they can peek into the Foster apartment. Lucy sees Ricky putting the pearls on Grace, but in the end she has egg (and paint) on her face!

The Fosters now live in apartment 2A.

In this episode the Ricardos' anniversary is on the nineteenth. No month is specified. Lucille Ball and Desi Arnaz had two marriage ceremonies—the first on November 30, 1940, at the Byram River Beagle Club in Greenwich, Connecticut. Nearly nine years later, on June 19, 1949, they renewed their vows in a Catholic ceremony at Our Lady of the Valley Church in Canoga Park, California, near their home. They always celebrated the November 30th date, however, and the last time they spoke to each other was on November 30, 1986, two days before Desi Arnaz died.

Ethel and Lucy call the apartment furnace pipe "the snooper's friend."

THE HANDCUFFS

Lucy wants Ricky to stay home one evening, so while he rests she handcuffs herself to him. Unfortunately, instead of Fred's trick handcuffs, she used his old Civil War shackles! When the locksmith can't get them undone, Ricky is left to make a TV show guest appearance with one hand tied behind his back.

Ricky needs the handcuffs off so that he can appear as the special celebrity guest on a star-studded television show called "Guest Stars."

Fred was given the handcuffs when he performed in a police benefit.

Mondays are Ricky's only night off.

Mr. Walters, the locksmith who comes to undo the handcuffs, lives in Yonkers, New York.

[109]
Locksmith Mr. Walters says his favorite Ricky Ricardo song is _____.

[110]
What three songs does Ricky say he has recorded recently?
a) "Similau"
b) "Yucatan"
c) "Babalu"
d) "In Santiago, Chile"

[102]
True or False: Fred was given the antique handcuffs in 1927.

Ricky (handcuffed to Lucy): Well genius, what now? Are we gonna go through life like this?

Lucy: Now honey, remember when we were married you wanted to be joined together in matrimony. Ha ha ha.

Ricky: And as I recall it was 'til death do us part.

Lucy: Yeah, that's right.

Ricky: That event is about to take place right now.

THE OPERETTA

[112]

According to Lucy's books, how much money is in the club treasury?

BONUS: How much money is actually in the treasury?

[113]

Who plays what? Match the character with his or her part in the play.

Lucy	Squire Quinn
Ricky	Lily
Ethel	Camille
Fred	Prince Lancelot

[114]

What is the total number of scenes in the first act?

Ricky: Well, look honey, you know I Love Lucy, and she's a wonderful girl and she's got wonderful qualities but, confidentially, when she sings she hits a bad note once in a while.

Ethel: Once in a while?

Lucy has been secretly borrowing from the ladies club treasury and now she's in trouble. She decides to write and perform a play to make the money back but when she rents the sets and costumes using a postdated check (which bounces!) the gypsy Camille, Lily of the Valley, and all their singing friends get bounced off the stage.

In Fred's big number from *The Pleasant Peasant*, his character claims, "The stout makes him ail and the ale makes him stout."

Lucy and Ethel each vie for the lead role, but after hearing Ethel sing. Lucy sighs, "Where do I go to get my teeth snaggled?"

JOB SWITCHING

Who works harder, men or women? Lucy and Ethel will get outside jobs and Ricky and Fred will do the housework. Easier said than done—Lucy and Ethel's stint in the chocolate factory is no more of a success than Ricky and Fred's attempt to make dinner for four. Fudge anyone? A true classic, and one of Lucille Ball's favorites.

Ricky and Fred claim there are two kinds of people—earners (men) and spenders (women).

Lucy and Ethel end up at the Acme Employment Agency where they manage to completely frustrate its president, Mr. Snodgrass.

Ethel's checking account is never overdrawn.

The sign on the door of the wrapping department says "Kitchen."

Fred scorches three of Ethel's blouses and Ricky starches Lucy's stockings.

[115]
What does Ricky serve for breakfast on the first day of their bet?

BONUS: What paper does Lucy read at the breakfast table?

[116]
Ricky makes how much rice for dinner?
a) one pound
b) two pounds
c) four pounds
d) he doesn't make rice

[117]
Ethel claims she worked in _____ departments at Kramer's Kandy Kitchen.

LUCY:
YES, MA'AM, I'M A DIPPER FROM WAY BACK.

FOREWOMAN:
YES?

LUCY:
THEY USED TO CALL ME THE BIG DIPPER!

THE SAXOPHONE

[118]
Which one of these problems
is Ricky not worried about?
a) he can't get hotel reservations
b) his musical arrangements are missing
c) one of his musicians has the flu
d) his tuxedo won't be cleaned in time

[119]
True or False: In her attic trunk Lucy found a hat she had once worn in the Easter Parade.

[120]
Ricky caught a fish in what lake?

BONUS: What does Ethel call the fish?

Lucy (to band members): Greetings, Gates! Slip me some skin, boy. Hiya cats! Where do I sit, dad?

Ricky: Lucy, I want to speak to you.

Lucy: Later Gater. I wanna get up here and get my kicks man!

Lucy wants to join the band when Ricky is going on tour, but he can't afford to take her. If she is a member of the band, she can go! She dusts off her old saxophone, rehearses "Glow Worm" for hours and shows up at the club to audition. When that fails she tries to make Ricky jealous so he will stay home.

Lucy Ricardo attended high school in Celoron, New York, which is also true of Lucille Ball.

The town of Celoron is next door to Jamestown, New York, where Lucille was born and spent her childhood.

VACATION FROM MARRIAGE

After reading a book about marriage, Lucy decides the foursome is in a rut. To put some spark back into their lives Lucy moves in with Ethel, and Fred with Ricky. This soon grows old and the wives pretend to have dates to make the husbands jealous. Finally, they all end up on the cold roof and decide to stick it out together.

In this episode the Mertzes have been married twenty-five years. However, in the next episode ("The Courtroom") they celebrate their twenty-fifth wedding anniversary. Their neighbor, Miss Lewis, gives them a cake. A season before, in Episode 2 ("The Girls Want to Go to a Nightclub"), they had been married only eighteen years!

[121]
Ethel and Fred have a plaque in their bedroom that reads _____.

[122]
Name the neighbor that Lucy and Ethel try to contact from the roof.

[123]
What personal item does Fred always misplace?
a) his eyeglasses
b) his wedding ring
c) his wallet
d) his toolbox

BONUS: Where does he always find it?

Lucy: The four of us have allowed ourselves to deteriorate.

Ethel: Yes.

Lucy: We have become stuffy, moldy, and musty. We are knee-deep in a pool of stagnation. Now what are we gonna do about it?

Fred: Well, I don't know about the rest of you, but I'm gonna go and take a shower.

THE COURTROOM

For their twenty-fifth anniversary, the Ricardos give the Mertzes a new TV, but when Ricky manages to blow it up it and Fred retaliates on the Ricardos' set, they sue each other. In court each tells the judge the "real" story but after they reenact the drama using the judge's TV, they decide their friendship is worth more than the price of a TV.

[124]
What color wires did Ricky connect to try to make the Mertzes' new TV set work?

[125]
What was on the wall behind the judge in the courtroom?
a) the State Seal of NY
b) the Ten Commandments
c) the scales of justice
d) a portrait of George Washington

[126]
During her courtroom testimony, Ethel refers to Ricky as _____.

Ricky (practicing): Now Mrs. Ricardo, tell us in your own words, what happened on the night in question.

Lucy: Well, uh, we went down to the Mertzes and . . .

Ricky: No, no, no. In your own words that I wrote for you!

This episode features some of Desi Arnaz's best physical comedy as he tries to get the Mertzes' new TV set down a flight of stairs.

In court, Lucy claims Ricky is an "electronic specialist." Good thing she changed her story, since the penalty for perjury was $500 or ninety days in jail!

After kicking in the Ricardos' TV set and having a big fight, Ethel and Fred storm out of the Ricardo apartment. Watch how they leave—Fred stomps out to the right, and Ethel stalks out to the left.

REDECORATING

Lucy enters a drawing for a new home full of furniture. After Ricky gets tickets to a new show and Lucy won't leave her phone (for fear the contest might call) Ricky tricks her into thinking she won. So she sells all the old furniture and she and Ethel hang wallpaper with disastrous results. Good thing it turns out she really did win!

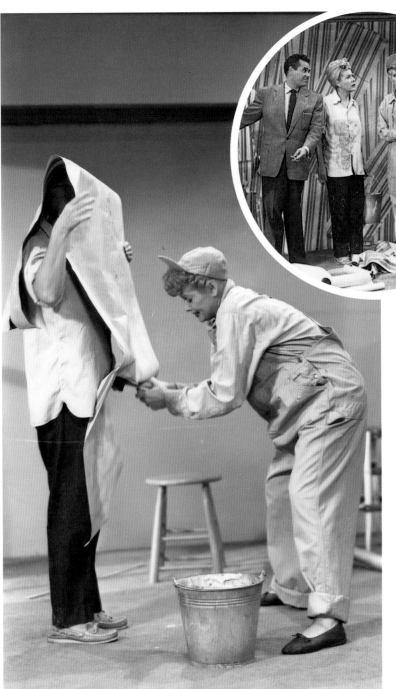

Lucille Ball wears huge painter's overalls to cover her pregnancy. When this was shot she was already four months pregnant.

This episode was the first time (but not the last) that furniture-buying played a major role in the plot of the story.

Fred and Ethel describe their furniture as "crummy," but they will not get anything new until the third season.

[127]
In order to shore up his nerves, what does Fred drink at the drugstore?
a) grape juice
b) a double chocolate malted
c) black coffee
d) a cherry Coke

BONUS: Name the waitress he ordered from.

[128]
True or False: Dan Jenkins, the used furniture man, first offers Lucy $75 for her furniture.

[129]
When hanging wallpaper Lucy asks, "How do you get the _____ out?"

Ricky (hatching a scheme): Well, Fred I'd be glad to do it. I'd love to do it, but she'd recognize my accent in a minute.

Fred: You're gonna use an accent?

RICKY LOSES HIS VOICE

[130]
Name the five breakfast items Ricky asks for in order to build up his strength.

[131]
Lucy thinks Ricky's sore throat looks like what American tourist site?
a) The Grand Canyon
b) The Carlsbad Caverns
c) The Rocky Mountains
d) The Mighty Mississippi

BONUS: What colors does she describe seeing?

[132]
_____ makes a surprise guest appearance in the finale of the "Flapper Follies" show at the Tropicana.

Ricky (trying to sing with sore throat): Babaluuuu. Babaluuuuuuuuuu . . .

Lucy: That's pretty Babalousy.

Just when the Tropicana is planning a grand reopening, Ricky comes down with a case of laryngitis. Lucy decides to stage the show herself with help from the Mertzes. They manage to pull off a vaudeville act using ancient showgirls and music from the Flapper era. Ricky's new boss, Mr. Chambers, loves the show and Ricky is saved!

Pianist Marco Rizo, a life-long friend of Desi Arnaz, often played himself on the show. In this episode he forgets who he is talking to and says, "Ok, Des," instead of "Ok, Rick."

This is the first time we see the *Home Show* furniture.

Fred says he performed his vaudeville routine at the Palace in Jamestown in 1927.

SALES RESISTANCE

In this flashback episode, Lucy buys a Handy Dandy Kitchen Helper, and when Ricky makes her return it she is stuck with a Handy Dandy Vacuum Cleaner! She tries to unload it to get her money back but her sales techniques fall short. All is forgiven when Ricky tries to return it and gets stuck with a Handy Dandy Refrigerator!

This was the first of the five "flashback" episodes that were taped in August and September 1952, and aired after the birth of Little Ricky, to allow Lucille Ball to recover from childbirth. In Episodes 45 and 46, it was explained that Lucy was still in the hospital.

After the original airing of this episode, an announcer mentions that the song, "There's a Brand New Baby at Our House," was released on a Columbia label with the *I Love Lucy* theme song on the flip side.

In this episode Lucille Ball makes a rare error. At first she says the Handy Dandy Kitchen Helper cost her $7.98. Later in the same scene she quotes the price as $7.95. Whatever its price, it was supposed to cut down on housework by two hours a day!

After failing at being a saleslady, a bedraggled Lucy returns to the apartment still carrying the vacuum, but minus her right shoe, which is "stuck in the door at 310 East 69th Street!"

[133]
What Handy Dandy appliance does Fred end up buying?
a) vacuum
b) refrigerator
c) dryer
d) dishwasher

[134]
Lucy is afraid that if Harry Martin returns to pick up the vacuum he'll sell her a Handy Dandy _____.

[135]
True or False: When Ricky finds the new vacuum in the closet, Lucy tells him it's his Christmas gift.

Lucy: And now ladies and gentlemen, I'm about to demonstrate the Handy Dandy Kitchen Helper. It's something you shouldn't be without. It peels and splices, cuts and rices, skins and dices, at lowest prices.

THE INFERIORITY COMPLEX

Lucy thinks she's no good at anything, so Ricky visits a psychiatrist who suggests a good dose of flattery from a handsome stranger would snap her out of it. He comes to the Ricardo apartment to do just that, but Ricky gets jealous and throws the doc out! Later he and the Mertzes convince Lucy she is a great joke teller, card player—and singer!

[136]
Ricky wants Lucy to have a lot of attention. What item doesn't he buy for her?
a) flowers
b) a dressing shawl
c) perfume
d) candy

[137]
What word does "Chuck Stewart" keep saying to Ricky?

[138]
Ricky looks for a psychiatrist in the phone book under the letter _____.

Ethel: I know something you do better than anybody in the whole world.

Lucy: What?

Ethel: There's nobody can get her hair the color you can.

Lucy: Thank you.

Ethel: That didn't come out the way I wanted it to.

Lucy: Neither did my hair.

This episode fully introduces a Lucyism to the American public. At one point she moans, "I don't need a complex. I really am inferior. Waaaaah!" She uses the "waaaaah" several times in this episode.

Lucy is convinced of her inferiority when she leaves the seeds in the juice, burns the toast, puts too much salt on the eggs, and breaks the toaster.

THE CLUB ELECTION

2/16/53

EPISODE

47

Ricky has a flashback to the time that Lucy and Ethel were both running for president of their ladies club. Lucy bribes a club member to give her a nomination, and she and Ethel both run for president. The husbands get involved and try to bribe the deciding voter. In the end the friends are tied and become co-presidents.

Lucy calls a caucus so that she can get nominated for office. Club members discuss the 1952 political candidates; although not mentioned by name, they were Dwight D. Eisenhower and Adlai Stevenson. The political conventions were first televised in 1948, but most families did not own a set. In 1952, most US citizens observed the political process for the first time. This is one of the few specific historical or political events ever discussed on *I Love Lucy*.

[139]
True or False: The Wednesday Afternoon Fine Arts League has never met on Tuesday.

[140]
Match the club member to the office she was nominated for:

Lillian Appleby   president
Marion Strong   treasurer
Ethel Mertz   secretary
Grace Munson   vice president

BONUS: Who nominates Lucy?

[141]
What item does Ruth Knickerbocker own that makes Lucy and Ethel want her in the club?

Ethel (angry): I'm gonna do that poster I decided not to do.

Fred: You mean, "With our club's welfare, do not tinker, Lucy Ricardo's a dirty . . ."

Ethel: That's the one!

THE BLACK EYE

Lucy is reading a mystery aloud to Ricky when the Mertzes overhear and suspect physical abuse! Later they see Lucy with a black eye. While the Ricardos deny there are any marital problems, Fred gets involved and ends up with his own black eye. When they all end up with shiners they realize that truth is stranger than fiction.

[142]
What man does Ethel think Lucy is in love with?

BONUS: Why?

[143]
According to Ricky, what happens when he reads a book aloud?

[144]
Ethel gave Fred a black eye by hitting him with _____.

ETHEL:

THIS IS ETHEL, YOUR FRIEND, TO WHOM YOU MAY TURN IN A MOMENT OF CRISIS.

LUCY:

ETHEL, HAVE YOU BEEN DRINKING?

Ethel calls Fred her "beautiful, fat, old goat."

Ricky is shown tossing a book to Lucy at waist height. How then does it manage to hit her in the eye? Later he asks the famous question, "Wha' happun?"

Lucy and Ethel both get hit in the left eye and Ricky and Fred in the right.

LUCY CHANGES HER MIND

Lucy can't choose a dress, a restaurant, a table, or an entree. When Ricky gets mad, Lucy decides to get even. To make Ricky jealous she finds and finishes a letter to an old boyfriend and leaves it lying around. When Ricky goes to confront the man at his fur shop, he finds Lucy flirting and dancing with a mannequin!

HENDERSON'S FURS

When this episode begins, Ricky tells Ethel and Fred that Lucy is out with the baby visiting Mrs. Jenkins. We have never heard of Mrs. Jenkins before, but one Mr. Jenkins is the furniture salesman from Episode 43!

Lucy and Tom Henderson (the fur store owner) went to college together.

After one table-change Ethel has three knives and Fred has three forks and two spoons.

[145]
Lucy changed her order several times during the evening. What was the original item each person ordered for dinner?

Lucy	lamb chops
Ricky	pork chops
Ethel	sirloin steak
Fred	roast beef

[146]
What does it say on the front of the menus at the Roof Garden restaurant?

BONUS: What is the name of the waiter?

[147]
The total number of restaurant tables the gang sits at is _____.

Lucy: I like Chinese food, but I'm crazy about Italian food, too.

Ricky: Well, maybe we can find a place that serves ravioli foo young.

Fred: Or chicken chow pizza.

LUCY IS "ENCEINTE"

Lucy goes to the doctor feeling "dawncy" and discovers she is going to have a baby! Try as she might, she can't seem to find the perfect moment to tell Ricky. In desperation she goes to the Tropicana and leaves an anonymous note for Ricky to sing, "We're Having a Baby, My Baby and Me." He finally realizes it's Lucy and the two dissolve into tears.

[148]
What special gifts does Fred give to Lucy for the baby?

[149]
Ricky wants to quit show business and move to
a) Connecticut
b) Cuba
c) California
d) New Jersey

[150]
Ethel wonders aloud whether she will become a _____ or a _____.

RICKY:
IT'S ME!

The French word enceinte was used here because the language of the day did not permit the use of the word "pregnant" on television. Lucy was said to be "expecting."

Reverend Clifton Moore, Rabbi Alfred Wolfe, and Monsignor Joseph Devlin were chosen to read the "pregnancy" scripts in order to filter out any objectionable material about the impending birth. None of them ever changed a word.

Desilu Productions received just over 200 letters disapproving of the Ricardo pregnancy. However, Lucille Ball and Desi Arnaz received over 30,000 congratulatory notes after their son was born.

The original ending for this episode is not the one we have all seen. The original script calls for Ricky to jump up and down, and yell in excitement. However, when the ending was first shot, Lucille and Desi were overcome by their own emotions, and both ended up in tears. Later, the directors shot the original written ending, but after viewing both choices they decided that the first take was the right one to use. Knowing that the real couple and the TV couple were experiencing the same feelings gives truth to this episode in a way that acting never could.

PREGNANT WOMEN ARE UNPREDICTABLE

Ricky wants to pamper his wife—he cooks her breakfast and brings her gifts, for the baby. She starts to think he only loves her because she's expecting. To make her feel special he invites her out for dinner and dancing. But when he doesn't mention the baby all night, she thinks that now he doesn't love the baby!

Lucy and Ricky went though many names for their baby—Scott or Pamela (the names of Lucille Ball's real niece and nephew), Gregory or Joanne, Philip or Cynthia, John or Mary, Romeo or Juliet, Pierpont or Sharon, Bob or Madelyn (the names of two of the Lucy writers). In real life there was only one choice for the name of the Arnaz son, Desiderio Alberto IV.

Ricky sends Lucy an orchid corsage and a box of candy, and he signs the card "Loverboy."

[151]
What item does Ricky not ask Lucy to help him find?
a) waffle mix
b) salt
c) waffle iron
d) eggs

[152]
When Ricky comes home from the club Lucy is practicing what baby-care skill?

BONUS: What time does Ricky come home?

[153]
What baby gifts does Ricky bring home to Lucy?

Lucy: Well, I'm not going to settle on just any old thing. I want the names to be unique and euphonious.

Ricky: Okay, Unique if it's a boy and Euphonious if it's a girl.

LUCY'S SHOWBIZ SWAN SONG

Ricky is putting on a Gay Nineties revue at the club and Fred and Ethel have parts. Despite her larger than normal form, Lucy wants a role too. When she and Ethel are turned down for their act, "By the Light of the Silvery Moon," Lucy decides to crash the barbershop quartet. When they discover her trick, the shaving cream flies!

[154]
What is the name of Fred and Ethel's singing act?

[155]
Ricky expected _____ to be in the barber's chair.

[156]
True or False: Lucy and Ethel call their act Ricardo and Mertz.

Lucy: We can work up a cute song-and-dance number.

Ethel: I hope you're not thinking of me as part of "we."

Lucy: Sure, we'll be a couple!

Ethel: A couple of what?

If you watch this episode very carefully, you can see Lucille Ball pulling the waist string as she turns in the dance, thus allowing her bloomers to fall and the laughs to start.

The "4 Santas" skit appeared again as part of a holiday trailer at the end of this episode.

The "*I Love Lucy* Baby" doll, produced in 1952, appeared in Episodes 52 and 54. This collectible is highly sought after today, and buyers will pay high prices for dolls in good condition. This was probably one of the first products produced and marketed for a television show. Fifty years later, almost every show has some sort of collectible product connected to it. *I Love Lucy* and Desilu also produced and marketed baby furniture, comics, his and hers pajamas, and many other items.

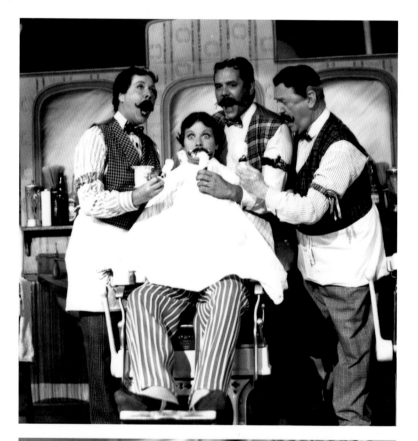

LUCY HIRES AN ENGLISH TUTOR

Lucy is ashamed of her English—and Ricky's! She hires Mr. Livermore to come and give the Ricardos and Mertzes lessons in proper grammar and speech so the baby will grow up knowing how to talk correctly. Ricky and the tutor make a secret deal: Mr. Livermore gets to sing his song at the club, and Ricky gets to end the lessons!

Mr. Livermore (sings): I tippy-tippy-toe through my garden, where all the pretty flowers dwell. There's a rare perfume in my garden, and I just love to stand there and smell. And as I tippy-tippy-toe along, all the pretty flowers seem to sing this song . . .

Ricky: Derry down pip pip

Lucy: Dilly dilly day

Ethel: Hey nonne nonne

Fred: Rippity pippity ay.

Fred: Derry down ding-dong

Ethel: Dilly dilly doo

Lucy: Hey nonne nonne

Ricky: Rippity pippity poo.

[157]
Mr. Livermore says they cannot say which three of these words?
a) okay
b) sure
c) lousy
d) swell

[158]
Lucy has cravings and sends Ricky out for what delicacy?

[159]
Ricky buys a _____, a _____, and a _____ for the baby.

In this episode, we learn that Lucy wants a girl who she can dress up in frilly clothes and fuss over, and Ricky wants a boy who will play football and box and win the jai alai pennant while attending Havana University. In real life, Lucille and Desi already had a girl (Lucie Desirée) and were hoping for a boy. They decided that the Ricardo baby would be a boy no matter what happened in real life with the Arnaz baby. Happily, nature complied with the script!

The writers make fun of Ricky's English with the words bough, rough, through, and cough. In real life, Desi Arnaz completed high school in Florida and was bilingual, speaking and reading both English and Spanish fluently.

RICKY HAS LABOR PAINS

Soon-to-be-mother Lucy is getting all the attention and Ricky feels left out. Fred decides to throw him a Daddy Shower, but Lucy and Ethel get suspicious that it's going to be more like a bachelor party and they decide to crash. Dressed as reporters from *The New York Herald Times Tribune*, they find it's all good clean fun.

[160]
Name the club where Fred hosts Ricky's Daddy Shower.

BONUS: What three animal heads hang on the wall?

[161]
After Lucy forgets to defrost the roast for dinner, what does she offer Ricky?

[162]
True or False: Lucy sends Ricky out for pistachio ice cream, hot fudge, and sardines.

Lucy (reads from newspaper column): Carrot-top Lucy Ricardo, formerly Lucy McGillicuddy, and currently one of show business's most beautiful wives, is infanticipating.

Lucy reads a *McCall's* magazine containing an article on *I Love Lucy*!

Ricky's doctor is Dr. Rabwin. The real Marcus Rabwin, M.D. was a dear friend and physician to Lucille and Desi.

In this episode, the reported discomfort between Vivian Vance and William Frawley appears to be at least partially true. While Lucy kisses Fred on the left cheek, Ethel barely manages to give him an air kiss on the right.

In June 1950, while on a vaudeville tour, Lucille Ball became pregnant. The lab that processed her test leaked word to gossip columnist Walter Winchell, who announced it to the country. Lucille and Desi heard it on the radio before they heard it from their doctor! Sadly, Lucille miscarried the baby.

LUCY BECOMES A SCULPTRESS

Lucy wants to surround the baby with artistic talent so she buys clay and commences to sculpt. Ricky thinks she has no talent but agrees to have an art critic come by and see her work. Lucy panics when she can't produce a good bust of herself so she covers her own head with clay. The art critic loves amazingly lifelike work of art and asks to buy it!

Lucy: Oh dear, surround him with music and art. If he wants to be a musician you can teach him. If he wants to be an artist . . . hey, who're we gonna get him to teach him about art?

Ricky: Well honey I wouldn't worry about it, it'll take care of itself somehow.

Lucy: Well now it's not that easy! Our child's artistic and cultural future is at stake. (pause while Ricky rolls his eyes) Well, there's just one thing for me to do.

Ricky: I know I shouldn't ask this, but what is it?

Lucy: I'll have to become an artist.

[163]
Name the art critic Ricky brings home to see Lucy's work.

BONUS: How much does he offer to pay for the bust of Lucy's head?

[164]
How much clay does Lucy buy?
a) 10 lbs
b) 20 lbs
c) 50 lbs
d) 75 lbs

[165]
Who does Lucy get to model for her?

Lucy and Ricky are again looking through Lucille and Desi's own scrapbooks and real photos. The childhood photos of "Lucy and Ricky" are true photos of Lucille and Desi—but the artistic-grandfather photo is not a real family member.

Lucy tells Ethel she has classic beauty, like the head on a Greek coin. Ethel is flattered, for a few seconds.

LUCY GOES TO THE HOSPITAL

Lucy is due any minute and the others are watching her like hawks. They calmly rehearse their duties, but when Lucy announces it's time to go, nothing goes as planned. Ricky has to leave the hospital to do his show. Fred waits in his place but when he calls Ricky to say, "It's a boy!" Ricky runs back in full voodoo make up!

[166]
What is the name of Lucy's obstetrician?

BONUS: What is her room number in the hospital?

[161]
Who does Ricky meet in the Father's Waiting Room?

[162]
True or False: Ricky calls Ethel to bring his makeup case.

Lucy (emerges from bedroom): Ricky, this is it.

Ricky/Ethel/Fred (pause, panicked): This is it!

Episode 56 is one of the classics of the series. Over seventy percent of the televisions in America were tuned in to see the show.

The riotous antics of Ricky, Ethel, and Fred when they are leaving for the hospital are truly amazing. That scene deserves to be in anyone's Hall of Fame. Pure comedy heaven.

Desi Arnaz, Jr. never appeared in this episode. The newborn baby was played by days-old James John Ganzer, and this was his only appearance on *I Love Lucy*.

Desi Arnaz, Jr. never appeared as Little Ricky at all. A four-year-old Desi was part of the crowd scene in the final episode of *I Love Lucy* ("Lucy Dedicates a Statue"). Contrary to myth, his sister, Lucie, was not.

NO CHILDREN ALLOWED

Neighbor Mrs. Trumble is complaining about Little Ricky's crying. Her lease says no children allowed. Ethel sticks up for Lucy, but when she tells everyone she meets about her good deed, it gets boring fast. When Lucy notes her bragging, a fight ensues and Little Ricky is left alone! Never fear, he is found safe—in the arms of Mrs. Trumble.

[169]
In the first scene, who manages to get Little Ricky to sleep?

BONUS: Who later wakes him up?

[170]
According to Lucy, to whom did Ethel relate her story of heroism?

[171]
Lucy says Ethel's scene has had "more performances than _____."

Vivian Vance slips while she is relating her story to the bridge club and calls the neighbor Mrs. Trimble instead of Mrs. Trumble.

Later Lucy, tired of hearing Ethel relate her story to everyone in town, argues with Ricky when he says Ethel did a nice thing. "Nice yes," she says, "but Ethel acts like she discovered penicillin!"

This is the first episode in which twins Richard Lee and Ronald Lee Simmons appear. They took turns playing the part of Little Ricky for the remainder of this season only, and earned $25 each per episode.

Ethel (arguing with disgruntled tenant Mrs. Trumble):
Don't worry Lucy. We can rent that apartment just like that. And even if we couldn't it wouldn't matter, because my friendship with the Ricardos means more to me than all the money on earth.

LUCY HIRES A MAID

New mommy Lucy is exhausted with caring for Little Ricky, so Big Ricky suggests they hire a maid to do the housework. Lucy doesn't pick well and ends up with a woman who does little and eats much. But how to get rid of her? Lucy and Ethel decide to mess up the apartment so she'll quit. They do, but find out later that Ricky already fired her!

[172]
What fabulous lunch does Mrs. Porter serve to Lucy?

BONUS: What does Mrs. Porter eat?

[173]
Ethel says the Ricardos owe how much back rent?
a) three months
b) two months
c) one month
d) they are all paid up

[174]
True or False: Lucy makes a paste of peanut butter, mustard, and molasses.

Ricky: Well, the father is the breadwinner. See, the father is supposed to get his rest at night so he can get up fresh in the morning, go out into the world, and make money for his family.

Lucy: You wouldn't tell me the rules before the game started. The next time we have a baby I get to be the father.

In Episode 58 there is a mug on the kitchen shelf that says "Lucy."

Lucy wants to give Mrs. Porter the following rules for working for her: she must cook, clean, do laundry and ironing, and help care for the baby. She can have Thursdays off and Sunday afternoons, she must come before 8 AM and cannot leave before 8:30 PM. Mrs. Porter, on the other hand, makes the following demands: she gets Wednesdays off and every weekend, she works from 9 AM–7 PM only and she will not take care of the baby or his laundry.

THE INDIAN SHOW

Ricky is staging a new show at the club, and guess who wants in? Ricky hires the Mertzes but says no to Lucy—she is a mother now and must stay home. Lucy makes a plan with singer Juanita to take her place in the song, "By the Waters of the Minnetonka." Ricky wants to know where Little Ricky is? He's being taken care of—papoose style!

[175]
When two actors dressed as Indians come to the Ricardo apartment, what do Lucy and Ethel do?

[176]
True or False: The afternoon is the only time Juanita can be with her baby.

[177]
What book is Ricky reading?

BONUS: Why does he say he is reading it?

RICKY (TO FRED):
LUCY'S A MOTHER NOW. SHE'S PERFECTLY HAPPY JUST STAYING AT HOME AND TAKING CARE OF THE BABY.

Fred comes over to fix the sink in the kitchen. Seems that particular sink needs fixing quite a bit—he just fixed it in Episode 10.

Lucy claims Little Ricky laughed aloud for the first time when she made a face at him.

Fred and Ethel do a number to the song, "Pass that Peacepipe."

97

LUCY'S LAST BIRTHDAY

Friend of the Friendless (relates his story): I didn't have a friend in the world. I was just a bit of flotsam in the sea of life, a pitiful outcast shunned by my fellow man. I was a mess.

Lucy thinks everyone has forgotten her birthday. After Mrs. Trumble fails to make her feel better with cake and confetti, Lucy goes out for a walk. She meets up with a group called Friends of the Friendless and decides to go to Ricky's club to tell her husband how upset she is. When she sees he has arranged a surprise party she is speechless.

Ricky is seen giving a round of applause for "Pugh and Carroll," a contortionist act. Of course, Madelyn Pugh and Bob Carroll, Jr. were two of the *I Love Lucy* scribes, who did occasionally appear in *I Love Lucy* episodes.

Ethel lies and says that she is going to dinner with the head of Fred's lodge.

At one point Lucy wails to Mrs. Trumble, "Sure I wanted him to forget my birthday. But he forgot my birthday!"

This is the first and only time that we hear the lyrics to the theme song, "I Love Lucy."

THE RICARDOS CHANGE APARTMENTS

The Ricardos need more space. Ricky says a larger place will cost too much, but Lucy finds a couple in the building who need a smaller place, so they decide to switch. Lucy, Fred, and Ethel switch all the furniture but are shocked later when it's switched back! Ricky unwittingly hired a moving man who came and undid all their work!

Ricky's pronunciation leaves a little to be desired when he tells Lucy he "won swish apartments."

Lucy complains to Ricky, "Little Ricky is gonna get awfully cramped sleeping in that crib until he's twenty-one years old."

The Bensons live in 3B, right down the hall from Fred and Ethel. Their apartment has one extra bedroom and a large living room window (so Lucy can crawl in and out when she needs to!).

[181]
What does Ethel come over to borrow from Lucy?

BONUS: Where does Lucy go to get it?

[82]
How many years has Ethel lived in the apartment building?
a) 14
b) 15
c) 16
d) 17

[183]
True or False: Fred offers to treat for ice cream after the moving is over.

Lucy (trying to get Ricky to switch apartments): Kiss me.

Ricky: I can't afford it.

Lucy: What do you mean, you can't afford it?

Ricky: That kiss will cost me $20 a month.

LUCY IS MATCHMAKER

Lucy sets up her friend Sylvia Collins with handsome, eligible bachelor Eddie Grant. When Sylvia can't make the date, Lucy goes to the meeting place to explain, but Eddie thinks Lucy wants to be alone with him! Lucy and Ethel wind up in Eddie's hotel room trying on the lingerie he sells when Ricky and Fred show up!

[184]
Where are Eddie and Sylvia supposed to meet?

[185]
Eddie's hotel room is number
_____ .

[186]
What was the retail price of the negligee Ethel wanted?
a) $129.50
b) $98.50
c) $115.50
d) $69.50

Lucy: We have to find Sylvia a husband.

Ethel: A husband?

Lucy: Yeah, it's our only chance. Now where can we find her a husband?

Ethel: I'll make the sacrifice. She can have mine.

When Eddie Grant calls Fred at his apartment he dials Circle 7-2099. Eddie is a friend of Fred's, although he is decades younger.

The bridge group complains about Sylvia, with one member saying, "You know she didn't even light her own cigarette once? Every time I looked up some man was racing across the room with a lighted match." Lucy chimes in with, "Looked like the start of the Olympic Games."

Lucy's negligee retailed for $139.50, more than double the price she usually pays for a dress.

LUCY WANTS NEW FURNITURE

Lucy buys new furniture without Ricky's consent. When Ricky finds out he blows his Cuban top. She can have the furniture when she has saved enough from her allowance. Lucy gives herself a home perm and tries to make a party dress. The results are disastrous, but Ricky takes pity and Lucy gets her furniture after all.

Lucy suddenly wants to get rid of her "ratty old couch." Funny, she got that couch six months before, when she won it in the "Home Show" drawing!

Ricky is referred to as Señor Tightwad.

In order to "save money" (or more likely to make Ricky so mad he gives in and lets her have the furniture) Lucy washes Ricky's new suit in the kitchen sink. After all, he told her to cut down on some of her 'stravagances.

Lucy left her home permanent on for five hours.

[187]
True or False: The sofa and coffee table Lucy bought cost $299.

[188]
What three items does Ricky ask Lucy to get in the kitchen?

[189]
After she made her own dress and did her own hair, who does Fred think Lucy resembles?

BONUS: What does Lucy think she looks like?

Ricky: Where's the butter?

Lucy: (surprised) Butter?

Ricky: Yeah butter.

Lucy: What do you want to do with it?

Ricky: I thought I'd put some on my bread.

Lucy: Butter on bread?

Ricky: Yeah.

Lucy: I'll never get used to your strange Cuban dishes.

THE CAMPING TRIP

Lucy wants to join Ricky on a "boys weekend," so Ricky takes her on a trial run camping trip to see how she likes it. Lucy schemes with Ethel to help out by bringing fish so Lucy won't have to catch them, and driving so Lucy won't have to hike. Ricky finds them out and in the end Lucy agrees that she's better off at home.

[190]
What couple is getting a separation?
a) Carolyn and Charlie
b) Marion and Norman
c) Jane and Steven
d) Joanne and Greg

[191]
During an evening conversation, Ricky tries to talk to Lucy about _____.

[192]
How many fish does Ethel bring to Lucy?

BONUS: What kind of fish are they?

Club member: Oh come now, Lucy. Every marriage reaches a point when the honeymoon's over.

Ethel: Yeah, our honeymoon was over on our honeymoon!

The partnership of Ricardo and Mertz won 25¢ at the ladies bridge game. Later Ricky bets Lucy $5 that he will beat her back to camp. Ai yi yi! When he stumbles into camp, breathless, there she is—relaxed and rested. Of course, she got back via a station wagon courtesy of Ethel, while Ricky spent three hours stumbling through the woods!

Ethel can drive in this episode, but less than a year and a half later she claims she never learned.

RICKY'S LIFE STORY

Ricky gets a spread in *LIFE* magazine, and Lucy wants some fame for herself. Fred convinces Ricky to show Lucy how hard show biz really is, so he puts her in a number at the club and rehearses her until she collapses. When she realizes what Ricky did she manages to get into another number and completely upstages him.

[193]
Name the title of the article about Ricky.

[194]
True or False: Lucy practiced her dance routine for a week.

[195]
Ricky's story got more pages than what other story?
a) "The Two-Headed Alligator"
b) "The Rebuilding of Berlin"
c) "The Dionne Quintuplets Turn 18"
d) "The Blind Bullfighter"

Lucy (complaining): I don't want my arm in there, I want my face in there. For heaven's sake. If I'd known what they were up to, I'd have held the baby in my mouth!

Watch this episode for the "challenge" dance routine with Lucy and Ricky. He is as cool as a cucumber while she collapses from the strain.

Lucy practiced her challenge routine six hours a day. Later, she is perfection as she stands behind him while he sings—performing magic tricks, gymnastic feats, and a tightrope act.

RICKY AND FRED ARE TV FANS

Lucy and Ethel are "boxing widows." They go out for a bite but find everyone at the drug store is watching the fights too! Lucy needs some change but no one helps her, so she reaches into the cash register and is arrested for stealing! What can she do now? The home phone is off the hook and Ricky's glued to the TV. Help!

[196]
Ricky reads the *TV Guide*—who is on the cover?

[197]
Name the counterman in the drug store where Lucy and Ethel get arrested.
a) Sam
b) Pete
c) Max
d) Charlie

[198]
Lucy and Ethel are accused of being criminals named _____ and _____.

LUCY:

MY HAIR IS NATURALLY RED. ISN'T IT ETHEL?

ETHEL:

UH, LOOK LUCY, LET'S NOT ADD PERJURY TO OUR OTHER CHARGES.

Ricky and Fred watch the fights. Fred has his money on a guy named Murphy, but we never hear the name of the other guy.

When Lucy asks Sergeant Nelson to call Ricky at home she gives the phone number MH5-9975.

Lucy and Ethel are hauled in to the 31st Precinct.

Lucy laments that the only way she and Ethel can get their husbands' attention is to "put on trunks and fight each other in the Garden."

THERE WILL NEVER BE ANOTHER SHOW AS GREAT AS *I LOVE LUCY*. There will never be another ensemble as great as Lucy, Ricky, Fred, and Ethel. There. That's all that needs to be said. But I promised a whole page, so here goes:

Everyone's always looking for the colorful side of life, but the Ricardos and the Mertzes proved to us that things are pretty hilarious in glorious black and white. I count myself among the hundreds of millions of "happy, peppy people" who have seen all 179 episodes literally dozens of times.

I know all the schemes, dreams, payoffs, and putdowns. And yet, as I now share the show with my kids, I can't help but feel the exhilaration of discovering true hilarity for the very first time.

What sets *I Love Lucy* apart from other shows is the feeling of believability. No matter how far out Lucy's antics get, we're there with her—selling the meat from a baby carriage, stealing John Wayne's footprints, out on a ledge as Superman, and so on. Thanks to Lucy, I learned the joys of stuffing my mouth with chocolates, stomping my own grapes for wine, and knowing not to stop at anything in my quest to "be in the show."

Ricky is the "I" in *I Love Lucy*. But for the past fifty years, it's clear that we love Lucy. And Ricky. And Fred. And Ethel. And Little Ricky. And Mrs. Trumble. And everyone and everything about this amazing show.

Believe me, if the day ever comes when I turn on the TV and there's no *I Love Lucy*, somebody's gonna have some 'splainin' to do!"

ROSIE O'DONNELL

THE THIRD SEASON

1953-1954

NEVER DO BUSINESS WITH FRIENDS

Ricky buys a new washer and the Mertzes buy his old one. Great deal, until the old one breaks down. Since the Mertzes never paid Ricky, they say he owns it. But he says they own it. When a handyman offers to pay $75 for it, everybody wants to own it! The four fight over it and it goes over the porch ledge—so no one owns it.

[199]
True or False: The Ricardos charge the Mertzes $35 to buy their old washing machine.

[200]
How much will Mrs. Trumble's nephew charge to fix the washing machine?
BONUS: What is his name?

[201]
What does Ethel want to do with her old washing machine?

Mrs. Trumble: Why Mrs. Ricardo, your temper is as hot as your red hair.

Lucy: And what about her?

Ethel: Oh mine's as cold as your dark roots!

Ethel complains that her washing machine was an old relic and probably one of the first ever made. In Episode 45 (broadcast only five months before) Fred had just bought her a new Handy Dandy Washing Machine!

This is the first episode in which Ricky uses his new phrase, "Honey, I'm home . . ."

110

THE GIRLS GO INTO BUSINESS

Lucy and Ethel buy a dress shop that they think is a gold mine. When it turns out to be a bust, and Lucy's check for the down payment bounces, they have to think fast. They sell the shop to a man who pays them $500 more than they paid. They think they are clever until they learn that he in turn sold it for thousands more!

While out shopping with Ethel, Lucy leaves her purse on the counter when she skips out of the store.

This episode was shot directly after Lucille Ball was cleared of being a communist by the House UnAmerican Activities Committee. During the 1950s, this Congressional group, lead by Senator Joseph McCarthy, ruined the careers of hundreds of left-leaning Hollywood actors, writers, producers, and directors. Lucille Ball (and her brother and mother) had registered

as a communist in 1936 to please her grandfather Hunt, although she had never voted for any communists. In December 1953, the *I Love Lucy* cast was invited to perform at the White House for Eisenhower's birthday, signaling to the country that the President had accepted Lucille's innocence.

This is the first episode in which the second set of twins, Joseph David and Michael Lee Mayer, appear as Little Ricky. The pair will play Little Ricky for three seasons.

[202]
What gift does Mrs. Hansen give to the two ladies who help her to "clinch the deal" with Lucy and Ethel?
a) sweaters
b) belts
c) scarves
d) handbags

[203]
What Spanish sentence does Ricky repeat to Mrs. Hansen over the phone?

[204]
Mr. Ralph S. Boyer buys the dress shop from Lucy and Ethel for $3,500 and then sells it for $_____.

Lucy: But Ricky, a dress shop is just the thing for you.

Ricky: Look, I already own a dress shop.

Lucy: What do you mean you already own a dress shop?

Ricky: Have you looked in your closet lately?

LUCY AND ETHEL BUY THE SAME DRESS

[205]
According to Lucy, Cuba's second biggest import is _____.

[206]
Match the club member with her special talent

Lou Ann Hall	recites the poem "Trees"
Jane Sebastian	impersonates Lionel Barrymore
Carolyn Appleby	plays piano
Rosalind McKee	does bird calls

[207]
Fred calls the Wednesday Afternoon Fine Arts League by what other name?

Lucy and Ethel are doing a duet in the talent show on TV, singing and dancing to the Cole Porter song, "Friendship." They buy identical evening gowns and each agrees to return hers and get something else. But, both in love with the gown, they each keep it and end up on TV in the same dress. Not for long—they begin ripping them off each other!

(Singing) Ethel: If you're ever in a jam, here I am.

Lucy: If you're ever in a mess, S.O.S.

Ethel: If you ever get so happy you land in jail, I'm your bail.

Both: It's friendship, friendship, just a perfect blendship, when other friendships have been forgot . . . ours will still be hot.

Ethel: If you're ever up a tree, phone to me.

Lucy: If you're ever down a well, ring my bell.

Ethel: If you ever lose your dough when you're out to dine, borrow mine.

Both: It's friendship, friendship, just a perfect blendship, when other friendships have been forgate . . . ours will still be great.

Ethel: If they ever black your eyes, put me wise.

Lucy: If they ever cook your goose, turn me loose.

Ethel: If they ever put a bullet right through your brain, I'll complain.

Both: It's friendship, friendship, just a perfect blendship, when other friendships have been forgit . . . ours will still be it.

Marion Strong announces that she was once Mistress of Ceremonies for the Senior Shenanigans at the Rappahanock School for Girls.

Ethel bought her dress at Macy's and Lucy bought hers at Gimble's.

The TV show is on from midnight until 12:30AM.

Ethel's middle name in this episode is Louise.

EQUAL RIGHTS

The wives want to be treated equally, so while dining out the husbands refuse to pay their checks, and Lucy and Ethel are forced to wash dishes. The girls get even by calling home and pretending they are being attacked. Ricky and Fred think it will be funny to trick back by pretending to be crooks—until the police arrive and arrest them!

This foursome can really eat! In this episode they go to dinner and order spaghetti and meatballs, pizza, steak, and salad.

When the episode opens Fred and Ethel are discussing a story about some land they owned in Miami, Florida.

When Lucy and Ethel call pretending they are being held up, Ricky is so frantic that he calls the police and yells in Spanish.

Lucy thinks there are so many dishes because the restaurant takes in all the dirty dishes from the other restaurants.

Ethel washes and Lucy dries.

[208]
When the women touch-up their make-up at the table, what do the men do?
a) laugh at them
b) comb their hair
c) shave
d) floss

[209]
According to Fred, women can now go everywhere except _____.

[210]
True or False: Lucy keeps everyone waiting while her hair dries.

Lucy: I don't know how you treat your women in Cuba, but this is the United States. And I have my rights.

Ricky: I'm not arguing about women's rights. I am the first one to agree that women should have all the rights they want, as long as they stay in their place

BABY PICTURES

The Applebys brag about Stevie and the Ricardos can't stand it. So Lucy drops by to visit Carolyn and insults both she and Stevie! Later Charlie Appleby calls to cancel Ricky's job on his TV show. To get Ricky's job back Lucy is forced to eat humble pie and have Ricky introduce the TV audience to the "world's cutest baby"—Stevie.

[211]
What was Ethel cooking that she burned?
a) pot roast
b) steak
c) pork chops
d) chicken

[212]
What amazing feat did Little Stevie Appleby accomplish?

BONUS: How old is Stevie?

[213]
Ethel grumbles, "The way the Applebys act, you'd think they _____."

LUCY:

WHAT KIND OF SHOW? WHEN'S IT GONNA BE? WHO'S GONNA BE IN IT?

RICKY:

VARIETY, NEXT THURSDAY, AND NOT YOU.

Charlie Appleby tells everyone to be on the look-out for some great new talent—Conway Turrell and Mable Norman, actors on his TV station.

Lucy gets mad at Ethel and says, "One more remark like that and you can turn in your Godmother suit."

Lucy claims Little Ricky speaks Spanish—but only when he's mad.

Carolyn implies that Little Ricky is fat.

LUCY TELLS THE TRUTH

Ricky and the Mertzes bet that Lucy can't go twenty-four hours without telling a lie. The next day at bridge she has to tell her real age, weight, and hair color. When she auditions for a movie, she can't fudge her way out of her lack of résumé. She does get a chance to be part of a knife-throwing act, but bolts when the daggers start flying.

The bet is for $100—Ricky bets $50 and Fred and Ethel each bet $25.

The Applebys have done some fast redecorating—in the previous episode they had early American furniture and in a week changed the whole apartment to Chinese modern.

The new Lucy calls Ethel, "Old Sneaky," and says Fred is a tightwad, Ethel is a tacky dresser, and Ricky is hammy, stubborn, and a coward.

[214]
Lucy says about Carolyn's new furniture: "Looks like a dream you'd have after _____."

[215]
During the bridge game, Ethel, Carolyn, and Marion get an earful from the newly honest Lucy. According to her, what are their faults?

[216]
Ricky is surprised to receive flowers. Who sent them?

BONUS: Why?

Carolyn: Lucy, how old are you?

Marion: How much do you weigh?

Ethel: What color would your hair be if you didn't dye it?

Lucy: 33, 129, and mousy brown.

THE FRENCH REVUE

After being embarrassed in a French restaurant, Lucy hires waiter Robert DuBois to give her lessons *en français*. DuBois's fee is that he be allowed to audition for Ricky. Ricky blows his top, but later decides to stage a French revue that features DuBois, which Lucy tries to crash as a lamp shade, a cello case, and a rotund madame!

[217]
How long was Fred in France during World War I?
a) three days
b) three weeks
c) three months
d) three years

[218]
In the French restaurant the gang places an order for four servings of _____.

[219]
Name the French song everyone has on his lips.

Lucy: Listen, Carolyn said that the menus are all written in French. Do you know how to read French?

Ricky: Sure I can read it.

Lucy: Oh good.

Ricky: But I can't understand it.

Lucy has bet Ricky she can sneak into the Tropicana to be part of the show. She dresses up as a janitor carrying a lamp (with the shade over her head), as a worker with a huge painting that needs to be hung (with a wig over her face), as a bass instrument case, and as an old dumpy French lady. This is five minutes of comic genius from all the actors involved.

REDECORATING THE MERTZES' APARTMENT

Ethel is ashamed to hold club meetings at her home so Lucy offers to redo the Mertzes' living room by holding a painting-and-reupholstering party, but before the paint is dry on the walls the feathers from Fred's favorite chair start flying! Waaaaah! The Mertzes inherit the Ricardos' furniture and Lucy and Ricky get a new set.

Lucille Ball makes a rare mistake when she says, "paint the furniture and reupholster the old furniture." Desi covers for her nicely.

In this episode the Mertzes have lived in the apartment for twenty years. The previous season, in Episode 61, they had only lived there for sixteen years.

Fred is called a "penny-pinching old goat." At the end of the episode we learn what happened to the mink Lucy was going to get from Ricky—it turned into her new living-room furniture.

[220]
Mrs. Trumble charges _____ for an hour of babysitting.
BONUS: How much does she charge for overtime?

[221]
What is Fred having for breakfast when he and Ethel are fighting?

[222]
What color does Fred think would be nice for the living room walls?
a) orange
b) yellow
c) white
d) blue

Ricky (talking about the mink he is buying for Lucy): I wish you wouldn't make such a point about how 'spensive it's gonna be. After all, I'm getting it wholesale.

Lucy: Shhhhh. No one's supposed to know that but you, me, and the mink.

Ricky: What's the difference who knows?

Lucy: I want people to think you love me retail, not 40% off.

TOO MANY CROOKS

Cat burglar "Madame X" is on the loose. Lucy and Ricky decide to buy Fred a suit for his birthday, but when Lucy sneaks into the Mertzes' closet to borrow a suit for measurements, Ethel assumes the worst! Lucy spots Ethel in disguise and thinks she is the thief! Ricky catches the real robber and everyone breathes a sigh of relief.

[223]
What does Ethel buy as a gift for Fred's birthday?

[224]
Who owns the silver service that Madame X tries to steal from Lucy's closet?
a) Lucy
b) Ethel
c) Lucy's mother
d) Ricky's mother

[225]
What is engraved on Ricky's silver cigarette case?

Ricky: What's a pretext?

Lucy: Well, it's when you want someone to do something but you don't want them to know that you want them to do that particular something, so you make up something else. Then they think they're just doing that something else, but in reality they're doing the something that you want them to do, but don't want them to know that you want them to do.

When this episode opens the Ackermans' apartment has just been robbed. In real life, Harry Ackerman was a CBS executive who worked closely with Lucille and Desi.

Mrs. Trumble is the one who sees Lucy sneaking out of the Mertzes' apartment with Fred's suit.

CHANGING THE BOYS' WARDROBE

Lucy and Ethel are disgusted with their husbands' choice of clothing, so they scheme to get rid of the old stuff on the sly. At the same time Ricky is named one of the ten best-dressed men. Ricky asks Lucy and Ethel to come to the club all dressed up, but they arrive in the boys' rags—just in time to have their picture snapped. Waaaaah!

[226]
At what store does Ricky pretend he bought his "new" clothes?
a) Lord and Taylor
b) Brooks Brothers
c) Allen's Clothing for Men
d) Fauntleroy's

[227]
To what store do Lucy and Ethel "donate" their husbands' old clothes?

[228]
Ricky's sweater says _____ on the back.

Ethel shows Lucy Fred's old sweater that says Golden Gloves 1909. That sweater is over forty years old!

Fred looks so awful in his old clothes that Ethel calls him "Raggedy Andy."

Lucy and Ethel lie and say that they cleaned the old clothes in gasoline and they burned up!

Ethel wants to wear her blue crepe dress to the club, but Lucy convinces her to wear the old clothes.

Lucy: Honestly, I don't know what's taking so long, I guess he's having trouble getting those old blue jeans off without breaking them.

Ethel: He's really attached to those pants isn't he?

Lucy: Sometimes I think it's vice versa. You know he doesn't hang 'em up in the closet, he stands 'em up in the corner.

LUCY HAS HER EYES EXAMINED

[229]
Translate the following:
Parker Preps Prod for Pitt
Preme.

[230]
When Lucy sends Ricky out
to buy ice cream, who gives
it to him instead?
a) Mrs. Trumble
b) Miss Lewis
c) Mrs. Benson
d) Ethel

BONUS: What kind does Lucy
want?

[231]
True or False: Mr. Parker
wants Fred and Ethel for the
graduation scene in his play.

Fred: Whad'ya want?

Ethel: I wanted to
tell you to be sure
and sandpaper that
new banister you put
in before some idiot
runs his hand down
it and picks up a
splinter. Whadda you
want?

Fred: I was wondering
if you'd help me get
this splinter out of my
hand.

Lucy and the Mertzes find out a producer is about to cast a new musical, and they manage to wrangle an audition! Meanwhile, Lucy drags Ricky to the eye doctor, but it is she who needs her vision checked. The doc dilates her pupils and the world becomes a big blur. After that her jitterbug audition is, shall we say, Lucy-esque.

The Mertzes are hired as actors in *The Professor and the Co-Ed.* For their audition, they do a great Charleston dance to the music of "The Varsity Drag." Ethel wears a fringed dress and sequined flapper cap while Fred looks jaunty in his stripped jacket, argyle socks, and plus-fours! However, even though their audition is flawless and Mr. Parker wants them in the show, it is never mentioned again by anyone.

RICKY'S OLD GIRL FRIEND

While taking a marriage quiz, Lucy teases Ricky with a list of all her former beaus. Ricky teases back with Carlota Romero, a woman he thinks he made up, but who turns out to be real and in town! Lucy gets angry and her jealousy-meter goes off. But when Carlota comes to dinner, Lucy can see she has nothing to worry about.

[232]
When Ethel suggests playing cards, Lucy says they can't because Little Ricky ate the _____.

[233]
Which one of these men did Lucy not date before she met Ricky?
a) Charlie
b) Argyle
c) Jess
d) Bennett

[234]
In Lucy's dream, how many weeks is Ricky and Carlota's act held over?

Lucy (crying about Carlota): Well, she's here now. I'll bet they're planning to stir those old embers again.

Ethel: Be kind of hard to stir embers into a flame after fifteen years.

Lucy: She doesn't look like her pilot light would ever go out. Waaaaah!

The Ricardos are reading the *New York Gazette*. The headline is "Bond Issue Defeated." The marriage quiz is called, "How to Rate Your Marriage, OR Is Your Spouse a Louse?"

After this episode originally aired, the famous "4 Santas" skit was aired. This is the third and last time this happened.

Fred is called the king of the bellyachers.

Ricky actually worked with the Five Romero Sisters fifteen years ago in Havana.

THE MILLION-DOLLAR IDEA

[235]
While trying to avoid Ricky's questioning of her overdrawn bank account, how many pastries does Lucy eat?
a) six
b) ten
c) twelve
d) all of them

[236]
How many tablespoons full of salt does Ethel add to each batch of salad dressing?

BONUS: How much did all the groceries cost?

[237]
"Average housewife" Isabella Klump (a.k.a Lucy) asks, "Aunt _____, Old _____, salad _____?"

Lucy has used her allowance for the next twenty-five years, so to make extra money she and Ethel plan to sell homemade salad dressing on TV. They are great salesladies and get hundreds of orders but Ricky explains they are losing money on each jar! It's back to the drawing board, and the TV station, with hilarious results.

Ethel: You sound just like Fred Mertz.

Lucy: Fred?

Ethel: Yep. Ever since we've been married he's been trying to think of one idea worth a million dollars.

Lucy: Oh, none of his ideas any good huh?

Ethel: Oh, he had some good ideas, but somebody always got to the Patent Office first. He's still mad at Edison for beating him to the electric light. And he's never forgiven Ford for scooping him with the horseless carriage.

It's Fred's idea to sell the salad dressing.

Lucille Ball makes a rare mistake when in one part of a scene she states they have completed 1,153 orders, but a few moments later tells Ricky she has only 1,133 jars.

The jars of dressing the girls bought at the market cost 50¢ each, and they are selling them for 40¢ each. This is a total loss of $115.30 for Lucy and Ethel.

In this episode, Ethel's middle name is Roberta.

RICKY MINDS THE BABY

Ricky has a week off and wants to spend it with his son. Lucy is thrilled at first but then experiences severe separation anxiety. When Ricky and Fred get wrapped up in a TV show and Little Ricky wanders off, Lucy decides to teach Daddy Ricky a good lesson. But as with most of her schemes, Lucy is the one confused in the end.

By 1954, *I Love Lucy* was seen by US Armed Forces all over the globe.

In this episode Mrs. Trumble has a cat. In later episodes Lucy and Ricky will get in trouble for having a dog, although Fred had one in Episode 4.

When Little Ricky is missing and Lucy calls to speak to him, Ricky stammers, "Little Busy's Ricky now."

Desi Arnaz shines early in this episode with his minutes-long pantomime of "Little Red Riding Hood," which he performs for Little Ricky in Spanish.

The Mertzes now claim to have been married only twenty-three years.

Lucy: I can arrange for you to spend seven glorious days at 623 East 68th Street. The cuisine is wonderful, the rates are reasonable, and we have facilities for all the popular sports such as vacuuming, washing dishes, hanging diapers out to dry.

Ricky: Now, Lucy . . .

Lucy: Besides, there's a gentleman who lives in the neighborhood who's just dying to meet you. He's heard a lot about you and I think it's high time you two got together.

Ricky: Who's that?

Lucy: His name is Ricky Ricardo, Jr.

Ricky: You mean Little Ricky?

Lucy: Oh, then you have heard of him!

[238]
Why does Ricky have a week off from work?
a) they are recarpeting the club
b) he gave the band the week off
c) they are redoing the club's kitchen
d) they are repainting the club

[239]
Ricky makes what breakfast for himself?
BONUS: What does he feed Little Ricky?

[240]
What were Ricky's original plans for his vacation?

THE CHARM SCHOOL

[241]
What scores did Ethel and Lucy get on Phoebe Emerson's free charm analysis?

[242]
True or False: Eve Whitney is an actress.

[243]
Miss Emerson pays Ethel a "compliment," saying she is "_____."

Lucy: Wait a minute, look around you.

Ethel: Whatsa matter?

Lucy: It's happened again.

Lou Ann Hall: What has?

Lucy: The great divide. Same thing happens every time we have party. Look in here. (The ladies go to the kitchen, see men inside talking about golf.)

Lucy: See what I mean? Women in one room, men in the other.

Ethel: Well?

Lucy: What do you mean well? Why does it have to be that way? Why aren't we all in here talking together? Give me one good reason.

Ethel: We're married.

Lucy and Ethel decide that they need to "glam up" a bit. They check into Phoebe Emerson's charm school for a crash course in putting on the ritz. Ricky and Fred, however, are less than charmed when they see what their wives have become. In the end they agree to go back to being "four natural, lovable slobs."

Ricky, Fred, and Tom Williams discuss the coming of color TV. In 1954, CBS considered shooting future *I Love Lucy* episodes in color, but the idea never came to be. Legend has it that Jess Oppenheimer nixed the idea, saying that color was useless for comedy shows unless it enhanced the comedy. At the time, color TV sets were very expensive (about $1,200 each).

Eve Whitney is played by Eve Whitney Maxwell, wife of Eddie Maxwell (co-writer of the song "There's A Brand New Baby at Our House").

SENTIMENTAL ANNIVERSARY

Lucy would like to spend a quiet evening alone with Ricky to celebrate their thirteenth anniversary. The Mertzes, however, have planned a surprise party! As soon as Lucy and Ricky sit down to exchange gifts (both prove to be horrible peekers), the Mertzes arrive to set up! In the end, the party goes off without a "hitch."

Desi Arnaz loved to play golf—in 1953 he built a home in Palm Springs alongside a golf course so he could play on weekends.

In this episode the Ricardos were married thirteen years, also true for Lucille and Desi.

Lucy and Ricky reminisced about their marriage, again using real Arnaz scrapbooks and photos.

[244]
Where has Ricky hidden Lucy's anniversary gift?
a) at the Mertzes
b) under the bed
c) in the piano bench
d) in the closet

BONUS: What did he buy her?

[245]
To throw the Mertzes off the scent, Lucy tells them she and Ricky are having dinner with what famous couple?

[246]
Ricky says Lucy made _____ for their first anniversary dinner.

Ricky: These have been the best fifteen years of my life. (He goes to kiss Lucy but she pulls away.) Whatsa matter?

Lucy: We've only been married thirteen years.

Ricky: Oh, well I mean it seems like fifteen.

Lucy: What?!

Ricky: What I mean is, it doesn't seem possible that all that fun could have been crammed into only thirteen years.

FAN MAGAZINE INTERVIEW

Lucy and Ricky ham it up for an interview about a happily married couple. Then Ricky's agent comes up with a scheme to invite hundreds of women to the Tropicana to make Ricky look popular. Lucy finds one of the invitations and thinks Ricky has a girlfriend. Once Lucy meets the woman though, she smells a rat.

[247]
How many invitations to the Tropicana did Jerry send out in Ricky's name?
a) 3,000
b) 1,333
c) 2,300
d) 3,033

[248]
Complete this Lucy quote:
"_____ is the basis of every happy marriage."

[249]
What did Lucy serve for dinner when the reporter was there?

Lucy: If some woman was trying to take Fred away from you, you'd sing another tune.

Ethel: Yeah, "Happy Days Are Here Again."

Before this episode aired for the first time, Lucille and Desi made a public service announcement for fans across the country to send their dimes into the March of Dimes. They said that if each of their 45,000 viewers sent in only one dime apiece, they could collect $4.5 million. The address given was, "*I Love Lucy* March of Dimes, Hollywood 46, California."

This episode brings up the controversial Kinsey Reports on human sexuality, which came out in 1948 and 1953.

OIL WELLS

New neighbors from Texas move into the apartment building. The Ricardos and Mertzes buy shares of stock in an oil well and immediately start dreaming about the future. Later a detective drops by looking for the Texans and Lucy gets the idea that the well is going to be a bust. The minute they sell the shares back, the oil starts gushing!

[250]
How many shares of stock did Fred Mertz buy from Mr. Johnson?

BONUS: How much did they cost?

[251]
Thinking he was coming into millions, Ricky inquired about a custom built, periwinkle blue Cadillac with a horn that plays _____.

[252]
What are the first names of the Johnsons?
a) Susan and Frank
b) Nancy and Sam
c) Sally and Tom
d) Millie and Bud

Ethel (angry with Ricardos): If you're the kind of people we would have had to associate with if we were millionaires, I'm glad we were wiped out!

Ricky contemplates buying a brand new Cadillac with all the trimmings. Price tag? $12,000.

Ricky utters the famous line, "Don't cross your chickens before your bridges is hatched."

After this episode originally aired, Lucy and Desi did a quick pitch for their new movie, *The Long, Long Trailer*, which was released in early 1954 and was an immediate hit.

RICKY LOSES HIS TEMPER

Lucy buys yet another hat and Ricky is furious! His loss of temper leads to a bet—can Ricky control his temper longer than Lucy controls her urge to shop for hats? Lucy loses the bet when she passes a hat shop, but then tries to trick Ricky into losing his temper. Ricky finally calls off the bet, but when he finds out Lucy cheated—ai yi yi!

[253]
What is the name of the hat shop and who works there?

[254]
What is the color of the hat Lucy buys after she bets Ricky she won't buy anymore?
a) pink
b) black
c) cream
d) turquoise

[255]
Name three things that Lucy does to try to irritate Ricky and get him to lose his temper.

Ricky: Now dun't cry!

Lucy: Every time I spend a little money you lose your temper.

Ricky (yelling): What do you mean I lose my temper? I never lose my temper!

Lucy: Well you're the first person I ever saw whose veins bulge just because they have a good disposition.

There is some great physical comedy from Desi Arnaz in this episode when Lucy is trying to get him to lose his temper. Watch especially the kitchen scene when the tomato juice runs down the front of his white dinner jacket, and then Fred comes by with the ruined golf club. His calm demeanor does work to his advantage when he is able to hire an act for $250 instead of $500.

At the end of the episode Ricky claims that he is going to be "the happiest, calmest man in the whole world." That lasts for all of two minutes.

HOME MOVIES

Ricky is miffed that Lucy, Ethel, and Fred do not want to watch his home movies for the hundredth time. When he tells them they cannot be part of his TV pilot film, they decide to make one of their own. Lucy edits the two films together, along with the home movies of Little Ricky, and to Ricky's surprise, the TV exec loves it!

Lucy claims to have visited Hollywood before.

The TV exec tells her, "Mrs. Ricardo, you are married to a genius!"

The film that Ricky shows is beautifully done—upside down shots, slow motion and reverse motion—and the real editors at Desilu should be commended for this piece of comedy.

Ricky titles his film *Ricky Ricardo Presents Tropical Rhythms.*

[256]
While trying to get Ricky off the subject of home movies, Fred talks about the milkshake he had that day. What flavor was it?

[257]
Name the TV executive who is coming to view Ricky's TV pilot.
a) Lou Nicoletti
b) Harry Ackerman
c) Bennett Green
d) Maury Thompson

[258]
True of False: Ethel's role in the western is named "Nevada."

FRED:
I'M JUST DYING TO SEE THOSE LOUSY MOVIES AGAIN.

BONUS BUCKS

A newspaper has a contest to match the numbers on dollar bills. Ricky finds a winning buck but Lucy gives it away in change and Ethel ends up with it. After much fighting, they decide to split the prize money, but Lucy's half goes out to the laundry! After Lucy falls in the vat of starch at the laundry and racks up $299 in expenses, the deal is all washed up.

[259]
What item does Ricky not find in Lucy's purse?
a) a baby toy
b) paper clips
c) a library card
d) a change purse

[260]
The name of the laundry the Ricardos use is _____.

[261]
How much money does Lucy owe the grocery boy?

LUCY (GRABBING DOLLAR):

NOW YOU HEARD WHAT FRED SAID— POSSESSION IS NINE POINTS OF THE LAW, AND I'M POSSESSED!

The "bonus buck" Ricky finds in his pocket is numbered B78455629G, and is worth $300 if they can get it to the newspaper office by 3 PM.

Ethel is known as Miss Walkie Talkie.

The gang had to pay $29 for the taxi plus a $25 tip, $10 for overalls, $50 fine for speeding, and $185 for damage caused at the laundry.

Ricky mentions that there are 8 million people living in New York City.

RICKY'S HAWAIIAN VACATION

Ricky is going to Hawaii, and Lucy and the gang want to go. Ricky says no, so Lucy gets mixed up with the *Be a Good Neighbor* TV show. Fred and Ethel (along with their ancient "mother") will get a free trip to Hawaii if Lucy performs a series of stunts. When Ricky gets wind of the plan, the trio waves aloha to Hawaii.

Hawaii was a very special vacation spot for the Arnaz family.

Mrs. Cleo Morgan, mentioned as a "good neighbor" for Mrs. Weston, is the name of Lucille Ball's cousin, who was later the producer of the *Here's Lucy* show.

They call Lucy "Mother Mertz" even though she is supposed to be Ethel's mother.

Ricky calls his sidekicks the Dead Weight Trio.

[262]
What prizes did Freddy Fillmore award to Mrs. Weston and her family?

[263]
True or False: Ricky is making very little money on this trip.

[264]
Name the one item which is not dumped on Lucy's head during Be A Good Neighbor:
a) tea
b) honey
c) eggs
d) water

Ethel: I told you to watch out for a trick. I'm not going to Honolulu as Lucy's mother, that's what's wrong with that.

Fred: Oh, listen, if it'll get us to Honolulu, I'll go as her mother!

LUCY IS ENVIOUS

Lucy's wealthy former school chum calls and asks her to donate "five" to charity. Lucy and Ethel each agree, not knowing that "five" means $500! To make money they answer an ad for "two girls with courage" to go to the top of the Empire State Building dressed as Martians and abduct an Earthling. "Zorch! It's a moo-moo."

[265]
Name Lucy's school friend.

[266]
Where did Lucy and Ethel find the ad for the job?
a) *The New York Times*
b) *Billboard*
c) *Variety*
d) *The Daily News*

[267]
Tourist Martha is looking for _____ through the telescope viewer.

Ricky: There you go again, wanting something that you haven't got.

Lucy: I do not, I just wanna see what it is I haven't got that I don't want!

The rich friend calls Ethel "Mrs. Hertz."

In their quest for extra cash Lucy found 51¢, a button, a nail file, and a piece of old Christmas candy in the couch; Ethel found 76¢ in one of Fred's old coats.

Lucy tells her rich friend that to make their "yacht" fit in the West Palm Beach harbor they "crank down the smoke stack and squeeze in the poop deck."

LUCY WRITES A NOVEL

Lucy writes her first novel and Ricky, Ethel, and Fred are less than amused. The novel is chosen to be published, but later the publisher reveals that a mistake was made and Lucy's novel did not make the cut. Later a writer offers to print portions of it in a book about how to write a novel in the chapter, "Don't Let This Happen to You."

In this episode you will see Ricky Ricardo eat his straw hat.

Lucy's publisher, Mr. Dorrance, asks her to call a writer, Mel Eaton, at Plaza 5-2099.

This episode is the first time the Ricardo fireplace has been used during the series. Ricky, Ethel, and Fred light a fire to burn Lucy's manuscript.

Dorrance Publishing Company, Inc. is located in Pittsburgh, Pennsylvania.

[268]
Where do Ricky, Fred, and Ethel find Lucy's manuscript?
a) under the couch cushions
b) in a hat box
c) in the linen closet
d) in the kitchen blinds

[269]
What is the publisher's excuse for the mix-up in "accepting" Lucy's book?

[270]
Lucy names her first novel

_____.

BONUS: What does she call her second novel?

Ricky (reading from Lucy's manuscript): His voice charmed millions, his guitar playing made women swoon, so it's a small wonder that . . .

Ethel (reads from next page): . . . he turned into such a big ham, you could stuff him with cloves.

[271]
How much is left in the club treasury?
a) 14 cents
b) $14.14
c) $1.14
d) $4.14

[272]
Match the club member with her musical instrument:

Lucy   violin
Carolyn   trombone
Neeva   drums
Marie   saxophone
Jane   trumpet

[273]
True or False: Fred persuades Ricky to help the girls' band rehearse.

Ricky: Lucy!

Lucy: Oh, honey I forgot. I promise I will never hum, whistle, sing, or reproduce in any manner "Twelfth Street Rag" in your presence as long as I live.

LUCY'S CLUB DANCE

The club treasury is nearly empty again, so the members decide to form an all-girl band and host a dance. When the best they can do is make a happy ragtime song sound like a funeral march, Ricky steps in to help and does the only thing he can think of. He dresses his musicians like women and goes on with the show!

Once again, Ethel has forgotten how to play the piano. She was a wiz in Episodes 18 and 38, only two years prior.

A newspaper ad announcing Ricky Ricardo and His All Girl Orchestra runs in the *New York Gazette*. It has the exact same headline as the paper that appeared in Episode 78.

In the opening scene Lucy and Ethel are studying French books for "the trip," although they haven't even heard about the European trip yet.

The club plans to charge $5 a couple for the dance.

THE DINER

Ricky wants out of show biz, so the Ricardos and Mertzes buy a diner together. Unfortunately, Ricky and Lucy have all the fun, and Ethel and Fred do all the work. They split the diner down the middle and form two teams, but neither couple has any customers. When a drunk stops by to order hamburgers—watch out!

[274]
Ethel and Fred worked in a diner once when they were stranded in _____.

[275]
Name the ingredients for the "Little Bit of Cuba Special."

[276]
How much does Mr. Watson pay them to buy the diner back?

BONUS: How much did they pay him originally?

The Ricardo kitchen sink is leaking again.

Ethel says Ricky only knows two songs: "Babalu," and "You Got the Know-How, I Got The Name Blues."

Ricky and Lucy call their side of the diner "Little Bit of Cuba," while the Mertzes call their side "Big Hunk of America."

Lucy says Ricky is as grumpy as a kangaroo with a porcupine in his pouch.

Ethel: Sure, this is just perfect for the four of us. Fred and I have the know-how, and Ricky has the name and Lucy has, uh, Lucy has, uh . . .

Lucy (pointing to Ricky): My name is the same as his!

135

THE BLACK WIG

Lucy loves the short Italian haircut she saw on the actresses in a foreign film, but Ricky says no way. So Lucy tricks him with a wig she gets from her beautician. Ricky is wise to her ways, but flirts with her just to go along with the gag. Lucy and Ethel make dates to meet Ricky and Fred, but the joke is on them at the end.

Lucille Ball's hairdresser was Irma Kusley.

Ricky flirts with the disguised Lucy and tells her he will "titch her to rumba." According to Desi Arnaz's autobiography, *A Book*, when Desi first spoke to Lucille he said, "Would you like me to teach you how to rumba?"

Ethel's costume is a mix between Eskimo, Japanese, and Native American. Lucy says she looks like "an ad for a trip around the world."

[277]

Name Lucy's hairdresser.

BONUS: Name the male hairdresser in the salon.

[278]

What is the name of the restaurant where Lucy and Ethel plan to meet Ricky and Fred?
a) Pete's
b) Joey's
c) Tony's
d) Dominick's

[279]

What time does Fred go to bed every night?

....

Ricky: All people in the world are divided into two groups, men and women.

Lucy: I know, it's a wonderful arrangement.

Ricky: Now, men have short hair and women have long hair. That's the difference between them.

TENNESSEE ERNIE VISITS

Lucy gets a letter from her mother saying that Lucy and Ricky will be getting a visitor from down south. Ernie moves right in and Lucy and Ricky don't have the heart to throw him out. In a last-ditch attempt, Lucy dresses as a "wicked city woman" to scare him away. But Ernie is unafraid—in fact, he likes it!

Lucy's mother thinks Ricky's name is Xavier.

Ernie is the middle boy of a cousin of an old college roommate of a friend of Mother McGillicuddy. What a connection!

Tennessee Ernie Ford would reprise his role twice more, in Episodes 95 and 112, more than any other *I Love Lucy* guest star.

At the time of his appearances, Ernie Ford was best known as a nightclub performer and

recording artist. Born in Bristol, Tennessee, on February 13, 1919, Ernest Jennings Ford began his career in 1939 as a ten-dollar-a-week radio announcer. After serving in the US Air Corps during World War II, he relocated to California where he developed a large radio following. In 1954, he was made the host of the TV show *The College of Musical Knowledge*. From 1956-61, he starred in another TV show, *The Tennessee Ernie Ford Show*.

[280]
When playing Scrabble, how does Ricky spell the word "local"?

[281]
True or False: Ernie sold his guitar for $50.

[282]
Which of Ricky's musical instruments did Ernie ruin?
a) conga drum
b) guitar
c) piano
d) maracas

BONUS: Who gave it to Ricky?

Ernie: You must be Cousin Lucy. And there's Cousin Ricky, too. How're you?

Ricky: How are you? Did you say cousin?

Ernie: Oh yeah, it's just a habit. Down in Tennessee everybody calls everybody else cousin.

Ricky: Oh.

Ernie: 'Course down in Tennessee, everybody is everybody else's cousin.

TENNESSEE ERNIE HANGS ON

[283]
Fred and Ethel claim the Ricardos are how much behind in their rent?
a) 6 months
b) 2 months
c) 7 months
d) 12 months

[284]
Name the TV show Ernie books them all on.

BONUS: What does Ernie call his little group?

[285]
True or False: One appearance on the show earns Ernie $200.

Ethel: Well, how are you going to get rid of him now?

Lucy: I'm not even gonna try. I give up.

Ethel: Oh Lucy, he'll stay here forever!

Lucy: Well, we'll get used to him through the years. Who knows, someday we may even adopt him.

Lucy and Ricky can't get rid of Ernie. He is eating them out of house and home, but he has no money for a ticket back to Tennessee. Lucy schemes to make him think that Ricky has lost his job and they are broke. Instead of just leaving town, Ernie saves the day with a guest spot on a TV show, making enough money to go home to Bent Fork.

The last few minutes of this show are classic. Watch our gang dressed like hillbillies, Lucy playing the washboard, Fred and Ethel square-dancing, and Ricky cringing through each moment.

Lester Bike is the host of the TV show.

Ethel and Fred play along with Lucy's scheme by visiting and bringing food and old clothes.

THE GOLF GAME

Lucy and Ethel are fed up with their husbands' obsession with golf. Their motto is: if you can't beat 'em, join 'em. So Ricky and Fred give them golf lessons full of made-up terms and rules. Lucy and Ethel find out the truth of the shenanigans from a real golf pro, and then it is their turn to put one over on the boys. Fore!

[286]
Lucy and Ethel play what game in the Ricardo living room?

[287]
How long did it take the foursome to get to the first green?
a) 30 minutes
b) 60 minutes
c) 90 minutes
d) 120 minutes

[288]
An angry Lucy deduces, "There's a rotten Cuban in _____."

Ricky: Now let's see, uh, Lucy shot first. And her ball went farther down the fairway than the third player's ball so . . . Lucy gets to carry all the bags!

Jimmy Demaret was a famous American golf pro. He was born in 1912, turned pro as a teenager in 1927, and won the prestigious Masters tournament in 1940, 1947, and 1948. At the time this episode was shot, he was still playing golf on the pro circuit.

Ricky and Fred are playing in a tournament to benefit the USO and the National Golf Fund.

THE SUBLEASE

Ricky and his band get a job in Maine for the summer, so he wants to sublet the apartment and make a profit. The Mertzes want a cut of the action too. They finally make a deal, but then the trip is cancelled and the renter won't leave! The Ricardos and the Mertzes find the good neighbor policy is not all it's cracked up to be.

[289]
Ricky and Lucy pay the Mertzes $125 a month for their apartment. How much does Mrs. Hammond say she can get on a sublease?

[290]
Why are Mr. Beecher's nerves shot?
a) his wife left him
b) he was fired from his job
c) he witnessed a murder
d) he is being followed by a hit man

[291]
All the apartments Lucy looks at will take _____ but not _____.

Mrs. Hammond: Well, I think that the Mertzes are going to sublease your apartment and then sub-sublet it to someone else.

Ricky: Ohhhh! They're trying to make us look at this thin' through a sweater!

Lucy: Oh! You mean they're trying to pull the wool over our eyes!

Mr. Beecher pays his entire two months rent up front.

Lucy Ricardo claims she was twenty-two when she married.

The Ricardos have lived in the Mertzes' building for twelve years.

In the end Ricky gets a call from his agent saying he has been booked for the summer in Del Mar, California. The Arnaz family spent most summer breaks on the beach in Del Mar; Desi Arnaz was living there when he died.

WHY WAS *I LOVE LUCY* SUCH AN UNEQUALED HIT?
The answer lies in that elusive combination of luck and talent that television producers have been searching for ever since. The unavailability of both Bea Benaderet and Gale Gordon retrospectively proved to be a real stroke of luck. Not to take away from their talents, but the unexpected casting of Vivian Vance and William Frawley proved to be genius. Of course, Lucy's talents are obvious, and one could go on and on. Those not familiar with the history of *I Love Lucy* tend to underestimate Desi's contributions. But without his input, who knows how many weeks the show would have lasted? And of course, without the brilliance of the three Bobs and Madelyn, and certainly Jess Oppenheimer, the show may very well not still be rerun in every country in the world. Take away any one of these components, and it wouldn't have been nearly as good. That's where luck and fate came into the picture. Thank you, Guardian Angels of Comedy! When I say *I Love Lucy*, I must qualify that with I love *I Love Lucy*. Lucy. Ethel. Ricky. Fred. 1951–1957. I think most fans would agree.

MELODY THOMAS SCOTT
ACTRESS, *THE YOUNG AND THE RESTLESS*

THE FOURTH SEASON
___
1954-1955
___

LUCY CRIES WOLF

Lucy decides to see whether Ricky loves her. She ransacks the apartment and calls Ricky at the club. The Mertzes rush over and find it was a trick. Lucy does it again and this time no one can find her until a neighbor calls to say she is out on the ledge! Ricky gets her back, but later she is really kidnapped and no one believes her.

[292]
Ricky says he will wait how long to remarry?

[293]
True or False: Ricky will give Ethel Lucy's clothes and furs.

[294]
Name the neighbor who tattles on Lucy.

Ricky (knows Lucy is listening): On second thought I don't think I'll call the police. It'll be bad publicity for me.

Ethel: That's right, Ricky.

Ricky: And after all, what can the police do? If she's gone, she gone, that's all. I'll just have to get used to it.

Mr. and Mrs. Craig were robbed of $5,000 worth of jewelry, silver, and furs.

While staying in a Chicago hotel in 1950, Lucille Ball was robbed of jewelry, including a 40-carat aquamarine engagement ring given to her by Desi.

When Ricky, Ethel, and Fred sit down to play bridge, Fred deals four hands instead of three.

THE MATCHMAKER

Lucy tries to help her friend Dorothy "trap" bachelor Sam. Ricky thinks she should "mess out" of the matter. This leads to a huge fight that ends in Ricky storming out of the apartment. After he does not return home, Lucy cries and wonders if her marriage is over. Ricky comes home with flowers and candy and apologies abound.

[295]
How long have Dorothy and Sam been dating?
a) three months
b) three years
c) three weeks
d) three days

[296]
Why does Ricky want to be in bed by 10PM?

[297]
True or False: Dorothy and Sam decide that marriage is not for them.

Watch the last scene when Fred is sleeping in Lucy's bed and Ricky comes in to apologize to "Lucy." Absolute hilarity.

Ricky tells Dorothy and Sam that he started in show business when he was twelve years old.

Ricky is so mad he starts to leave the apartment in his pajamas.

At least he remembered his hat!

Lucy: Anyway, I have a plan. We are going to show Sam what it's like to be married. First, I'm gonna serve a delicious home cooked meal, and then we'll all tip-toe in and take a look at the baby sleeping peacefully in his little crib, and then we'll all come out here and sit around a big fire and listen to romantic music.

Ethel: Oh, that'll be nice.

Lucy: Won't it?

Ethel: Yeah. . . . When are you gonna show him what it's like to be married?

147

[298]
How much does Lucy charge at the corner market?

[299]
Complete Lucy's compliment to Mr. Hickox: "Did anyone ever tell you you look like _____?"
a) Maurice Chevalier
b) Clark Gable
c) William Holden
d) Charles Boyer

[300]
Ricky sees Lucy's note to buy "Can All Pet." What stock does he think it stands for?

BONUS: How much does he make buying and selling the stock?

Lucy (to the business manager): Five dollars to buy food and have my hair dyed? Done! Well, at least I have a choice. I can be a thin redhead, or a fat brunette.

THE BUSINESS MANAGER

Ricky hires a business manager to make sure Lucy pays the bills. This leaves Lucy with only $5 extra a month! She comes up with a scheme to buy groceries for the neighbors, charge it to her account, and pocket the cash. Ricky, thinking she is playing the stock market, buys some good stock and fires the manager. Help!

Andrew Hickox was a Desilu employee.

Charles Lane, who played Mr. Hickox, later played miserly banker Mr. Barnsdahl on *The Lucy Show*.

When Mr. Hickox first came on the scene, Lucy owed $20 for the milk bill, $11.25 for the phone bill, $8.75 for gas and electric, $15 for cleaning, and $187.50 for back rent.

MR. AND MRS. TV SHOW

Lucy meets an ad agent who is looking for new TV talent. Ricky gets the job and as usual Lucy wants to be part of the act. Ricky says no, but the agent says yes, so Ricky has to swallow his pride and beg Lucy to take part. Ricky tells his beloved the husband and wife show was his idea, but watch out when she finds out he lied!

William Frawley makes a rare mistake when he flubs the words during the second rehearsal of the Phipps song, but Vivian Vance covers for him.

Lucy sings her famous signature song, "Sweet Sue."

Originally slated for broadcast on November 1, 1954, this episode aired months later (in the middle of the "Hollywood" episodes). Its broadcast was postponed in most parts of the country when the Republican Party aired a political announcement a week before the 1954 national elections.

[301]
Name the ad agent Lucy meets at "21."

BONUS: Name his agency.

[302]
Ethel thinks Lucy is as subtle as a _____.

[303]
What is the title of the Phipps TV spot?
a) Phipps Presents Lucy and Ricky
b) Breakfast with the Ricardos
c) Breakfast with Ricky and Lucy
d) Shopping at Phipps with Lucy and Ricky

Ethel and Fred (sing): Oh, when we go on shopping trips, where else would we go but Phipps? From the top floor to the bottom, if it's bargains, Phipps has got 'em. Down at Phipps your credit's great. Ask today for a Phipps-a-plate. First on your list of shopping tips put . . .

Lucy: P-h-i-p-p-s, Phipps.

149

MERTZ AND KURTZ

[304]

By what name was Fred and Barney's act known?

[305]

What does Barney really do for a living?

a) sells newspapers

b) cooks in a restaurant

c) ushers at a movie theatre

d) sells peanuts at the ball park

BONUS: In what city is his job located?

[306]

Barney's grandson lives in Indianapolis, but his train will arrive at _____ in New York.

Ethel: Let's see now, what else can I borrow that looks better than what I've got?

Lucy: How 'bout Ricky?

Ethel: That's a thought.

Fred's old vaudeville partner, Barney, is in town and Fred and Ethel want to impress him, so they put on quite a show. When Fred confesses to the truth, Barney confesses that he is no longer a star either. But when Barney's grandson comes to New York to see his grandfather act on stage, it's Ricky to the rescue once again.

Lucy portrays Bessie, the Mertzes' maid. She serves beef, gravy, potatoes, beans, and rolls.

Fred brags that he owns several apartment buildings, two cars, and employs a chauffeur!

During dinner Ethel mentions an actress named Venus Jones, which is the name of Vivian Vance's real-life sister.

RICKY'S MOVIE OFFER

Ethel is nervous about a chain of robberies in town, so when a stranger drops by she and Lucy knock him out cold. It turns out he is a talent scout who wants to see Ricky about a movie screen test! The neighbors find out and they all come by the Ricardos' hoping to be "discovered." But Ricky outfoxes them and auditions solo.

Poor Fred is installing new door locks again. He just put in new ones a year ago.

Watch Lucy and Ethel try to prop up the unconscious talent scout—they straighten his tie, comb his hair, give him a cigarette, and sit next to him laughing and waiting for him to come to.

Mrs. Trumble comes over to borrow a cup of sugar, but leaves without it when she finds out the talent scout is not there.

Lucy dresses like Marilyn Monroe and Fred and Ethel are a Spanish dance team.

[307]
The talent scout is named

_____.

[308]
Lucy almost misses her dentist appointment. How many weeks did she have to wait to get it?
a) six weeks
b) five weeks
c) four weeks
d) three weeks

[309]
True or False: Pete the grocery boy plays the trombone.

Lucy: Honestly, this has been going on all morning.

Ethel: What has?

Lucy: People calling up and wanting to audition tonight.

Ethel: No kidding.

Lucy: How did they find out?

Ethel: I dunno. I didn't tell anybody, did you?

Lucy: Certainly not. I didn't tell a soul, and they all promised to keep it a secret.

RICKY'S SCREEN TEST

Ricky is going to make a screen test and Lucy is all ready to move to Hollywood. She decides that if Ricky is going to be a star, so is she! When Ricky asks her to read with him during his screen test she is sure she will be discovered. She tries her best to get her face on camera but is foiled over and over by Ricky. Roll 'em!

[310]

Lucy says she wants her Hollywood pool to be shaped like a _____.

[311]

Lucy tells Ethel there is a vacant lot right next to what star's house?
a) Clark Gable
b) William Holden
c) John Wayne
d) Jack Benny

[312]

What is the budget for the movie, *Don Juan*?

Lucy (to Ethel and Fred): Well now it just might happen sorta like this; we make the test here in New York, they send it out to the coast, they show it at the studio, my face comes on the screen, just for an instant, but that's enough. The head of the studio sees it, he jumps up and says, "That face! That face! Get me that girl!" "But sir, she's an unknown, a nobody." "I don't care, find her, get that girl! I want to make her a star!" And the rest is motion picture history.

Ricky is set to star with many of the actresses of the day, including Marilyn Monroe, Jane Russell, Ava Gardner, Yvonne DeCarlo, Arlene Dahl, Lana Turner, and Betty Grable. Desi Arnaz dated some of them before he met Lucille.

In the first scene, Lucy tries to get Little Ricky to dance and act so he can be a big star like Jackie Coogan, one of the most popular child film stars of the 1920s. Jackie Coogan married Betty Grable in 1937.

In *Don Juan*, Ricky's love interest is married to Count de Renzo.

LUCY'S MOTHER-IN-LAW

Ricky's mother is coming from Cuba! Lucy prepares for the visit, but the non English-speaking Mrs. Ricardo arrives unexpectedly. Things go wrong from the start so Lucy schemes to impress with her Spanish. Trouble is, she is faking, and doesn't really know a word of the language. Mama finds out the truth, but loves Lucy for trying to please.

[313]
Name the man who does the mind-reading act.

[314]
What nickname does Lucy say she was called in grade school?
a) Droopy Drawers
b) Rhode Island Red
c) Bird Legs
d) Big Foot

[315]
True or False: Lucy ruins Mama Ricardo's dress in the washing machine.

Fred did not appear in this episode.

Mrs. Ricardo tries to pay her cab fare in pesos.

Watch Lucy use charades to describe that she is making *arroz con pollo* for dinner.

This is the first time Grandma Ricardo has seen Little Ricky, and she thinks he looks like an angel.

Lucy: Oh Ethel, I haven't done anything right since Ricky's mother came to visit us.

Ethel: Oh honey, you have too.

Lucy: I have not. The day she arrived the apartment was a mess, my hair was up in curlers, the closet exploded in her face, and I burned the dinner.

Ethel: Yes, I know but . . .

Lucy: And then the next day I took her shopping and I lost her in the subway.

Ethel: But someone turned her in to Lost and Found . . .

153

ETHEL'S BIRTHDAY

It's Ethel's birthday and Lucy and Ricky are treating her to dinner and the theater. But when Lucy buys a gift for Fred to give to Ethel, all plans are off. Ethel hates the gift, and Lucy is insulted. At the theatre the ladies get sentimental, the best friends cry, hug, and make up.

[316]
What gift does Ethel say she wants for her birthday?
a) an ironing board
b) a toaster
c) a radio
d) a coat

[317]
What is the "emergency present" Ricky gives to Lucy?

BONUS: What do the "emergency" cards say?

[318]
Name the play they attend.

Ethel (holding up pants): What are they?

Lucy: Well, they're hostess pants. You wear 'em when you give smart dinner parties.

Ethel: Oh, I was wondering what to wear to all those smart dinner parties I give.

Lucy: Well, I saw them last month in *Harper's Bazaar.*

Ethel: Well, they're certainly bizarre!

Lucy: Well now, wait a minute Ethel, look. You get yourself a little black, off the shoulder blouse, and a big crushy belt and little ballet slippers and you're all set.

Ethel: What for, Halloween?

Vivian Vance was forty-five years old when this episode was taped.

In this episode the Speedy Cleaners turns forty and Goldblatt's Delicatessen turns fifty.

Lucy wants Fred to fix that kitchen sink again—it's been leaking for four months!

The theater tickets are a bargain by today's standards at $6.60 a piece.

Last year for her birthday Ethel shopped, cooked, and cleaned up while Fred rested.

We never see Fred pay for the tickets after they devise their little scheme.

RICKY'S CONTRACT

Ricky is going crazy waiting for Hollywood to call. Fred thinks it's a good idea to leave a phone message saying Ricky got the part. Lucy finds it by mistake, thinks it's true, and calls Ricky! The three come up with a plan to tell Ricky the truth, but he comes home to say that Hollywood really did call and he really *did* get the part!

Ricky has been waiting for Hollywood to call for more than two weeks.

Fred has a secret hiding place where he puts all the rent money. He thinks Ethel doesn't know where it is but she does.

Ricky takes the boys out to celebrate at Lindy's.

Fred says he left his autograph book in Indiana.

The phones all have very long cords and Ricky is never without a phone in his hands. At one point he leaves the apartment and walks out the door with the phone, cord and all!

[319]
By what name does Fred call his stomach?
a) Sam
b) Pat
c) Scottie
d) Charlie

[320]
Lucy does an imitation of what dog?

[321]
Ricky gives Lucy, Ethel, and Fred the charter to the _____.

Ethel: Any word?
Lucy: Not yet.
Ethel: Wonder why?
Lucy: Who knows?
Ethel: How's he?
Lucy: Just awful.
Ethel: No kidding.
Lucy: Getting worse.
Ethel: What are you talkin' short hand?

GETTING READY

How will the Ricardos get to California—by plane, train, or bus? They decide to buy a car and the Mertzes can go along too! Fred has a friend in the used car business and he buys an old, broken-down jalopy. Ricky and the girls tell him to take it back, but they are afraid he won't get his money back so they devise a scheme which fails as usual.

[322]
Name Fred's friend who has the used-car business.

[323]
The Cadillac touring car Fred bought was made in what year?
a) 1936
b) 1921
c) 1923
d) 1919

BONUS: How much did Fred pay for it?

[324]
Ricky and Lucy will be in Hollywood for how long?

Fred: I'll tell you, this car is in good shape and it drives beautifully. Now jump in and I'll take you for a spin.

Ricky: Well, what've we got to lose?

Lucy: Our lives, that's what!

The number for the car business is Nevins 8-2098. Lucy gives a fake phone number to Fred's friend—Murray Hill 5-9099.

Marion Van Vlack saw the movie Sabrina five times.

Lucy called Fred a pinch-penny because he wouldn't chip in for gas or oil. He will supply all the water though.

Ricky is willing to carry his wife and son across the country piggy-back if Lucy will only decide how she wants to travel.

This was the last episode in 1954.

LUCY LEARNS TO DRIVE

Ricky has bought a brand-new Pontiac convertible and Lucy can't wait to learn to drive! Her first lesson goes badly, but she decides she can teach Ethel how to drive too! Ethel accidentally steps on the gas and the Cadillac and the Pontiac get hooked together. It will take a miracle—or Lucy—to get them apart.

Less than two years ago, Ethel knew how to drive.

This is the first episode to be sponsored by a company other than Philip Morris. *I Love Lucy* was now also sponsored by Proctor and Gamble. The companies took turns sponsoring the show. Cheer laundry soap was the first product Proctor and Gamble promoted on *I Love Lucy*.

It's strange that there is no traffic on a busy Manhattan street. Not one car goes by the Ricardo apartment!

[325]
Fred's mechanic friend, Joe, says he can fix the Cadillac enough to get it running. How much will he charge?
a) $50
b) $40
c) $30
d) $20

[326]
When Lucy made a U-turn in the _____, traffic was backed up all the way to _____!

[327]
What is the horsepower on the new car?

Lucy (to Ethel):
Look, if Fred comes back, you tell him that the man came for the Cadillac, and that Ricky has the Pontiac downtown. If the man comes for the Cadillac, you tell him that Fred has it out for one last farewell spin. If Ricky comes home you tell him the man came for the Cadillac, and Fred took the Pontiac downtown to have it washed. Okay?

CALIFORNIA HERE WE COME!

[328]
Match the characters to their desired tourist spots:

Ethel	The Grand Canyon
Ricky	Cincinnati and Niagara Falls
Fred	Ozark Mountains and Carlsbad Caverns
Everybody	New Orleans and the Rockies

[329]
Mrs. McGillicuddy calls Ricky by what name?

BONUS: How much did Fred pay for it?

[330]
Why does Mrs. McGillicuddy want to go to Hollywood?

Ethel: Nothing's the matter. Go ahead and have a nice trip. And don't forget to drop a line to Mr. and Mrs. Fred Horninsky. Or as we are more commonly known, the Tag-Along Mertzes.

Fred: Bon voyage!

Everyone is set to go west until Lucy gets a letter from her mother saying that she is going too! Ricky says no way and everyone gets upset. Once they make up, it's time to leave and Fred and Ricky pack the car. Sort of. They decide to ship most of their belongings ahead of them and Mrs. McGillicuddy will fly with Little Ricky.

In order to fulfill everyone's sightseeing plans, they will have to go through New York three times on the way to Chicago.

Lucy's mother has never been west of Youngstown, Ohio.

Marion Van Vlack is a real-life childhood friend of Lucille Ball.

Mrs. McGillicuddy mentions Hunt Road, which is a real road in Jamestown, New York, named after Lucille's maternal ancestors.

FIRST STOP

Ricky drives all day and everyone is starving. They finally stop at an old run-down cafe. They decide to spend the night there, and end up in a rickety set of bunk beds and a double bed that has a ditch a mile wide in the middle! After the train passes through and the bed moves across the room, they decide to make a run for it!

Mr. Skinner: What'll it be?

Lucy: I think I'll have the steak sandwich, rare, with the French fries.

Ethel: Uh, steak sandwich, I'll have that too.

Fred: I'll have the same.

Ricky: Me, too.

Mr. Skinner: We're all out of steak sandwiches.

Ethel: Oh, you are? Gee, I had my mouth all set for one.

Lucy: Well, I think I'll have the roast beef, rare, with a baked potato.

Ethel: Roast beef, that's for me.

Fred: I'll vote for that.

Ricky: Make it four.

Mr. Skinner: We're out of roast beef, too.

Ricky: Well, let me see here, uh, hey that fried chicken with biscuits sounds good.

Lucy: Any point in running that chicken around the table?

[331]
When Ethel looks in the picnic basket, what two items are left?

BONUS: Which does Fred choose?

[332]
Lucy is dying to know, "I wonder if this bed stops in _____?"

[333]
Name the restaurant that served turkey dinner with all the trimmings for $1.
a) Aunt Sally's Cafe
b) The Golden Drumstick
c) The Turkey-in-the-Straw Diner
d) The Wild Turkey Tavern

Fred thinks George Skinner's place is like Lower Slobovia.

They are traveling west on Route 48 in Ohio.

Mr. Skinner's establishment is called the One Oak Cafe and Cabins.

Their bill for the four cheese sandwiches comes to $4.80—80¢ for the entertainment tax! The cabin costs $16 for the four of them.

Mr. Skinner lures them back with a sign that says, Good Accommodations, Wonderful Food, 5 miles.

TENNESSEE BOUND

With Lucy driving, the foursome takes a detour to Tennessee, home of Ernie Ford. When they get a speeding ticket and old big mouth sasses the sheriff, they end up in the pokey. It takes a visit from good old Cousin Ernie, some country singing, a marriage proposal, and a square dance to get them back on the right road.

According to Ernie, the sheriff is about as popular as a skunk at a picnic.

The role of the country boy is played by a very young Aaron Spelling, who went on to be a famous television producer and director. His company produced Lucille Ball's last series, *Life with Lucy*.

The original idea for this episode was to have a taffy pull and tie the sheriff and his daughters up with taffy, instead of the rope they eventually used.

[334]
What is the population of Bent Fork?
a) 52
b) 53
c) 54
d) 55

[335]
The speed limit in town is _____; Lucy claims they were going _____.

[336]
True or False: The sheriff fines them $35 for speeding.

Country Boy: Shucks, you're in Tennessee!

Lucy: Tennessee?

Ethel: Tennessee?

Ricky: Tennessee?

Fred: Tennessee?

Country Boy: You got a bad echo in that car!

ETHEL'S HOME TOWN

The gang stops in Albuquerque, New Mexico, to visit Ethel's father. Apparently Ethel has been writing letters which indicate that she, not Ricky, is going to star in a Hollywood movie. Ethel is feted all over town while Ricky gets no attention at all. This all changes at Ethel's stage show, when the other three steal the spotlight.

Ethel had three middle names—Louise, Roberta, and Mae, depending on the episode.

The Albuquerque Little Theatre where Ethel performs is the name of the real theatre where Vivian Vance began her acting career.

Irving Bacon, who plays Ethel's father, was born in 1901. Vivian Vance was born in 1909 and William Frawley was born in 1887. That makes Fred fourteen years older than his own father-in-law and Ethel only eight years younger than her own dad!

Fred plays "Chopsticks" on the piano.

[331]
Mr. Potter's store motto is: "You can lick our cones, but you can't beat our _____."

a) sodas
b) prices
c) egg creams
d) sundaes

[332]
True or False: Ethel and Fred eloped.

[333]
Chronicle headline reads: "Ethel Mae Potter, We Never _____."

Mr. Potter: Well, how come you're on your way to Hollywood to star in a movie?

Ethel: Uh . . .

Ricky: Star in a movie?

Ethel: Uh, Daddy, you misunderstood. Ricky's going to be in the picture!

Mr. Potter: Oh are you gonna be in it, too?

Ricky: Well, I wouldn't exactly put it that way.

Mr. Potter: Oh, now don't worry. If Ethel says you're gonna be in her picture, you're gonna be in her picture!

L.A. AT LAST

[340]
Bobby the bellboy recently played a part in the movie
_____.

[341]
Where does Ricky first meet William Holden?
a) the studio commissary
b) the movie set
c) Mr. Sherman's office
d) the hotel
BONUS: What was Ricky wearing at the time?

[342]
How did Lucy finally put her nose out?

Bill: That's it, that's where I saw you! The Brown Derby. She was sitting in the next booth and, uh, I asked the head waiter who the beautiful redhead was.

Lucy (shocked): You did?

Bill: Yes, I wanted to find out your name and come over and tell you that you should be in movies. But, uh, you left before I had a chance. (winks)

Finally, the gang has hit Tinseltown. At the Brown Derby restaurant, Lucy, Ethel, and Fred see many actors. Lucy gets caught spying on her idol, William Holden, and causes a pie to hit him in the face as she flees in embarrassment. Later Ricky brings Bill home to meet her! What else can a girl do but set her own nose on fire?

William Holden appeared courtesy of Paramount Pictures. He mentioned his latest film, *The Country Girl,* also starring Grace Kelly and Bing Crosby.

In the Brown Derby, Lucy notices the sketch of actor Eddie Cantor, who starred in Lucille's first movie, *Roman Scandals.*

The foursome is staying at the Beverly Palms Hotel.

DON JUAN
AND THE STARLETS

Lucy sees the green-eyed monster when Ricky gets his picture taken with beautiful young starlets. Later he attends a premiere with the ladies, but without Lucy. Lucy sleeps through his arrival home and his departure in the morning, leaving her to think he was out all night! Ricky pleads his case, but is lost until the maid stops by.

Ricky: Honey, you know I had nothing to do with this. Don't get mad.

Lucy: Mad? Me, mad? Why, why should I be mad? On the contrary, I'm glad, very glad. Why when those four girls walked in here today it was the happiest day of my life. And when they didn't want me to be in the pictures I wanted to jump for joy!

Ricky: Lucy . . .

Lucy: And my goodness, when you all put on those bathing suits and trooped down to the pool, I just felt as if my fondest dreams had come true.

Ricky: Now, honey . . .

Lucy: And you thought I was mad. Why I wasn't mad, I was happy, happy. H-A-P-P-Y. Happy!

[343]
What two things did the maid do to ruin Ricky's alibi?

[344]
Ethel complains, "I sleep on the couch lots of nights. Fred _____."

[345]
What does Ricky promise to give the maid?
a) flowers
b) movie tickets
c) a studio tour
d) a box of candy

Lucy claims that fifteen years ago, Marion Strong asked if she would go on a blind date with a Cuban drummer.

Ricky got home at 2:38 AM and left again at 5:30 AM.

The program for the premiere was on the desk all along, and could have cleared Ricky.

PR man Ross Elliot says the movie *Don Juan* is all about love, "it has nothing to do with marriage."

Lucy and Ethel spot movie star Robert Taylor sunning by the hotel pool.

LUCY GETS IN PICTURES

Lucy has been writing postcards home that say she is going to be in a movie. She is distraught when even Ethel and Fred get roles, so Ricky promises to try to get her a bit part. She lands the role of a showgirl who is shot dead on the staircase, but she causes so much trouble that in the end only her feet make it on to the screen.

[346]
Lucy goes to Schwab's Drugstore to try to get discovered. Name the long list of treats she orders there.

[347]
Name Ethel and Fred's old vaudeville chum who gives them parts in his movie.
a) Jimmy O'Brien
b) Jimmy O'Connor
c) Jimmy O'Reilly
d) Jimmy O'Shea

[348]
Lucy writes _____ on the bottom of her shoes.

Bobby the bellboy: Hey, you're great!

Lucy: Yeah, well thanks a lot. I'm afraid my light's always gonna be hidden under a bushel.

Bobby: What about your husband? Can't he help you get in pictures?

Lucy: You mean Ricky Ricardo, the Cuban bushel?

Ricky says he has a lunch date with Mr. Minnelli. He must have been referring to Vincente Minnelli, director of Lucille and Desi's MGM film hit, *The Long, Long, Trailer*.

Lucy actually only messed up four takes before the director came up with the "new concept" of having her dead when the scene opens.

Lucy found Schwab's Drugstore on Sunset Boulevard, where legend has it that Lana Turner was discovered.

Lucy writes a postcard to Lillian Appleby, not Carolyn Appleby.

THE FASHION SHOW

Ricky says Lucy can buy a dress at Don Loper's swanky salon. While there she hears about a fashion show for Hollywood wives and wrangles a spot in the lineup. But later she gets a terrible sunburn, Ricky finds out her dress cost $500, and Don Loper asks her to wear a tight tweed suit in the show! If she'll do it, her dress is free.

Lucy: Oh Ricky, I would dearly love to have just one dress from an exclusive salon like Don Loper's.

Ethel: Oh yes, it'd just set you up for life if you could open up your closet door and see one Loper label. Eh, what's the sense of dreaming?

Fred: Well, now wait a minute, honeybunch. Maybe we can figure something out.

Ethel: Who said that?

Lucy: It sounded like Fred but I don't believe it.

Ethel: Fred, do you really mean it?

Fred: Sure!

Ethel: Oh!

Fred: What do you think he'd charge for one label?

[349]
Fred wants to sell the apartment building and buy an _____ in Pamona.

[350]
How many dresses does Lucy see before she chooses one?
a) two
b) three
c) four
d) five

[351]
True or False: Lucy wears a size-ten dress.

The other actor's wives in the fashion show are Sheila MacRae, Brenda Holden, Jeanne Martin, Frances Heflin, Marylin Tucker, and Mona Carlson.

Don Loper's new collection is called Facade and Lucy's suit is called French Dandy.

The charity Share Incorporated is hosting the fashion show.

Lucy takes Francis McCrea's place in the show.

THE HEDDA HOPPER STORY

Mother McGillicuddy has set up a tea with a "newspaper lady" she met on the plane. Meanwhile Ricky's press agent is trying to get him in Hedda Hopper's column. He devises a plan in which Lucy jumps in the pool and Ricky saves her. But Hedda never shows up to see it—she is in the Ricardo hotel suite with Mrs. McGillicuddy!

[352]
Bobby brings up a telegram addressed to Mrs. _____.

[353]
Flight number 930 is due in at 1:55PM from what city?
a) Bombay
b) Stockholm
c) Paris
d) Madrid

[354]
True or False: Mother McGillicuddy waited for them at the airport.

Lucy: Well, at least she sent us a wire and told us she's arriving at 9:30.

Ricky: Hooray for Mother. AM or PM?

Lucy: She doesn't say.

Ricky: What day?

Lucy: She doesn't say.

Fred: What airline?

Lucy: She doesn't say.

Ricky: Whatever happened to that woman's brain?

Lucy: She doesn't say.

Ricky and company have been in California for five weeks, already one week longer than the original plan.

After this episode, Lucille and Desi did an announcement for the benefit of the U.S. Olympic team, which was in need of funds for the 1956 summer games in Melbourne, Australia. They mention that teams behind the "iron and bamboo curtains" are funded through their governments, but that American athletes have to rely on private donations.

Hat-enthusiast Hedda Hopper was born Elda Furry on June 2, 1890, in Hollidaysburg, Pennsylvania. Hopper was an actress, radio host, and newspaper columnist. A staunch anti-Communist, Hopper once said that no one whose name was mentioned before a Congressional committee investigating communists should be allowed to appear on the screen again. She must have changed her mind after Lucille's 1953 scare.

DON JUAN IS SHELVED

Ricky's picture is canceled! Lucy, Ethel, and Fred try various means to let the studio know how popular he really is. They finally hire an "actor" to play a producer to make the MGM executive think that Ricky is wanted for work at another studio. The plan goes awry when Ricky arrives and blows everyone's cover.

MGM production chief Dore Schary was set to play himself in this episode but had to back out because of sudden illness. Born Isadore Schary on August 31, 1905, in Newark, New Jersey, his first job was as a junior writer for Columbia Pictures. He left MGM in 1956. Since Schary was ill, Vivian Vance's husband, Phil Ober, played the part instead.

The good news for Ricky is that MGM is going to pick up his option and find a new picture for him.

[349]
How many fan letters do Lucy, Ethel, Fred, and Mother write?
a) 200
b) 300
c) 400
d) 500

BONUS: Why don't they ever get mailed?

[350]
How much does Lucy agree to pay "George Spelvin" to impersonate a producer?

[351]
True or False: Production on *Don Juan* hasn't even started.

Fred: Did you see Mr. Schary today?

Ricky: No, but they're shovelin' the picture.

Fred: What if they do shovel it? Maybe they'll put you in another one.

Ricky: Oh sure, yeah. Maybe they're gonna use me in one of the Marx brothers pictures. You know—Chico, Harpo, Groucho, and Floppo.

BULL FIGHT DANCE

Ricky is going to emcee a TV special for the Heart Fund, and Lucy is writing a magazine article about being married to Ricky. She lands a part in the TV show by threatening to give less than flattering answers to the magazine questions. When Ricky gives her a part she doesn't want, she changes the number, and even Ricky has to laugh.

Lucy writes an article entitled "What It's Like to Be Married to Ricky Ricardo."

Lucille and Desi were often the subjects of movie and TV magazine articles such as, "Lucy Loves Desi," "The Real Lowdown on Lucille Ball," and "Lucy and Desi's Happy Ending."

[358]
Ethel and Fred take Ricky to Will Wright's for an ice cream soda. How many flavors do they have?

BONUS: How many has Ethel tasted?

[359]
In the skit Ricky plays _____ The Matador and Lucy plays _____ The Terrible.

[360]
Which magazine is doing the article on Ricky?
a) *Spotlight*
b) *Photoplay*
c) *Movie Life*
d) *Silver Screen*

Lucy: Ricky, about the television show, I have a question for you.

Ricky: Well, I'm pretty sure what it is, and I have an answer for you.

Lucy: Well, I'm pretty sure what your answer is, but let me ask it anyway.

Ricky: All right.

Lucy: Can I be on the show?

Ricky: No.

Lucy: Ten seconds, that's the fastest we've ever done it.

HOLLYWOOD ANNIVERSARY

Ricky can't remember the date of his anniversary! He pretends he knows and says he has a party planned. He telegrams the town hall in Greenwich, Connecticut, to get the date, and Lucy is happy—until she finds the telegram! Lucy refuses to go to the party with Ricky, but shows up later and is serenaded by her apologetic hubby.

This episode was the first to be sponsored by a new Proctor and Gamble product—Lilt Home Permanent.

The Ricardo anniversary is now on "the 7th." There is no month specified.

Ricky's full name is Ricardo Alberto Fernando Ricardo y de Acha.

[361]
What is the date of Fred and Ethel's anniversary?
a) February 3
b) March 3
c) April 3
d) May 3

[362]
Ricky looks at his _____ to see if the date is written down.

[363]
At what Hollywood nightclub does Ricky hold the party?

Ricky (sings): Tonight is our night, and here we are, but it's not the way that I planned. I told you I'm sorry, you know how I feel. Darling say you understand.

Tell me I may always dance the anniversary waltz with you.

Tell me this is real romance, an anniversary dream come true. Let this be the anthem to our future years, to millions of smiles, and a few little tears.

Tell me I may always dance the anniversary waltz with you . . .

169

THE STAR UPSTAIRS

Lucy has seen ninety-nine Hollywood stars. She finds out that Cornel Wilde is staying in the hotel penthouse and wants him to be number one hundred. She manages to sneak into his suite, but gets stuck out on the locked balcony. She tries to escape by climbing down, but falls and lands on a palm tree. Later she hears Mr. Wilde has left because there were prowlers on his balcony!

[364]
Where did Lucy see Robert Taylor?

BONUS: What did he sign for her?

[365]
Cornel Wilde is convinced that Bobby the bellboy has what talent?

[366]
True or False: Cornel Wilde invites Ricky up to his room to play cards.

Ethel: I hate to point this out, but Ricky told you to just forget that Cornel Wilde is up there.

Lucy: Well, for once in my life, I'm not gonna do what Ricky tells me.

Ethel: For once in your life? You never do what he tells you!

Lucy: So why spoil a perfect record?

Van Johnson was originally chosen to guest-star in this episode.

Watch Vivian Vance shine in this episode when she tries to keep Ricky from seeing Lucy swinging from the balcony.

Cornel Wilde was born October 13, 1915, in New York, and entered college at age sixteen, intending to study medicine. He soon turned to the theater, however, and began working regularly in Broadway plays. In 1940 he made his first movie in Hollywood, entitled *The Lady with Red Hair.*

IN PALM SPRINGS

Those annoying habits are getting on everyone's nerves, so the spouses decide to separate for a week. Lucy and Ethel go to rainy Palm Springs. Ricky and Fred miss them, so they travel down and convince Rock Hudson to tell a sad story about a married couple and their annoying habits. It works, the couples kiss, and all is forgiven.

This episode promotes Rock Hudson's new film, *Captain Lightfoot.*

Hollywood star Hudson was born Roy Sherer, Jr. on November 17, 1925, in Winnetka, Illinois. He served in the U.S. Navy during World War II, and

was discovered by a talent agent in 1947, when he was working as a truckdriver. He made his first film, *Fighter Squadron*, in 1948.

Adele Sliff, the wife in Rock Hudson's story, was a script supervisor for *I Love Lucy.*

[367]
Match the character with the annoying habit:

Lucy   chews loudly
Ricky   stirs coffee
Ethel   jingles keys
Fred   drums fingers

[368]
Lucy gets Ricky to come to Palm Springs by calling and pretending to be whose secretary?

[369]
Ethel laments, "For twenty-five years I felt like I was married to the _____ man."

Lucy: Let's call 'em and tell them to come down right away, huh?

Ethel: Oh. Oh wait a minute, you can't do that.

Lucy: Why not?

Ethel: Well, if you call 'em up it'll just be admitting that we were wrong and that we miss 'em.

Lucy: Well, we were wrong and we do miss 'em.

Ethel: You can't tell a husband a thing like that—you'll set wives back 2,000 years!

HARPO MARX

Lucy has told Carolyn she is hosting a big party for the stars and now she is in a pickle. She and Ethel arrange to have Carolyn "lose" her glasses so she can't tell the difference between the real movie stars and Lucy in movie star masks! But when the real Harpo (and his harp) shows up at the door, things get interesting.

[370]
Name the star who Lucy does not impersonate.
a) Gary Cooper
b) Clark Gable
c) Van Johnson
d) Jimmy Durante

[371]
What song does Harpo play for Ethel and Carolyn?

[372]
In the last scene Ricky and Fred run in dressed as _____ and _____ Marx

LUCY:

RICKY, I'M NOT ASKING FOR MUCH. ALL I WANT IS A HALF A DOZEN MOVIE STARS FOR A COUPLE OF HOURS.

In 1938 Lucille Ball made the movie *Room Service* with the Marx Brothers—Harpo was her favorite. Born Adolph Marx on November 23, 1893, in New York, Harpo was the second of five brothers. He quit school after kindergarten and helped to support his family with his job as a delivery boy. His musical talent was developed, in part, by learning to play his grandmother's beloved harp. In 1922, he and his brothers left vaudeville to star on Broadway, and after that landed in Hollywood where they made movies together in the 1930s and '40s.

The "mirror" pantomime by Harpo and Lucy was based on a scene from the Marx Brothers' movie *Duck Soup* (1933).

Episode 124 was filmed before Episode 125, although as far as the *I Love Lucy* plot line goes, Episode 125 comes first (and was aired first).

THE DANCING STAR

5/2/55

EPISODE

125

Uh-oh, Carolyn Appleby is in Hollywood! Lucy has been lying about hobnobbing with movie stars, and now she has to produce. On bended knee she pleads with Van Johnson to let her rehearse his dance number with him so she can fool Carolyn. But when Van's partner gets sick, he asks Lucy to fill in for real.

Marco must have come to California with Ricky since he is also Van's pianist in this episode.

Van Johnson met Desi in 1939, when they acted together in the Broadway play *Too Many Girls*. Johnson was born August 25, 1916 in Newport, Rhode Island. Hollywood first discovered Van in the movie version of *Too Many Girls* (1940). His first big hit was *Murder in the Big House* (1941).

[373]
Who is Van's regular dancing partner?

[374]
True or False: Lucy and Ethel have seen Van's show fourteen times.

[375]
What happened to Carolyn's glasses?
a) she left them on the plane
b) she left them in New York
c) she broke them
d) she needs a new prescription

Lucy: Oh what am I going to do? I know she's probably on her way over here right now and I haven't even got an idea. You think of something.

Ethel: Listen, if Einstein can't work out a problem you don't hand it to Mortimer Snerd.

RICKY NEEDS AN AGENT

MGM still hasn't found a picture for Ricky. Hoping that she can light a fire under Dore Schary, Lucy decides to impersonate Ricky's agent and pretend that Ricky has another offer to star on Broadway. She is more than surprised when Metro decides to let Ricky out of his contract. After all, they don't want to hold him back!

[376]
Which of the following has Ricky not done?
a) dedicated a new freeway
b) judged a cat show
c) opened a supermarket
d) crowned the queen of an automobile show

[377]
Lucy the "agent" visits _____ at MGM.

[378]
What does Ricky do when Lucy tells him what she did?

Ethel: Oh Lucy, what are you going to do?

Lucy: I don't know.

Ethel: Oh honey!

Lucy: I thought maybe I'd dye my hair black and move to Mexico. But first I'm gonna swim to Catalina to throw him off the scent.

Ethel: Oh honey!

Lucy: There's just one thing I can do, Ethel.

Ethel: What?

Lucy: I'm just gonna have to face him with what I've done.

Ethel: Oh you know Ricky's temper.

Lucy: Yeah, we've met.

Desi Arnaz had his first acting job in the Rogers and Hart musical *Too Many Girls* on Broadway.

Lucy Ricardo is seen looking through Lucille Ball's real scrapbooks again.

Trying to convince Walter Reilly to keep Ricky, Lucy mentions he could star in such remakes as *Gone with the Cuban Wind, It Happened One Noche,* and *Meet Me in St. Ricky.*

THE TOUR

Lucy and Ethel decide to take a bus tour of movie star homes. Lucy annoys the driver with her constant chatter and bragging, so when she asks to be let out to pick a Richard Widmark grapefruit, the bus takes off. And when Lucy falls over the guard wall, she has no choice but to sneak inside and try to get out the front door.

Lucy and Ethel take tour bus number 134. The tour goes from the Hollywood Freeway to downtown, up Wilshire Boulevard to the beach, to the Pacific Palisades and through Brentwood, Bel Air, Holmby Hills, and Beverly Hills.

Richard Widmark promotes his new film, *Prize of Gold*. Widmark was born December 26, 1914, in Sunrise, Minnesota. His first Hollywood film, *Kiss of Death* (1947), catapulted him into celebrity stardom. In many of his early films, he played the gangster role, but he later broadened his talents and acted the part of the hero.

[373]
Where does Ricky have lunch with Richard Widmark?
a) Perrino's
b) The Brown Derby
c) The Farmer's Market
d) Romanoff's

[374]
True of False: Rock Hudson's house was on the tour.

[375]
Where does Lucy hide when Richard Widmark comes home?

BONUS: Who discovers her there?

Ricky (to Richard Widmark): Well, I'll tell you Dick, the way I look at it is this way, you know everybody has a problem. There are some people that have financial problems, and then there are people that have health problems. Everybody has something, you know. Well, there it is (points to Lucy), my problem. But I love her . . .

I HAVE FOND MEMORIES OF *I LOVE LUCY*.
My parents grew up watching the show, and their love for the Ricardos and Mertzes was passed on to my sister and me. I remember watching episodes in the afternoons when I got home from school. My whole family would laugh hysterically at Lucy's predicaments, and those fun times are etched into my childhood memories. The great feelings that *I Love Lucy* brought during those special moments are the reason I will always love Lucy. Music and film have always been a part of my life, and *I Love Lucy*, with its humor and lovable characters, helped to fuel my own desire to perform. From the musical influence of Ricky and his band, to Lucy's star-struck adventures in Hollywood, the show had a huge impact on my life.

LANCE BASS
'N SYNC

THE FIFTH SEASON

1955-1956

LUCY VISITS GRAUMAN'S

Ricky's picture has just been wrapped up, so it's time to head east. Lucy and the Mertzes beg for one more week. Lucy decides she just has to get one more souvenir: John Wayne's footprints from in front of Grauman's Chinese Theatre! Lucy steps in the bucket of cement, and later the footprints break into a million pieces. Ay carumba!

[382]
How much does Ethel pay for caviar for Ricky's celebration?
a) $2.50
b) $10.00
c) $5.00
d) $8.75

[283]
What star's feet does Fred think are the same size as Ethel's?

[284]
When Ricky walks in to the Mertzes' hotel room, Lucy pretends to be _____.

Lucy: I'm gonna take home a souvenir to end all souvenirs— John Wayne's block!

Ethel: Well, you'll need it cause when Ricky finds out, he'll knock yours off!

This is the first episode to have a new sponsor— General Foods. Their signature product was Sanka coffee.

The name of Ricky's new film is never mentioned.

The Grauman's marquee promotes *The Tall Man*, starring Jane Russell and Clark Gable.

Conveniently, Ricky finds a hammer on Fred's dresser, and he is able to smash the cement on Lucy's foot.

John Wayne was born Marion Michael Morrison on May 26, 1907, in Winterset, Iowa. During a college break, Wayne got a job as a prop boy at the Fox Film Corporation and met director John Ford, who cast him in the film *Hangman's House* (1930). During the filming of *The Big Trail* in 1931, his director changed his name to make him more appealing for the cowboy roles he would play throughout his career.

LUCY AND JOHN WAYNE

Lucy and Ethel have made the morning paper! Police are out combing the streets for the thieves who stole John Wayne's cement block from the forecourt of Grauman's Chinese Theater. Ricky is furious and his career might be on the line. He calls his friend John Wayne and asks if he will do him a favor. Mr. Wayne graciously consents to re-do his footprints—over and over again!

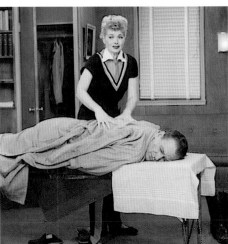

John Wayne's new picture is *Blood Alley*, produced by Warner Bros. Wayne received scale for his work ($280) on *I Love Lucy*.

Fred calls John Wayne "Count" instead of "Duke."

Fred calls himself "Bone-Crusher Mertz."

The Millers have the hotel suite directly under the Ricardos.

[385]
The newspaper describes Lucy as a _____ redhead, and Ethel as a _____ blonde.

BONUS: Name the couple that saw them loitering.

[386]
What is the total number of blocks of footprints that John Wayne made?
a) 7
b) 6
c) 5
d) 4

[387]
True or False: John Wayne's masseuse is named Steve.

Lucy: Have you gone crazy? How can we take it back—it's broken into a million pieces!

Ricky: He says if I bring it back undamaged he will protect me. Otherwise it's a case for the police!

Lucy: Ehhhhh!

LUCY AND THE DUMMY

The studio wants Ricky to be in a show for the MGM executives, but he is determined to go fishing. Lucy tricks them into letting her do the show with "Ricky" (actually a life-sized dummy with a sculpted Ricky head on it!) The number is a flop, but the execs think it is so funny they offer Lucy a studio contract!

[388]
Ethel teases that Fred "gets queasy if I have too many _____ in my hair!"

[389]
Who calls from MGM to ask Ricky to be in the show?
a) Matt Reeves
b) Chip Jansen
c) George Lewis
d) Steve Johnson

[390]
True or False: Ricky thinks his head sculpture should be made into a lamp.

Ricky (to Lucy):
Angry? Honey, why should I be angry? Just because you took a dummy over to the studio and made him pass as your husband? Why honey, that is exactly what any normal, red-blooded, American girl would've done

During the original airing of this episode, the television audience was treated to a short preview of the new MGM musical, *Guys and Dolls*, starring Marlon Brando, Frank Sinatra, and Jean Simmons.

Ricky gets Lucy to turn down the contract by telling her that he will show Little Ricky her picture every night, and she will be able to come home for a whole day at Christmas.

RICKY SELLS THE CAR

Ricky sells the car and plans to go home on the train, but he forgets to buy train tickets for the Mertzes! They are so insulted they buy an antique motorcycle, intending to drive it all the way back to New York. Ricky agrees to buy their tickets, but Lucy gives them the wrong ones and is forced to try to "steal them back."

In Episode 128, the Mertzes' hotel room was on the left side of the Ricardos' suite. In this episode, it is on the right.

The name of the train they are taking is the City of Los Angeles. Ricky buys the train tickets on the family plan—one for him, one for Lucy, and one for Mother McGillicuddy. Little Ricky doesn't need one.

The Ricardos travel in compartments; the only tickets Ricky could get for the Mertzes are for upper berths.

[391]
Ricky's friend _____ buys the Ricardos' car.

[392]
What does Lucy ask Fred to get her from the store?
a) tissues
b) baby powder
c) Q-tips
d) hand cream

BONUS: What does he actually buy?

[393]
Ethel gets a ticket for what offense?

Ethel: I presume that when Ricky sold the car, the back seat went with it.

Lucy: Well naturally, what are you getting at?

Fred: Well, we were rather attached to that back seat. That's the way we came out here and that's the way we planned on going home.

Lucy: Is that what you're upset about?

Ethel: You'd be upset too if you just had your backseat shot out from under you!

THE GREAT TRAIN ROBBERY

The gang is set to head back east but the usual mishaps prevail. First Lucy leaves her purse at the station, then Mother and Little Ricky switch compartments, and finally Lucy gets involved with a jewelry heist! Through it all our redheaded heroine manages to stop the train, drive the conductor out of his mind, and save the day.

[394]
How many times does Lucy pull the emergency brake handle?
a) 3
b) 4
c) 5
d) 6

[395]
What compartment are Mother McGillicuddy and Little Ricky supposed to be in?

[396]
The jeweler's name is Mr. _____.

CONDUCTOR:
MADAME, DID YOU STOP THIS TRAIN BY PULLING THAT HANDLE?
LUCY:
WELL, I DIDN'T DO IT BY DRAGGING MY FOOT!

The train's first stop is in Riverside, California.

After the second emergency stop, the conductor bet the engineer $5 that Lucy would pull the brake again. Can you guess who wins the bet?

Character-actor Frank Nelson is brilliant as the beleaguered train conductor in this episode. In 1963, he would reprise his conductor role on *The Lucy Show* in the episode titled "Lucy Visits the White House".

The Hollywood trip, which was to last a month, ended up lasting ten months.

THE HOMECOMING

King Ricky has returned to his kingdom and he is amazed that all his friends are now his fans. They hang on his every word—even Ethel and Fred. And Lucy! Determined to get his old life back, Ricky acts the part of a star, ordering Lucy around, demanding she fulfill his every wish. Until she comes back to earth, that is!

[397]
What is the name of the taxi cab company that brings the Ricardos and Mertzes back home?

[398]
When Mother McGillicuddy forgot to cancel the paper, Mrs. Trumble puts them all in the _____.

[399]
What is the title of Nancy Graham's story about Lucy?
a) "The Movie Star's Wife"
b) "My Life with Ricky"
c) "Now I Am His Slave"
d) "I Devoted my Life to Him"

Ricky makes a mistake when he says he and Richard Widmark had lunch at Perrino's; they ate at Romanoff's.

There were 160 million people living in the United States at the time of this episode.

Fred nearly faints when he learns that Mrs. Trumble turned on the furnace but couldn't turn it off. It's been running for two weeks!

Lucy (to Ricky): And I'm not gonna lift a little finger to help you anymore. You can answer your own phone, shine your own shoes, type your own lyrics, light your own cigarettes, and knock off your own ashes. And if you want another roast pig you can crawl into the oven yourself, you big ham!

185

FACE TO FACE

Ricky's new agent thinks he should move into a swanky apartment. Ricky and Lucy say no, they are happy where they are. But the Mertzes think they should move to help Ricky's career. After a series of misunderstandings, the two couples become mortal enemies. It takes an appearance on a TV show for them to see the light.

[400]
Ricky's new agency is _____ and his new agent is _____.

[401]
Name the host of Face to Face.

[402]
True or False: Lucy looks at new apartments that cost $11,000 a year.

Ethel: Now let's see, how does a landlord get a tenant to move out?

Fred: Well suppose we give 'em a lot of bad service—no heat, no repairs. Think that'll work?

Ethel: It hasn't for fifteen years!

Ricky's new agent is played by a good friend of William Frawley.

Ethel calls her Aunt Martha and Uncle Elmo at Gramercy 3-8098.

During the TV interview, Fred takes his jacket off to show his shirt that reads "Call Fred Mertz Plaza 5-6098."

Mrs. Schyler calls Ethel to get a reference for Lucy and Ricky.

LUCY GOES TO A RODEO

Fred's lodge is going to put on a western show and Lucy and Ethel are in it. Meanwhile Ricky thinks he is booked to do a radio show, but it's really a *rodeo* show! When he can't find any real talent, the gang comes to his rescue. They help him put on a great show full of singers, dancers, and bell ringers. Yee-haw!

Ricky sings "Texas Pete," a western version of his famed "Cuban Pete."

Ricky says he was born in West Havana.

Lucy is introduced as Lucy "Cannonball" McGillicuddy.

When they first hear of Fred's lodge show, Lucy and Ethel suggest they reproduce their famous operetta, *The Pleasant Peasant*.

[403]
Fred's old buddy is named _____ Jones.

[404]
At what famous New York spot does Ricky's rodeo show take place?
a) Madison Square Garden
b) Radio City Music Hall
c) The Palace Theatre
d) Central Park

[405]
True or False: Ricky pays the gang $100 to do the show.

Lucy: Did I hear someone say that they had to get a show together?

Ethel: Lucy, you were way out in Little Ricky's room, how'd you hear him say that?

Ricky: Listen, when it comes to hearing about show business, Lucy has a special sense. Something that the Navy later developed and called radar.

187

[406]
What condition does Lucy claim to be suffering from?

[407]
Lucy has been reading a book by _____ ever since Little Ricky was born.

[408]
Little Ricky has had tonsillitis _____ times.
a) 3
b) 4
c) 5
d) 6

Lucy (to Ricky): After breakfast I put on his snowsuit, I pull on his galoshes, I slip on his mittens, I walk him to the park. He chases the pigeons, I chase after him, he runs after the squirrels, I run after him, he gets on the swing, I push the swing, we go on the teeter-totter, he teeters, I totter. Then we leave the park and we walk home, and I pull off his galoshes and I pull off his mittens, I pull off his snowsuit, I fix his lunch, I put him down for his nap and he sleeps for a whole half-hour!

NURSERY SCHOOL

Ricky thinks Little Ricky should go to nursery school but Lucy is afraid of losing her baby. After the first day of school Little Ricky gets another case of tonsillitis, and the doctor schedules surgery. Little Ricky comes through fine, but when Lucy is told she can't spend the night, there is nothing this mother won't do to be with her son.

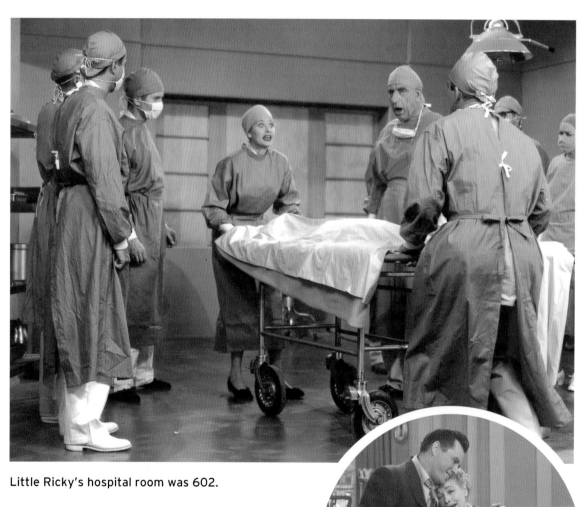

Little Ricky's hospital room was 602.

In nursery school Little Ricky paints a picture of an elephant sailing a houseboat.

The hospital nurse tells Ricky they are looking for a "screwball redhead nurse who has gone berserk."

Ricky does some English-mangling with his new saying: "Spin the beans out of the cat bag."

RICKY'S EUROPEAN BOOKING

Ricky just signed a deal for a three-week European trip. Lucy and Ethel can only go if they raise the $3,000 themselves, so they devise a plan to hold a raffle. Trouble is, the D.A.'s office catches wind of the scheme and they could go to jail for fraud. Luckily for Lucy, the charity is for real, and then Ricky finds out they can go for free after all!

Lucy found $9.73 in the chairs and sofas: $29.25 in the sugar bowls, and $28.16 in the piggy banks. Ethel found lint and a Woodrow Wilson button.

Hazel Pierce won the raffle with ticket #2725. Hazel was Lucy's stand-in and a regular extra on the show.

During the episode, Ricky and the Pied Pipers sing the song "Forever Darling," which helped to promote Lucy and Desi's new film of the same name.

The original script names for Mrs. Wolbert and Mr. Feldman were Mrs. Osborne and Mr. Mellman.

[409]
How much money did Lucy and Ethel find around the house?
a) $213.76
b) $205.82
c) $198.54
d) $200.16

BONUS: What does "GTHP" stand for?

[410]
How many raffle tickets does Ricky buy from Lucy?

[411]
Ricky gives the band manager job to _____.

Ricky: Now, if I promise her a wonderful trip later on, I think she'll be reasonable.

Fred: My Lucy has red hair and blue eyes. What does your Lucy look like?

THE PASSPORTS

The gang needs passports and Lucy can't find her birth certificate. Is there no record of her birth? She tries to get an old friend and her pediatrician to sign letters on her behalf, but the friend chickens out, and after Lucy locks herself in a trunk, the doctor can't identify her! All is well when good old Mom sends the birth certificate.

[412]
What important document does Ricky need from the safe deposit box?
a) his old passport
b) his Cuban birth certificate
c) his naturalization papers
d) his Social Security card

[413]
What name did Helen call Lucy when she was little?

BONUS: What is Helen's new last name?

[414]
When she was young, Lucy was bitten by _____'s cat.

Lucy: If I'd known Jamestown was gonna be that careless I'd've been born somewhere else.

Ricky: Well, honey, you need your birth certificate if you wanna get a passport.

Lucy: Well, what'd you want me to do? They never heard of me!

Fred: Well, maybe you were never born.

If there is no written proof of your birth, it is possible to get a passport by obtaining affidavits from people who witnessed your birth.

Lucy Ricardo was born in 1921 in West Jamestown, New York. There is no West Jamestown, New York, only Jamestown, where Lucille Ball was born in 1911.

Dr. Peterson was probably named after Lucille's stepfather, Ed Peterson.

The original itinerary had the group traveling to London, Paris, Venice, Holland, Madrid, and the French Riviera—all in three weeks.

STATEN ISLAND FERRY

Lucy and Ethel hate their new passport photos, but time is running out for them to get their passports. Meanwhile, Fred expresses his concern over seasickness so Lucy takes him for a ride on a New York ferry. Fred takes seasick pills and feels great. Lucy takes them and falls asleep! She barely wakes up enough to get her passport.

The gang is sailing on the SS *Constitution*.

Fred has learned the words to order nine different kinds of beer. Lucy has learned to ask, "How much is that dress in the window," and "Wrap it up; I'll take it!"

Lucy calls her friends Marion and Norman Van Vlack, who were real-life friends of Lucille Ball.

At the end of the original episode, they aired an announcement for "Truth Dollars," which were purchased to help Radio Free Europe broadcast behind the Iron Curtain.

[415]
Lucy, Ricky, Ethel, and Fred are all studying different languages for their trip. Match the character to the language:

Lucy   Italian
Ricky   German
Ethel   English
Fred   French

[416]
In search of better photos, Ethel and Lucy hire their own photographer and each has _____ more photos taken.

BONUS: The same photographer once took photos of Lucy for what other important event?

[417]
True or False: Fred took two seasickness pills.

Lucy and Ethel (looking at photos): AHHHHH!

Lucy: I look like Frankenstein!

Ethel: Well, shake hands with your bride.

BON VOYAGE

The gang is finally off—or so they think. At the last minute Lucy runs off the ship to give Little Ricky one last kiss. She gets her skirt stuck in a bicycle chain and the ship pulls off without her. She misses the pilot boat, and has only one other chance of getting on board—she will be flown out by helicopter and lowered onto the deck!

[418]
What French product does Mrs. Trumble ask Lucy to bring back for her?

[419]
Lucy has to get the helicopter at which airport?
a) Idelwilde
b) La Guardia
c) Stewart
d) Newark

[420]
True or False: After she misses the pilot boat, the dock agent tells Lucy she can sail on the *Queen Elizabeth II*.

LUCY (TO HELICOPTER PILOT):

YOU HOVER OVER WHERE AND LOWER WHO ON A WHAT?

I Love Lucy writer and European traveler Bob Carroll, Jr. appears in this episode as a ship passenger.

The Ricardos are in room 0785.

The SS *Constitution* had a ballroom, a theater, shops, and elevators.

After the original episode aired, Lucy and Desi announced the release of the new "Forever Darling" record, the title song of their new movie.

SECOND HONEYMOON

The lovebug has bitten Fred Mertz and he and Ethel are on their second honeymoon. Poor Lucy has been left behind because Ricky has to work all day and all night, so she schemes to lock Ricky in for the night. But when she finds out he has the night off, she calls for Ethel through the porthole and gets herself stuck!

[421]
Name Lucy's winning } partner.

BONUS: The pair received a trophy for winning what shipboard contest?

[422]
How many days will the gang be aboard?
a) 4
b) 5
c) 6
d) 7

[423]
A surprised Lucy says, "The love bug? I thought Fred had been _____."

Lucy: Ethel, what's the name of this boat?

Ethel: The SS *Constitution*, why?

Lucy: Well, from the way everybody's paired off I thought it was the SS *Noah's Ark*.

The captain's name is Captain Jacobson.

Lucy wants to do all the activities on board—tea dances, shuffle board, deck tennis, and ping pong, to name a few.

There is a large bloodhound on board named Rocky.

Ethel has a new nickname for old Freddie—Tiger!

LUCY MEETS THE QUEEN

The Yanks have landed on the British shore, and Lucy wants to see the queen. Told they will be presented to the queen, Lucy and Ethel get leg cramps when they practice curtsying. Later Ricky allows Lucy to be in his show in the circus pony act. After her dance Lucy cramps up, but nothing will stop her from meeting Her Majesty!

[424]
The Fab Four is staying in what hotel
a) Wimbledon Hotel
b) Wiltshire Hotel
c) Wimbleshire Hotel
d) Wellington Hotel

[425]
At what famous London venue does Ricky perform?

[426]
True or False: Fred gives Ethel ten dollars to spend.

Lucy: Gee, I don't know how to address a queen. What do I say? Hello Highness? Good evening, Elizabeth?

Ethel: Maybe you just call her Mrs. Mountbatten.

Fred: Oh you make so much of this. You just walk up, slip her the grip and say, "Hi ya, Queen."

Buckingham Palace has over five hundred rooms.

Queen Elizabeth II was born April 21, 1926, in London, and became England's royal ruler upon the death of her father, George VI, in 1952. At the time this episode was filmed she had only two children, Charles and Anne.

In 1956 a British pound was worth about $2.80 in American currency.

Nancy Kulp, who would later star as Miss Hathaway on *The Beverly Hillbillies*, appeared in this episode as the hotel maid.

THE FOX HUNT

The American foursome has been invited to an estate for the weekend where they will take part in a foxhunt. Lucy is jealous of the estate owner's daughter, a young, beautiful, single actress. When Ricky joins the foxhunt, so does Lucy. It takes her several tries to get on the horse, and once she does she doesn't stay on for long!

Lucy said she took Boring Talk 1A in high school. She also told Ricky she rode horses at Girl Scout camp.

Ricky says that "Ai yi yi" is an expression that translates to the British "blimey."

Lucy's horse is named Danny Boy.

At the end of the original episode, Lucille and Desi announced the world premiere of their movie *Forever Darling* in Jamestown on April 7, 1956. Desi said this was his first try at being a movie producer.

[427]
Name the man who invited the Ricardos to his estate for the weekend.

BONUS: Name his estate.

[428]
Angela Randall would like to "borrow" Ricky for the afternoon to attend Cecily Higgins' _____.
a) coming-out party
b) croquet match
c) luncheon
d) lawn party

[429]
After she is thrown from the horse, where does Lucy land?

Ethel: Lucy, why did you say you'd go on a foxhunt? You've never been on a horse in your life!

Lucy: Well, I don't care, I'm not letting them out of my sight. The fox isn't the only thing she's hunting!

LUCY GOES TO SCOTLAND

Lucy dreams that she is a Scottish lass visiting the town of her ancestor Angus McGillicuddy, when she is kidnapped by the townsfolk to be fed to the horrible two-headed dragon! Ricky appears as Scotty MacTavish MacDougall MacArdo and falls in love with her. He plans to save her from her fate, but chickens out in the end.

[430]
How often does the fearsome dragon eat?
a) every 30 days
b) every 30 weeks
c) every 30 months
d) every 30 years

[431]
Scotty MacArdo's great-great-great-grandfather sailed to Scotland with the Spanish Armada. His name was _____ Ricardo.

[432]
Fill in the blanks: "Fee Fi Fo _____, I smell the blood of a _____."

Lucy (singing): I'd give you my Davy Crockett hat, my shillings, my fillings, my cricket bat, my candied yams, my brandied quince, my TV antenna, my henna rinse!

Lucy and Ricky never actually visited Scotland on camera.

This episode was filmed in color with Desi Arnaz's personal home movie camera, and the footage still exists today as part of the family's private home movie collection.

Lucille Ball was part Scottish.

Lucy's full name is Lucille Esmerelda McGillicuddy Ricardo.

Vivian Vance and William Frawley are comically perfect as the two-headed dragon that can't decide between a McGillicuddy burger or McGillicuddy foo young!

PARIS AT LAST!

When Lucy unknowingly exchanges her U.S. dollars for phony French francs the trouble begins. After she insults a chef by asking for ketchup for her escargot, she tries to pay with counterfeit money and then ends up in the Paris police station. Only a drunk who speaks Spanish and German stands between her and the Bastille!

[433]
Lucy expects to get 7,000 French francs for her $20. How much does the counterfeiter offer her?

[433]
Name the "artist" who sells Lucy a painting.

[435]
At what hotel is the gang staying?
a) Hotel Royale
b) Hotel Parisian
c) Hotel Montmartre
d) Hotel Louis XIV

LUCY:
WAITER, THIS FOOD HAS SNAILS IN IT!

Lucy sings the French song "Alouette" as she waits for her meal.

Lucy pays only 400 francs for her "specialite de la maison"—just over $1! She pays less than $3 for the painting by the unknown "artist" she meets on the street.

Fred complains about the forwarding of Christmas cards, although the gang left several weeks after Christmas.

Writers Madelyn Pugh and Bob Carroll, Jr. appeared in this episode, sitting at the table in the cafe next to Lucy.

At the end of the original broadcast of this episode Lucille and Desi did an announcement to alert people about Heart Month.

LUCY MEETS CHARLES BOYER

When Lucy spots French star Charles Boyer at a cafe, he insists he is an out-of-work actor named Maurice DuBois. When Ricky pretends to be jealous of Boyer, Lucy hatches a scheme with "DuBois" to pretend that she is not interested so Ricky will feel better. When DuBois is exposed as Boyer Lucy's antics ruin his day, not to mention his wardrobe.

[436]
How much does Lucy offer to pay "DuBois"?
a) 1,000 francs
b) 5,000 francs
c) 3,500 francs
d) 10,000 francs

[437]
True or False: Lucy eats a banana while "DuBois" is trying to woo her.

[438]
Ethel laments: "Fred wouldn't smolder if he backed into a _____."

Lucy: I have a big problem! Ricky is insanely jealous of Charles Boyer!

Ethel: Ha-ha-ha!

Lucy: He is! You should have seen him—he was so mad he was snorting like a bull, and his eyes bugged out something awful!

Ethel: Worse than they usually do?

The gang eats at the Cafe Du Monde.

An article about Ricky's lunch with Boyer appears in the *Paris Tribune*. (Copies of the Paris edition of the *Herald Tribune* were flown in for use in this episode.)

Desi Arnaz shows his talent for comedy in the scenes in which Ricky pretends to be jealous of Boyer.

Born August 28, 1899, in Figeac, France, Charles Boyer was a natural for stage and screen. Blessed with a phenomenal memory and an acute sense of style, he won worldwide acclaim for both his film and stage work. His well-known Hollywood films include *Gaslight* (1943) and *Nana* (1957).

LUCY GETS A PARIS GOWN

Lucy wants a Jacques Marcel dress and she is willing to starve to get one. At last Ricky buys her one, but takes it back when he realizes her "strike" was a hoax. Ricky and Fred cook up a scheme to teach the girls a lesson by having a tailor sew up some potato sack dresses for them, which they wear in public on the streets of gay Paris.

Ricky: Oh honey, forget about the fashion show, let's have some lunch. What'd you want?

Lucy: Nothing.

Ricky: What do you mean nothing?

Lucy: I am going on a hunger strike.

Ricky: Oh no.

Lucy: Until you buy me a Jacques Marcel dress, no food will pass my lips.

Ethel: Oh don't you think that's carrying things . . .

Ricky: Leave her alone. If that's what she wants to do, it's all right with me.

Fred: Yeah, that hunger strike's a good idea, Ethel, why don't you . . .

Ethel: Oh shut up.

On February 28, 1955, Lucy made a written statement that read: "If Ricky buys me a Don Loper original, I will never ask him for another expensive dress as long as I live." Of course, we know that Lucy got the Don Loper dress for free. Ricky, however, is still in the dark.

Big spender Ethel bought a handbag in Paris that cost 1,000 francs—or $2.85.

One of the sack dresses that appeared in this episode still survives and is owned by the Arnaz family.

[439]
Match the food with the place Lucy has hidden it:

bologna	in the atomizer
lettuce	in a book
mustard	in a vase
milk	under a lamp
	skirt

[440]
Lucy complains: "If I stay on this hunger strike much longer I'll be _____."

[441]
What is the lowest price of a Jacques Marcel dress?
a) $250
b) $500
c) $750
d) $1000

LUCY IN THE SWISS ALPS

To get Ricky's mind off of his missing musicians, Lucy plans an afternoon of mountain climbing in the Swiss Alps. After a lovely lunch on top of the world, the gang heads down and straight into a snow storm. They get snowed in, while taking refuge in a mountain cabin but are rescued hours later by a leiderhosen-clad oom-pa band.

[442]
Fred sent the band to _____, but they were supposed to go to _____.

BONUS: How did the plans get messed up?

[443]
Locked in the cabin, Ethel confesses she was nineteen when she married. Fred says no, she was:
a) 18
b) 20
c) 22
d) 24

[444]
What food does Lucy find hidden in her backpack?

Lucy: Well, actually the whole thing is Ricky's fault.

Ricky: My fault?

Lucy: Yeah, if you hadn't left Cuba and come to America, we wouldn't have gotten married and we wouldn't be in Switzerland in the first place!

Fred confesses that he charges the Ricardos $10 more a week than all the other tenants. Ethel confesses that she has always given it back to them. This doesn't seem possible, since Fred rarely allowed Ethel to even touch the rent money.

While in the cabin the gang discussed the movie musical *Seven Brides for Seven Brothers*, in which all the brides and brothers are stuck in one house together until the spring thaw!

LUCY GETS HOMESICK IN ITALY

Fred books the gang into a no-star hotel. The elevator is broken, the beds are like stone, and the only phone is in the lobby. Desperate to speak to her son on his third birthday, Lucy is thwarted at every turn. When a local boy says "it's-a his" birthday too, Lucy throws a party for the boy and his friends, who later sing to Little Ricky.

[445]
How much does Fred owe the furnace man for fixing the apartment furnace?

[446]
Besides candy and a party, what gift did Lucy give to Giuseppi?

BONUS: Why wouldn't he accept it?

[447]
Lucy and Ricky are in the fourth-floor "bridal suite." Fred and Ethel are a floor above in what Ethel calls the bridal suite for _____.

LUCY:
THAT ELEVATOR, SHE'S-A NO BUST, SHE'S-A POOPED!

Lucy and Ricky are in room 47 in the Hotel Grande in the town of Florence.

Little Ricky did turn three in 1956, but he was born on January 19th, not in April.

The hotel manager is named Señor Nicoletti, probably after Desi's longtime friend and *I Love Lucy* extra, Lou "Nick" Nicoletti.

Lucy pretends to call Benjamin Franklin at Pallazio 8000.

Bart Braverman, who played little Giuseppi, went on to have a career in television.

This is the last time the Mayer twins would be seen as Little Ricky, and Mrs. McGillicuddy would not return again until, briefly, the twelfth episode of *The Lucille Ball-Desi Arnaz Show.*

LUCY'S ITALIAN MOVIE

On the train to Rome, Lucy is "discovered" by an Italian film director who wants her to act in his new film, *Bitter Grapes*. In order to get a feel for the grape industry, Lucy disobeys Ricky's order and spends a day at a local vineyard. She is chosen to do the "stomping," and ends up getting stomped on by her co-worker in the vat!

[448]
What time does the train arrive in Rome?
a) 8 PM
b) 10 AM
c) 3 PM
d) 6 AM

[449]
Fred compares the Roman Colosseum with what New York landmark?

[450]
Vittorio Phillippe wanted Lucy for the part of a _____, and when she came home all stained with grape juice, he hires _____ for the role.

Lucy: All I wanna do is soak up a little local color so I know what I'm acting about. What could possibly happen to me?

The Ricardos are in hotel room 605.

This is one of the most famous and popular *I Love Lucy* episodes. "Job Switching," another fan favorite, takes place in Kramer's Kandy Kitchen, and also involves food throwing.

The grapes used in the filming were grown in California, not Italy.

Fred is on the lookout for Italian movie queen Gina Lollobrigida.

Lucy is seen reading the Italian movie magazine *Teatro*.

LUCY'S BICYCLE TRIP

It's time to say *arrivedercci* Italy and *bonjour* France. Lucy wants to take the cross-border trip on bicycles. After staying overnight in an Italian farmer's barn, they arrive at the border. Ricky, Ethel, and Fred pass through but Lucy has forgotten her passport! Is it locked in her trunk? Where is the key? It could take a miracle to get Lucy to Nice.

The bikes used were courtesy of Arnold Schwinn and Company.

Bicycling is a popular sport in Europe; every summer France hosts a three-week long international race called Le Tour de France.

In this episode, Lucy tries to cross the border by pretending to be a rider in the "Festival de Nice" bike race, which was taking place April 23-25.

Fred called Lucy "Miss Crazy Quilt."

The Italian farmer serves a "continental breakfast" to the group—bread, cheese, and very fresh milk (that Lucy "collects" herself)!

Ricky: Fred wants to go to Nice by bus.

Fred: The train's faster, but I vote for the bus because it's cheaper.

Ricky: Well, I vote for the train.

Ethel: And I vote for the train.

Lucy: I vote for bicycles.

LUCY GOES TO MONTE CARLO

[454]
How much money does Fred now claim they made in Rome?
a) $3
b) $30
c) $300
d) $3,000

[455]
True or False: Ethel claims Fred hides his money in his underwear drawer.

[456]
Lucy tells Ricky and Fred that Ethel's rich French Aunt _____ left her the money.

Lucy (on the hotel phone): Ethel, listen to me now, Ricky's gone downstairs, it's my only chance to talk to you. Ricky found all that money in your suitcase and thought Fred had been juggling the books, so I told him it was your money.

Ethel: What'd you do that for?

Lucy: Well I didn't want him to think Fred was an embezzler, and I didn't want him to find out I'd been gambling, and you were the only one left—I ran out of people!

While strolling though a casino, Lucy finds a chip on the floor, throws it back on the table, and wins! She keeps her chips on the table and she keeps winning! Afraid that Ricky will be furious that she gambled, Lucy hides the money. Ricky finds it in the Mertzes' hotel room, and thinks Fred has been embezzling the band's money!

Lucy writer Bob Carroll, Jr., appears in this episode as a gambler.

At the time this episode was filmed, one U.S. dollar was worth about 350 French francs, so Lucy's 875,000-franc jackpot would have been worth about $2,500. No wonder Fred is so thrilled when he thinks the money belongs to Ethel!

RETURN HOME FROM EUROPE

Needing to get home in a hurry to play at the Roxy, Ricky makes plane reservations. Everything except clothing will have to be shipped, but Lucy is determined to take a 25-pound Italian cheese to her mother. Since Ricky won't pay extra for it, the only "logical" thing to do is disguise the cheese to look like a baby so it can fly for free!

Mrs. McGillicuddy makes a mistake when she forwards Ricky's important telegram via regular mail. It arrives so late that Ricky almost misses his chance to play at the Roxy.

Desi Arnaz publicly announced his marriage to Lucille Ball during his show at the Roxy Theatre in New York, the same day they eloped.

Doris Singleton, who plays Mrs. Bigsby in this episode, had been a regular as Carolyn Appleby in previous episodes.

Ricky says the airlines will only allow sixty-six pounds per person on the plane and every pound over costs $2. Lucy's "baby" ends up costing 10 percent of the regular fare, or about $30.

Ricky refuses to sit next to his wife, claiming, "I am not the father of that cheese!"

[451]
What does Lucy say is the name of her "baby"?

BONUS: What is the name of Mrs. Evelyn Bigsby's baby?

[452]
Ricky admits, "Being married to you is not easy, but it sure is _____."

[459]
True or False: Mrs. Bigsby adds cod liver oil to her baby's formula.

Lucy: What do they take on the plane for free?

Ethel: Only the clothes you're wearing.

Lucy: Oh, well that's no good. Very few people wear cheese.

I FEEL LIKE I'VE KNOWN LUCY ALL MY LIFE.

She was one of my first baby-sitters from the moment I discovered her on television. As I got a little older, I loved Lucy's scheming to become part of Ricky's show. She was so determined to perform, and Ricky was just as determined to keep her off the stage. When she and Ethel would get into very elaborate situations that would always get messed up, I would laugh my head off. I think Lucy invented "Girl Power"!

I only have to think of Lucy and I start to smile. She can do that to me whenever I feel sad. I can always count on Lucy to cheer me up. Lucy inspired me to become an actress and try to make people laugh. She is definitely my role model.

Dressing up in '50s style dress, high heels, and a red wig, and "becoming Lucy" was one of my biggest thrills as an actress. It was so cool to go back in time and try to create an *I Love Lucy* moment. I don't think there will ever be another Lucy, but luckily she'll always be on TV for every future kid to discover why *I Love Lucy*!

AMANDA BYNES
ACTRESS, *THE AMANDA SHOW*

1956-1957

LUCY AND BOB HOPE

Ricky bought the Tropicana and renamed it Club Babalu. He wants to get Bob Hope for the opening night, and Lucy tries to help. She sees Mr. Hope at a baseball game and manages to get him beaned with a baseball. When she cries that Ricky never lets her be part of the act, Bob says he won't do the show if she can't. Famous last words!

[460]
Uncle Fred compares Little Ricky to what famous baseball player?
a) Babe Ruth
b) Lou Gehrig
c) Mickey Mantle
d) Joe DiMaggio

[461]
Lucy takes over the job of _____ at Yankee Stadium in order to get close to Bob Hope.

[462]
True or False: Lucy wears the number 22 on her Cleveland Indians uniform.

Bob Hope (to the tune of his signature song, "Thanks for the Memory"):
Hey, thanks for the memory, of being here with you, at your Club Babalu, and through it all I had a ball, in spite of you-know-who. How lovely it was . . .

This is Keith Thibodeaux's first appearance as Little Ricky.

Bob Hope plugs his newest movie, *The Iron Petticoat.*

Bob Hope owned a part of the Cleveland Indians team.

Lucille acted with Bob Hope in several films during her career, and Desi was hired by Hope to serve as musical director for Hope's radio show in 1946. Born Leslie Townes Hope on May 29, 1903, in Kent, England, Hope came to the U.S. in 1908 when his family settled in Cleveland. In 1933, he married wife Dolores and together they raised four children. Starring in dozens of movies, TV shows, and specials, Hope is particularly loved for his dedication to entertaining the armed service troops around the globe, in wartime and in peace.

LUCY MEETS ORSON WELLES

It's cold in New York and Lucy wants to go to Florida. She changes her tune when she hears Orson Welles wants her to perform with him at a benefit. She thinks she is going to recite Shakespeare with the great thespian, and invites her high school teacher to come witness the event. Alas, alack, she is only to be part of his magic act.

The original broadcast of this episode fell on the fifth anniversary of the first *I Love Lucy* broadcast.

Ellen Corby, who in later years portrayed the beloved Grandma Walton on *The Waltons*, played Lucy's high school drama teacher, Miss Hannah.

Famed actor and director Orson Welles was born May 6, 1915, in Kenosia, Wisconsin.

He graduated from high school at age fifteen, after which he took off for Ireland, where he landed his first theatrical role. An accomplished Shakespearean actor, Welles is perhaps best-known for his temperament, his 1938 sensation "War of the Worlds" radio broadcast, and his 1941 cinematic masterpiece *Citizen Kane*.

[463]
When Lucy meets Orson Welles in the department store, what product is he autographing?
a) his autobiography
b) his record album
c) his movie poster
d) his photo
BONUS: What is Lucy wearing at the time?

[464]
What play is Miss Hannah's class producing when Lucy calls?

[465]
Lucy played Juliet to _____'s Romeo.

Ethel: Well, winter is officially here. We've had our first cold wave, Fred's put on his red flannels, and you've started your annual "Let's Send Lucy to Florida" campaign.

LITTLE RICKY GETS STAGE FRIGHT

The gang is so nervous at Little Ricky's first music recital that their sympathy stage fright rubs off on him. He refuses to go on, or even to play the drums anymore. His music teacher says he must get back on stage, so Ricky arranges for Little Ricky and his band to play at Club Babalu. When one band member gets sick, Lucy fills in for the youngster.

[466]

Everyone is nervous! Match the character with his or her symptoms:

Lucy	forgot to put on pants
Ricky	got dressed and then took a shower
Ethel	put ice cubes in oven
Fred	couldn't eat breakfast

[467]

What instrument does Lucy play in the recital at the club?

BONUS: Name the little boy who was supposed to play it.

[468]

True or False: Fred comes over to fix the kitchen sink again.

Lucy: From here on he could develop a fear of all sorts of things. He might be afraid to go to school, he might be afraid to meet people, appear in public. Why if we don't conquer this right now it might ruin his whole life!

Ricky: Well, that makes a lot of sense. Boy I'm glad that you're the mother of my child.

Lucy: Well, thank you dear.

Ricky: When I thin' of all those other women I might have married.

Lucy: Yeah, you sure were lucky . . . all what other women?

Just like when Lucy went to the hospital, each adult was responsible for a piece of Little Ricky's drum set, but they walked out the door without Little Ricky!

Vivian Vance and William Frawley are great as they nervously search for each other all over the apartment building.

This is the first time five-year-old Keith Thibodeaux performs on the drums on *I Love Lucy*. Watch for his solo!

Episode 156 was filmed a week before Episode 157, although Episode 157 aired first. This may have been because in Episode 156, Little Ricky is ready for a concert, and in Episode 157 he has never even had a lesson.

LITTLE RICKY LEARNS TO PLAY THE DRUMS

Ricky wants his son to be a musician and Lucy wants him to be a physician. They undermine each other until it becomes clear that the boy possesses musical ability. But when Little Ricky's steady beat begins to drive everyone crazy, the adults get into a fight. They all come together again to find Little Ricky when he runs away.

Angry at Fred and Ethel, Lucy and Ricky beat out the "Nertz to the Mertz Mambo" on pots and pans.

Watch the kitchen scene during which Lucy and Ricky do everything to Little Ricky's beat, including cracking eggs, squeezing oranges, beating eggs, eating, and vacuuming.

Ricky asks for two eggs but Lucy gets so carried away that she cracks nine!

Fred calls Ethel "Miss United Parcel." Lucy calls Fred "Freddie the Fritzer." Lucy still calls her son "the baby."

This is the last time Mrs. Trumble would be seen.

[469]
How many years are left on the Ricardos' lease?
a) 97
b) 99
c) 96
d) 95

[470]
Ricky buys his son a drum at _____ Music Company.

[471]
True or False: Playing with his doctor's kit, Little Ricky diagnoses his dad as needing to have his tonsils out.

Ricky: Hey, it looks like he's gonna be a drummer!

Lucy: Well he certainly is not. That's that last thing I want him to be.

Ricky: What's so bad about being a drummer?

Lucy: It's just not good enough for a son of mine.

Ricky: Well it's good enough for a husband of yours.

Lucy: Well that's different.

Ricky: How is it different?

Lucy: He's my flesh and blood. You're just a close relative.

VISITOR FROM ITALY

[472]
Mario needs $_____ for a bus ticket to San Francisco.

BONUS: How much does he have when he arrives?

[473]
What mistake did Mario not make during his two short days working at Ricky's club?
a) throw garbage out the window
b) spill drinks on customers
c) drop a tray of dishes
d) trip a waiter who was carrying a cake

[474]
Name the pizza parlor where Mario was hired.

Mario: When I got off the boat this morning from Italy I said to myself, suppose the Ricardos don't remember me!

Lucy: Not remember you, oh, imagine not remembering!

Ricky: Yeah, now 'bout that, you. Ha-ha! How could we possibly forget you?

Lucy: Yeah, good old . . . you.

Lucy and Ricky have an unexpected guest—Mario Orsatti, the gondolier they met in Venice. Mario has come to the United States to see his brother Dominic. But Lucy thinks Dominic has gone to San Francisco. Mario doesn't have money for a bus ticket so he gets a job in a pizza parlor. When Lucy ends up filling in for him—*mama mia*!

Mario Orsatti is a gondolier on the Grand Canal.

The real Orsattis were great friends of Lucille and Desi.

Lucy claims that Mario gets the day off because of the "Taft-Hartley Visitors from Italy Who Work in Pizzerias Get Every Third Day Off Amendment."

By the time Mario leaves, Lucy owes $210.33 for bus fare, cleaning bills, broken dishes, and a burned-out pizza oven.

Lucille Ball actually studied the art of pizza-making at Micelli's Pizza Parlor on La Cienga Boulevard in West Hollywood in order to perfect this skit.

OFF TO FLORIDA

Lucy lost the train tickets, so she and Ethel have to "share" a ride to Florida. They sleep in swamps, eat watercress, and end up changing a tire! They manage to tough it out until they "discover" their driver is an escaped hatchet murderess. When she leaves them at a diner they have to hitch a ride on a chicken truck.

Ricky found the "lost" tickets in Little Ricky's wallet where Little Ricky had put them for "safe-keeping."

Ricky, Fred, and Little Ricky go down to Florida three days early to go fishing.

Actor Strother Martin, who played the diner waiter in this episode, went on to be a movie actor who starred in such classics as *Cool Hand Luke* and *Butch Cassidy and the Sundance Kid*.

[475]
Name the escaped hatchet murderess.

BONUS: Where was she finally caught?

[476]
Lucy and Ethel arrived at the North Miami train station _____ before the train.
a) 15 minutes
b) 30 minutes
c) 45 minutes
d) 60 minutes

[477]
Lucy thinks watercress sandwiches taste like _____.

Ethel: Who's gonna change the tire?

Mrs. Grundy: Well, after all, I've been doing all the driving. I'm sure you two wouldn't mind changing a tire! You'll find everything you need in the trunk.

Ethel: I hope we find a mechanic back there.

DEEP SEA FISHING

Lucy and Ethel spend too much money shopping in Florida, so to make up the cash they make a bet with Ricky and Fred. Whoever catches the biggest fish wins the money. Lucy ensures that the ladies will win by buying a huge tuna and stashing it in the hotel room. When the boys do the same, everyone is busted.

[478]
Lucy spent $ _____ on clothes and Ethel spent $ _____.

BONUS: What is the prize for the winner of the bet?

[479]
Lucy calls up the kitchen and asks for how many ice cubes?
a) 2,000
b) 3,000
c) 4,000
d) 5,000

[480]
True or False: Ethel catches the biggest fish.

Ethel: Well, let's put it somewhere. Moby Dick is getting heavy.

Lucy: We can't put it anyplace, we've got to hide it, and we've gotta hide it before Little Ricky comes home from the playground. I'd hate to have to explain this to him.

Ethel: Why would you have to explain it, isn't he used to having tuna around the house?

The Ricardos are in room 919 and the Mertzes are across the hall in 921.

They are staying at the swanky Eden Roc Hotel, where Ricky is performing with his band.

One of Desi Arnaz's favorite things to do was to fish in the ocean. He often went away for long fishing weekends with his friends.

Lucille and Desi owned a boat they called the *Desilu.*

DESERT ISLAND

Ricky and Fred are judges for a bathing beauty contest and Lucy and Ethel are not thrilled. Lucy arranges to have them run out of gas while on a boat trip, making it impossible for them to get back in time for the contest. They drift onto a nearly-deserted island and are "attacked" by "giant natives"! Will they be stranded forever?

[481]
Lucy puts extra gas in one jug; what does she put in the other?

[482]
Ricky is going to participate in a documentary film about
a) Florida
b) Latin music
c) Cuban culture
d) The Everglades

[483]
_____ was the first to spot the island.

Lucy: Now let me see, how can we keep them from judging that contest?

Ethel: Yeah, what awful thing are we gonna do?

Lucy: I don't know yet, but I've got a hunch it's gonna be a dilly!

On June 27, 1934, seventeen-year-old Cuban refugee Desi Arnaz arrived in Florida.

Ricky tells Fred he made a film with Claude Akins in Hollywood.

Lucy and Ethel go to get suntan oil. Didn't Lucy learn anything about sunburn when she was in Hollywood?

The *I Love Lucy* cast went on a publicity tour in 1956 and Florida was one of the destinations on their itinerary.

THE RICARDOS VISIT CUBA

Lucy is nervous about meeting Ricky's family, especially the formidable Uncle Alberto. She bungles her way through the introduction and manages to insult him, spill a drink on him, and squash his cigars. Determined to make it up to him, she almost gets arrested for stealing. All is forgiven when Little Ricky shines on stage.

[484]
Lucy screws up her Spanish and calls Uncle Alberto a big _____.

a) ugly bear
b) dirty moose
c) fat pig
d) skunk

[485]
The cigars Lucy wants to buy for Uncle Alberto cost $ _____.

BONUS: What is the brand name?

[486]
Uncle Alberto finally confesses, "Any mother of a boy like that is _____."

Lucy: If the first time I met you I said awful things, spilled stuff all over you, and acted like a first-class nincompoop, what would you have done?

Ricky: Just what I did—wait for my clothes to come back from the cleaners and then marry you.

Ricky says Uncle Alberto practically raised him.

There is no mention of Ricky's five brothers, but his mother is played by the same actress that played her in Episode 105.

Lucy says she took Spanish in high school.

Ricky was performing at the Casino Parisian at the Hotel National in Havana.

Desi Arnaz's middle name is Alberto.

LITTLE RICKY'S SCHOOL PAGEANT

Little Ricky's class is putting on a show and everyone gets to be in it. As Lucy, Ricky, Ethel, and Fred struggle with their roles, Little Ricky is given the lead. The part seems to be too much for the youngster to handle, but Lucy is determined that he will do it. The play goes off with just a few minor hitches, and Lucy steals the show.

The settings and the choreography for the play were courtesy of Pepito the Clown and his wife Joanne Perez, who ran a dancing school.

Lucy tells Carolyn Appleby that she learned how to do the cha-cha while in Florida and Cuba.

[487]
Fred is given the role of _____ the frog, and Ricky gets to play the _____.

[488]
Who gets to produce and direct the show?
a) Jimmy Wilson
b) Clifford Terry
c) Charlie Appleby
d) Bill Jacobs

BONUS: Why is he given the job?

[489]
True or False: The Mertzes' TV set is on the fritz again.

Lucy (as witch): I promise to be and kind and gentle and to love little children and all the birds and trees and the flowers and the animals, and I promise to laugh and sing and spread joy and happiness, and I promise never to cast an evil spell as long as I live!

SPECIAL
EPISODE

THE *I LOVE LUCY* CHRISTMAS SPECIAL

While trimming the tree Lucy, Ricky, Ethel, and Fred reminisce about their fifteen years together, and especially about the birth of Little Ricky. The next morning they are each dressed as Santa! They run into the kitchen so they don't confuse Little Ricky, but when they count there are five Santas! "Merry Christmas everybody . . ."

[490]
According to Little Ricky, how does Santa know the children are asleep?

[491]
How much did Fred spend on the first tree?

BONUS: How much did the replacement tree cost?

[492]
Ricky and Lucy give their son a _____ and a _____ set. Santa brings him a _____.

Little Ricky: Mama, there aren't any steps, how does Santa Claus get down the chimney?

Lucy: Yeah, how's he do that, Daddy?

Ricky: I took care of the why and the who. You take care of the how.

Lucy: Uh, how, huh? Well, um, now you see Santa Claus doesn't need any steps, honey. When he comes he brings the North Pole with him and he slides down like a fireman.

This is the first true flashback episode, in which the action is taking place today, and they flash back on memories. The others, broadcast during Lucille Ball's maternity leave, featured brief introductions, after which the rest of the episodes were seen as memories.

This episode was a longer version of the Santa tag, which appeared during the first few years of *I Love Lucy*, at the end of the episodes closest to Christmas (Episodes 9, 52, and 78).

This episode was considered to be a gift to the fans, and did not become part of the syndication package.

LUCY AND THE LOVING CUP

Lucy buys a new hat for a banquet but Ricky hates it. To get even she says she will wear the trophy Ricky is to present to jockey Johnny Longden, and puts it on her head. Trouble is, she can't get it off! She will need to see a silversmith to get the cup off, but when Ethel tries to take her— leave it to Lucy to get lost on the subway.

Lucy and Ethel take the Lexington Avenue local. Ethel gets off at the Bleecker Street station but Lucy goes past Spring Street and ends up at Flatbush Avenue.

Johnny Longden was born in England in 1910. He began racing in 1927 in Utah, and he won the Triple Crown in 1943 with his horse, Count Fleet. He won his five thousandth race in 1957,

the year this episode was first broadcast. In this episode, he was honored for being the "winningest jockey of all time—4,961 victories."

Desi Arnaz was a huge horseracing fan and when he retired from Desilu, bought the Corona Breeding Farm and bred his own racehorses for several years.

[493]
How much did Lucy spend on her new dress for the banquet?
a) $29.95
b) $39.95
c) $49.95
d) $59.95

[494]
On what New York street is the silversmith located?

[495]
Ethel confronts a fellow passenger: "What are you staring at? Haven't you ever seen a _____ on the subway before?"

Lucy (lost on subway platform): Pardon me, can you tell me where I am?

Man: Yeah, you're on earth!

Lucy: Pardon me, where am I?

Lady: Where are you? What are you?

LITTLE RICKY GETS A DOG

[496]
Match the pets to their names:

turtles   Hopalong
birds   Mildred and Charles
frog   Alice and Phil
fish   Tommy and Jimmy

[497]
Who gave the puppy to Little Ricky?

BONUS: What does Little Ricky name the dog?

[498]
Fred admits: I'd rather live with a little dog than a big _____!"

Fred: Now haven't I been lenient? Didn't I close my eyes when you got the turtles? Didn't I look the other way when the frogs and the goldfish arrived? And didn't I keep quiet when you got those two molting buzzards? I gotta draw the line someplace. That pooch has got to go.

Ethel: Oh Fred, you haven't seen him. He is the cutest thing.

Fred: One more word out of you, Ethel, and you go too!

Little Ricky is given a puppy but the lease says no pets. No one has the heart to send the cute pooch away. When a grumpy new tenant gives Fred a hard time, Fred says the dog will have to go. Lucy can't bear to do it though, and tries to hide the dog from Fred. In the end Fred decides to keep the dog—and throw the tenant out!

Lucy is caught with a box of dog biscuits and she eats one, saying they are a delicious treat.

Lucille and Desi loved dogs and always had several as pets.

This episode was the first in which Lucy mentions moving to the country.

Lucy tries to calm the dog at night by putting a clock in his bed—the ticking sound will soothe him. Trouble is, the alarm goes off—and so does the dog.

LUCY AND SUPERMAN

It's Little Ricky's birthday party and Lucy is competing with the Applebys, who are holding Stevie's party on the same day. When Lucy tells Carolyn that Superman is coming to Little Ricky's party, Carolyn bows out. But when Superman can't make it, it's up to Lucy to put on a cape, climb out on the ledge, and fly through the window!

Little Ricky is chronologically only four years old, but he is celebrating his fifth birthday. His birthday, January 19th, did actually fall on a Saturday in 1957, although Little Ricky was born on a Monday.

Keith Thibodeaux was six years old at this time, and remembers this as one of his favorite episodes.

Ricky says he and Lucy have been married fifteen years. When the episode was filmed Lucille and Desi were married fifteen years, but by the time it aired they had celebrated their sixteenth anniversary.

[499]
How much did Fred and Ethel spend on Little Ricky's party favors?
a) $2.97
b) $3.64
c) $4.86
d) $5.32

[500]
Little Stevie is having a _____, a _____, and a _____ show at his birthday party.

[501]
True or False: Fred is so desperate to rent the empty apartment that Ethel is afraid he will steal what precious item?

Lucy: But it makes much more sense for you to change, Carolyn, after all Stevie's birthday isn't on Saturday, it's on Thursday, isn't it?

Carolyn: Well, so what? Little Ricky's birthday isn't until next Monday.

Lucy: Well, Monday's much closer to Saturday than Thursday.

LUCY WANTS TO MOVE TO THE COUNTRY

[502]

What item did Lucy not bring home from her weekend in the country?

a) fresh milk

b) homemade jelly

c) fresh eggs

d) fresh butter

[503]

Ricky put down a deposit of $_____ to secure the Connecticut house.

BONUS: After Lucy's little stunt, how much more of a deposit does he have to pay?

[504]

What are the first names of the Spauldings?

Ricky: Mr. Spaulding, I know that it's very difficult for anybody to believe that anyone would pull a stunt like this, but you don't know my dizzy wife and her crackpot friends.

Lucy is hinting that she wants to move to the country. Ricky says no, but when he changes his mind and buys a house, Ethel cries so much that Lucy says she will never leave New York. In order to get Ricky's deposit back, Lucy decides to make herself appear "undesirable," but she almost gets everybody arrested in the process!

Ethel is afraid Fred will never spring for the $3.08 round-trip ticket from New York to Westport.

Lucy says the names of the Seven City Dwarfs are "Sneezy, Dusty, Stuffy, Drafty, Sniffly, Noisy, and Pasty."

Lucy and Ricky were visiting their friends, the Munsons, in the country. Grace Munson used to be a member of the Wednesday Afternoon Fine Arts League.

LUCY HATES TO LEAVE

The Ricardos are almost ready to leave their city apartment and Fred wants to rent it before they do. A newlywed couple will take it, but only if they can move in right away. No problem—the Ricardos will move in with the Mertzes; after all, it's only for a couple of days. But a couple of days becomes a couple of weeks . . .

Lucy and Ethel walk around the apartment one last time, and while Ethel says it's just another apartment, Lucy laments the fifteen years of memories she is leaving behind. Actually, since the Ricardos changed apartments less than four years ago; the other eleven years are back in their first apartment.

Lucy mentions that Ricky has the "home-owner's heebie-jeebies."

Gene Reynolds, who played newlywed Mr. Taylor, went on to become a Hollywood producer.

[505]
Ricky will be _____ years old when the mortgage is paid off.

[506]
Name three changes Mrs. Taylor wants to make to the Ricardos' furniture.

[507]
True or False: Fred is saving Lucy and Ricky over $200,000 on their ninety-nine-year lease.

Ricky: If you wanna know the truth, I'm worried about that new house in the country.

Lucy: Ah, honey, now there's nothing to worry about. Mr. Spaulding accepted our offer, the bank's got all the papers; that house is ours.

Ricky: That's what I'm worried about—that house is ours!

LUCY MISSES THE MERTZES

[508]
How much did Ethel's new shoes cost?
a) $20
b) $16
c) $23
d) $12

[509]
What ancient tradition does Ricky perform when they first move in?

BONUS: What does Little Ricky do?

[510]
Fred spent $_____ on taxi fare and $_____ on train tickets.

Lucy: Oh gee, honey, I just can't believe we're really here. You know, we should be awfully happy in this house. It's so quiet and peaceful.

Ricky: Yeah, no noise . . .

Lucy: No dust . . .

Ricky: No traffic . . .

Lucy: No Mertzes . . .

Moving day is here and Lucy and Ethel are sobbing. After one night apart, Lucy and Ricky head for the city, and Ethel and Fred take off for the country. When neither duo can get a hold of the other, the Ricardos go home to bed, and the Mertzes let themselves in with their spare key. Now each thinks the others are burglars!

Lucy and Ricky are both thrilled and shocked to receive a fruit basket from the Mertzes, prompting Ricky to exclaim, "For Fred to spend ten dollars on a basket of fruit, he must have been hysterical!"

The Ricardos get so scared of the country noises on their first night that they all end up in one twin bed—including Little Ricky and his dog, Fred!

LUCY GETS CHUMMY WITH THE NEIGHBORS

Lucy's new friend, Betty Ramsey, takes Lucy shopping for new furniture. The trouble begins when Lucy goes way over budget and Ricky tells her to send it back. Betty gets mad at Lucy, her husband Ralph gets mad at Ricky, and even the children, Bruce and Little Ricky, get into a brawl. Is it back to New York for the Ricardos?

Lucy: Oh gee, that Betty Ramsey is a nice person. And so is Ralph, her husband. You're just gonna love him. We're sure lucky to have such good neighbors.

Ricky: Look honey, eh, I don't think it's a good idea to get too friendly with the neighbors too fast.

Lucy: Why not, we're going to be living here the rest of our lives. Why shouldn't we get friendly with the neighbors right away?

Ricky: That's just it—we are going to be living here for the rest of our lives, so I think that we should get chummy gradually.

Lucy: Oh well maybe you can get chummy gradually. With me it's instant chummy.

Lucy calls Fred and Ethel at Schyler 4-8098 and begs them to come to Connecticut before Ricky gets home and sees the furniture.

Mr. Ramsey offers Ricky a guest spot on a TV show that pays $3,500, but after he thinks Ricky is insulting Betty's taste, he rescinds the offer and he and Ricky end up fighting amongst the rosebushes.

[511]
How much does Ricky say Lucy can spend on furniture?

BONUS: How much does she actually spend?

[512]
Lucy tells Carolyn she wants to send all the furniture back because she thinks _____ furniture would look better.

[513]
True or False: Mr. Perry, the furniture dealer can get Lucy 40 percent off.

[508]
Nosy neighbor Betty Ramsey arranges for what famous national magazine to do a spread on the Ricardos' house?

BONUS: Ricky says they might make the next issue of
_____ .

[509]
Lucy says eggs cost how much a dozen?
a) 35¢
b) 50¢
c) 75¢
d) 99¢

[510]
Who will manage the apartment building for Fred and Ethel?

Lucy: A lot of people around here make extra money by farming. Now we could have apple orchards and grape vineyards and maybe some grain and wheat fields, and a herd or two of cattle maybe.

Ricky: Lucy, we only own two acres. What you're talking about would take the entire state of I-o-away.

LUCY RAISES CHICKENS

Ricky is frantic about the cost of country living, so Lucy suggests they raise chickens and sell the eggs to defray the costs. They hire Fred and Ethel to help with all the work, but when Lucy and Ethel pick up the baby chicks too early, and Little Ricky lets them loose to run around the house, Lucy looks like a big dumb cluck.

The Ricardos' bills are much higher in the country—heating is $52, phone is $23, electric is $18.75, water is $16, groceries are $88, and tree surgery is $50. Ricky says for the price of the tree surgery, he could have had his appendix taken out!

The baby chicks were quite loud. If you listen very closely you can even hear them cheeping when they are supposedly in the hen house.

This is the first episode sponsored by Ford. They run a long commercial, featuring Desi and Lucille, for their retractable hard top.

LUCY DOES THE TANGO

3/11/57

EPISODE
172

Ricky is upset because the chickens are not laying and he is losing money. Lucy and Ethel decide to "help out" by buying some eggs and stashing them in the hen house. They hide the eggs in their clothes and head for the hen house, but when Ricky wants to practice the tango number for the PTA show, Lucy's plans get all scrambled.

The minute after the tango's finale has been timed as the longest laugh on *I Love Lucy*. It actually lasted sixty-five seconds, and had to be edited for broadcast purposes.

Lucille and Vivian did not rehearse with raw eggs, making the moment of truth even more realistic.

[511]
Fred says they have to exchange the chicks for full-grown hens because they won't start laying until they are _____ months old.
BONUS: How many hens do they get for their 500 chicks?

[512]
Ricky says he should have raised something he knew about, like _____.
a) tobacco
b) mangoes
c) bananas
d) sugar cane

[513]
True or False: Lucy and Ethel buy three dozen eggs.

Lucy: Don't give up, we've got one more day.

Ethel: You don't expect those hens to lay a bumper crop of eggs overnight?

Lucy: You know they could if we helped them.

Ethel: Lucy, I have never laid an egg in my life, and I refuse to start trying now.

RAGTIME BAND

Lucy has promised that her husband will perform for the Historical Society's show, but Ricky says no. So Lucy forms a band with Ethel, Fred, and Little Ricky that is not quite ready for the big time. They finally convince Ricky to help with the rehearsals, but he quickly gives up and gives in. He will do the show—and they will all help.

[520]
Fred says the last time he played his violin was at a rally for what president?

[521]
Match the musician with the instrument:

Lucy	sinciro
Ethel	bongos
Fred	cuica
Little Ricky	ganarrya

[522]
What does Lucy serve for dinner when she is trying to "butter up" Ricky?

Lucy: She said on the strength of Ricky Ricardo's appearance tickets are selling like hot cakes.

Ethel: Oh dear. What'll they do when they hear the bad news? They'll have to change their name to the Westport Hysterical Society.

Lucy serve for dinner when she is trying to "butter up" Ricky?

Fred and Little Ricky are again playing Fred's favorite game—baseball.

Ethel has lost her memory again; she can no longer play the piano except for the song "She'll Be Coming 'Round the Mountain," which she plays very badly. Lucy can only manage a half-hearted attempt at "Sweet Sue." Her saxophone song used to be "Glow Worm."

LUCY'S NIGHT IN TOWN

Lucy blows it again! She has the theater tickets and she is there on the right evening—but her tickets are for the matinee! The show is sold out, so Lucy and Ethel watch the first act and Ricky and Fred will watch the second. But when Lucy finds two empty seats, the ladies sneak back in. That's fine, until the other couple shows up.

The musical *The Most Happy Fella* was partially financed by Desilu. The show opened in May 1956.

The Ricardos and Mertzes had great matinee seats—Row F, Orchestra seats 104, 105, 106, and 107.

Lucy goes out to get a glass of orangeade and ends up in the wrong box.

Fred's $500, which Ethel thought was in her purse, was actually with Fred the whole time.

[523]
What dinner does Lucy order for everyone?
a) roast beef and mashed potatoes
b) steak and baked potatoes
c) spaghetti and meatballs
d) pork chops and wild rice

[524]
The show is performed at Broadway's _____ Theatre.

[525]
How many tickets did Ricky end up paying for?

Ricky: I wonder what the story's all about?

Fred: Well, I can tell you one thing, the guy is not married.

Ricky: How do you know that?

Fred: Look at the title! (he points to the poster, *The Most Happy Fella*)

HOUSEWARMING

[526]

Ethel says she can't make Betty's next party because she and Fred are busy with the _____ Convention, the _____ Annual Ball, and the _____ Amalgamated.

[527]

Where were Ethel and Betty born?

BONUS: What were their childhood names?

[528]

True or False: Fred once darkened the whole Eastside of New York for forty-eight hours when he tried to re-wire his kitchen.

Betty: Oh, I was so flattered, Kay Bailey asked me for the recipe for my cake last night.

Lucy: Did she?

Betty: Yes she did. I told her the secret was your fresh eggs!

Lucy: Oh, thank you! You know, we're in the egg business together, so half of those eggs belong to Ethel. Isn't that right dear?

Ethel: Yes, the shells.

Ethel is upset that Lucy is spending so much time with her new friends, so Lucy decides to introduce her to Betty Ramsey. When Ethel and Betty find out they were childhood chums, Lucy is the one who is left out. Later Lucy hears Ethel discussing housewarming gifts over the intercom, and thinks they are planning a party for her.

Watch for the scene when Lucy and Ricky practice looking surprised. Desi Arnaz's timing is perfect.

The intercom and its potential for misunderstandings and miscommunications was a brilliant addition to the Connecticut house.

When the gang finally does show up for the (surprise) housewarming party, Fred is surprised to be caught in his PJs!

BUILDING A BARBECUE

Lucy decides to keep Ricky busy by having him build a barbecue in the backyard. But when she and Ethel are mixing the cement she loses her wedding ring. That night Lucy and Ethel take the entire barbecue apart, brick by brick, but find nothing. Ricky is furious when he sees his creation in ruins, but Lucy is more upset about her ring.

Ricky: Well, that's the easiest way in the world to lose your wedding ring.

Lucy: Well I've been doing it for sixteen years and I haven't lost it yet.

Ricky: Why do you have to take it off?

Lucy: Because dishwater is very hard on diamond rings.

Ricky: When we got married you said you will never take your ring off.

Lucy: When we got married you said that dishwater would never touch these lily white hands.

Ricky: Well, I bought you a pair of rubber gloves, didn't I?

[529]
Where does Lucy leave her ring every day?
a) on top of the kitchen radio
b) on the windowsill
c) in the soap dish
d) on her dresser

[530]
Happily, Lucy finds her ring in her _____.

[531]
Ethel wishes she could write, "Dear Diary: Tonight I went out in the backyard in my nightgown and _____."

When the episode begins, Lucy forgets that Ricky is on vacation. She sends him sleepwalking off to the train, but Ethel comes over to ask how the vacation is going. Lucy runs after Ricky, who has not gotten very far, leads him back to the house, and he stumbles off to bed.

Lucy and Ethel planned to get the boys to make the barbecue by pretending they were going to make it themselves.

Ricky comes to the conclusion that Hurricane Lucy and Hurricane Ethel ruined his masterpiece.

When Lucille Ball and Desi Arnaz eloped in 1940, the only ring he could find at the last minute was a brass one from Woolworth's. He later gave her a real platinum ring, but she always treasured the first one as much as her real jewels.

[532]
Diana dances with Ricky
_____ times, Fred
_____ times, and Ralph
Ramsey _____ times.

BONUS: Who does she dance
with first?

[533]
True or False: Lucy says
Ethel's hairdo makes her
look like Marilyn Monroe.

[534]
How much money did Fred
tip the orchestra so they
would keep on playing?
a) $2
b) $5
c) $10
d) $15

LUCY:

GLAMOUR TODAY IS NOTHING BUT A TIGHT SKIRT, LOOSE HIPS, AND WET LIPS.

COUNTRY CLUB DANCE

The men are complaining that they are being dragged off to another boring event, until the lovely, young, and shapely Diana Jordan shows up. The wives get jealous and decide to do something to make their husbands pay attention. They try new dresses, hairdos, and perfume, but the men decide they don't want glamour after all.

A twenty-two-year-old Barbara Eden appears as the vivacious Diana Jordan. More than seven years later, on September 18, 1965, she would premiere in her own long-running classic series, *I Dream of Jeannie*.

This is not the first time that Lucy and Ethel have employed methods of glamour to keep their husbands interested.

Lucille Ball has a very funny moment when she rips her dress on the way out of the dance.

LUCY RAISES TULIPS

Lucy is very proud of her tulip garden and hopes to win a local gardening contest. She asks Ricky to mow the lawn (using a borrowed riding mower), but when he skips out in the middle of the job, Lucy finishes it herself. When the mower goes berserk, she also finishes everyone's chances of winning the gardening prize.

Lucy calls Ricky by his whole name, which is now Enrique Alberto Ricardo y de Acha. In Episode 121 it was Ricardo Alberto Fernando Ricardo y de Acha. Fred's full name is Frederick Hobart Mertz.

The boys took Little Ricky to Fred's favorite hangout, Yankee Stadium.

The mower was borrowed from Ralph Ramsey.

Lucy replaces Betty's damaged tulips with waxed ones and later, when Ricky mows down Lucy's bulbs, he does the same thing.

[535]
What color are Lucy's tulips?

BONUS: What color are Betty Ramsey's?

[536]
Lucy and the lawn mower took a turn on the _____ Road.

[537]
True or False: Betty has won the Garden Club prize three years in a row.

Ethel: Lucy, was there much damage?

Lucy: Well, every lawn between here and town is half mowed.

THE RICARDOS DEDICATE A STATUE

Lucy is in charge of the Yankee Doodle Day celebration, and Ricky will unveil the new Revolutionary War statue. But when Little Ricky's dog, Fred, runs away and Lucy drives off after him, the statue looks like it's been through a war! There is nothing left for the master schemer to do but dress up like a statue and hope no one notices.

[538]
Ricky paid _____ for Fred's Dog Obedience School.

[539]
How long will it take Mr. Silvestri to make another statue?
a) two days
b) one week
c) ten days
d) two weeks

[540]
What three pieces of the statue does Lucy manage to save?

Lucy: Did you get the posters up all over town?

Ethel (exhausted): Yup.

Lucy: Did you nail 'em to the telephone poles like I asked you to?

Ethel: (shows her bandaged thumb)

Lucy: All right. Now let's see, did you call all the members of my committee and ask them to be here for luncheon tomorrow?

Ethel: Yup, I did.

Lucy: All of 'em?

Ethel: Yup, all of 'em.

Lucy: Did you check the man who's writing the special song about the Battle of Compo?

Ethel: Yup, I did that.

Lucy: Did you talk to Mr. Silvestri the sculptor, and make sure the statue will be ready the day after tomorrow?

Ethel: Yeah, uh-huh.

Lucy: Day after tomorrow?

Ethel: Yep, yep, yep.

Lucy: Did you rent the trailer to carry it?

Ethel: Yep, yep.

Lucy: Good. Oh boy! I'm never gonna be chairman of another committee! It's too much work!

The Battle of Compo Hill took place on April 28, 1777.

Desi Arnaz IV and family friend Suzie Meyer appear in the last scene of this episode.

Desilu hired Silvestri Studios to make the statue.

The last line uttered in the last episode was, "Shoot if you must this old redhead."

THE LUCILLE BALL-DESI ARNAZ SHOW

1957-1960

LUCY TAKES A CRUISE TO HAVANA

In this flashback episode, secretaries Lucy McGillicuddy and Susie MacNamara take a cruise and end up in Havana where they meet up with musicians Ricky Ricardo and his amigo Carlos Garcia. After dislike at first sight, Lucy and Ricky fall in love—only to let misunderstandings, drunken jailers, and pompous crooners almost get in the way.

[541]
How much did Lucy pay for the cruise?
a) $84.50
b) $76.50
c) $92.50
d) $105.50

[542]
Ricky and Carlos are offered $_____ to take Lucy and Susie out for the day.

BONUS: Who offers the money?

[543]
True or False: Lucy sees the movie Gone with the Wind aboard ship.

Susie: Hi.

Lucy: Hi, any luck?

Susie: I have searched this boat stem to stern, top to bottom, fore and aft, and

I haven't found one available man. I hate to tell you, Lucy, we're traveling on a floating YWCA.

Lucy: Brother, they weren't kidding when they said this ship was on its maiden voyage.

Lucy and Susie sail on the *Caronia*.

Lucy and Susie stay in hotel room 6B in Havana.

Ricky and Carlos fight Rudy Vallee in a cafe and do $235 worth of damage!

Fred and Ethel are on their honeymoon cruise, twelve years after their 1928 wedding.

Formerly frumpy Ethel has a new, sleek look and now appears to be at least as young as Lucy.

Cesar Romero, born in New York City on February 15, 1907, was a popular nightclub dancer in the 1930s. From there he went on to Broadway and Hollywood.

Singer Rudy Vallee, born Hubert Prior Vallee on July 28, 1901, in Island Point, Vermont, formed his own orchestra, the Connecticut Yankees, in 1927. By 1929 the radio had made his voice famous, and he had thousands of fans all over the country. He also appeared on the stage and in Hollywood movies.

Born January 2, 1912, in Valley City, North Dakota, Harriet Lake (a.k.a. Ann Sothern) made her stage debut in New York in 1930, and then went on to make films. From 1953 until 1957 she starred as Susie MacNamara in her own TV show, *Private Secretary*.

At the end of this show, Desi Arnaz came out to thank the audience, and also the *U.S. Steel Hour* for delaying the start of their program, "The Locked Door." The final version of this first *Lucy-Desi* show ran fifteen minutes too long, so Desi went to the head of U.S. Steel and asked him to delay their regular program until 10:15 PM. With Ford Motor Company paying for the extra fifteen minutes, Desi got his seventy-five-minute show and the *U.S. Steel Hour* got their highest ratings ever. The full seventy-five-minute version of this episode can be viewed at the Museum of Television and Radio in New York and in Hollywood. It has also been made available on CBS home video.

240

THE CELEBRITY NEXT DOOR

Actress Tallulah Bankhead moves in next door and Lucy sure makes a mess of things. She insults her, she ruins a dinner, and she sprays her with paint. Even after all of that, Tallulah agrees to star in the PTA play. When Lucy gets mad at Tallulah for ruining her best suit, Lucy decides to ruin the play too. But the audience loves it!

Lucy: Oh you know what I mean, she's a big celebrity, you're only a husband. Oh what am I gonna do?

Ricky: Well if you want a little advice from only a husband, you'll forget all this nonsense. It doesn't matter to Miss Bankhead whether we have help or not.

Lucy: Well, it matters to me. She already thinks I'm a snoop and a bungler. You don't want her to think I'm a fibber too.

Ricky: But you are!

Lucy: Well you know it, and I know it, but I don't see why Tallulah Bankhead has to know it too.

The play Tallulah stars in is called *The Queen's Lament.*

Tallulah Brockman Bankhead was born in 1902 in Huntsville, Alabama. She left home at fifteen to go to New York and make her name in the theater. She was briefly married to actor John Emery, who appeared in *I Love Lucy* Episodes 5 (as Harold) and 165 (as Mr. Stewart).

The sponsor for this episode was Ford. They introduced their 1958 cars with two long commercials—one showing the cars in Paris and another showing them in Turkey.

At the opening of the show, Desi Arnaz appears thanking viewers for the kind letters they sent after the first *Lucille Ball-Desi Arnaz Show* one month earlier.

Bette Davis, a former drama-school classmate of Lucille's, was the original choice to guest-star in this episode.

It was during rehearsals for this episode that Lucille Ball and Desi Arnaz made the decision to buy RKO Studios, where they had both been employed, and where they met in 1940. They paid $6.15 million for the purchase, $4.3 of which they had received from CBS, Inc. when they sold all their rights to *I Love Lucy* in 1956.

Lucy calls Fred "Fritzi Boy," which is a nickname Lucille called her brother, Fred Ball.

LUCY HUNTS URANIUM

Lucy wants to hunt for uranium in Las Vegas, but Ricky predictably says no. She prints up a phony newspaper about a local uranium strike to convince him and this time it works! The Ricardos and Mertzes join up with actor Fred MacMurray to find the rare element, and then race each other to see who can get to the claims office first.

[547]
How much will the U.S. government pay to anyone who finds uranium?
a) $1,000
b) $5,000
c) $10,000
d) $25,000

[548]
Fred MacMurray is very upset that he lost $ _____ gambling.

BONUS: Who does he say is going to "kill" him?

[549]
True or False: It costs Fred $50 to rent a Geiger counter.

Ethel: What's that?

Lucy: It's a Geiger counter to hunt uranium with while we're up in Las Vegas.

Ethel: A Geiger counter?

Lucy: Yeah.

Ethel: Now Lucy, I thought when you asked Ricky if you could go uranium-hunting he put his foot down.

Lucy: Oh, he's put down so many feet I feel like I'm married to a Cuban centipede.

Henry the Bellboy is played by Bobby Jellison, who played Bobby the Bellboy during the gang's stay in Hollywood.

The Ricardos stayed in room 236 in the Sands Hotel.

Guest star Fred MacMurray was born August 30, 1908, in Illinois. He was a saxophonist in a popular jazz band when he met a Paramount talent scout and talked his way into a screen test. He appeared in many movies, such as *The Caine Mutiny* (1954) and *The Shaggy Dog* (1959). MacMurray was married to actress June Haver and was the father of four children. The script had him call his wife Junie Bug, while she called him Freddie Bear.

MacMurray teamed with William Frawley again in 1960 when the hit TV sitcom *My Three Sons* was launched.

At the show's opening Lucille and Desi said they drive Ford cars. Tennessee Ernie Ford (no relation) also appeared in one of the Ford commercials during this episode.

LUCY GOES TO MEXICO

Lucy and the gang are in San Diego with entertainer Maurice Chevalier, and Lucy and Ethel want to shop in Mexico. They manage to get into trouble with customs, and when they are all arrested for smuggling Lucy sneaks away to find the American Consul at the bullfight. In order to escape the police, she becomes a matador!

Westinghouse sponsored this episode and promoted their new product, the "Fiesta." Perfect for newlyweds, it featured a TV and a phonograph with optional stereophonic sound. The set fit into small spaces and sold for $229.95.

At the end of the episode, Maurice Chevalier entertains aboard the USS *Yorktown*, a Navy aircraft carrier.

Maurice Chevalier was born September 12, 1888, in Paris. At twelve he was already performing professionally. He came to Hollywood in the twenties, but returned to France during World War II. In 1958, at the age of seventy, Chevalier starred opposite Leslie Caron in the film classic *Gigi*. In 1959, he was awarded a special Oscar for his lifelong commitment to entertainment.

[556]
How much does Ethel pay for her basket?
a) $1.50
b) $6
c) $7.50
d) $9.00

[557]
True or False: Maurice asks Lucy to buy him French perfume in Mexico.

[558]
The little Mexican boy they befriend in Tijuana is named

_____.

Customs officer: The Admiral's been kind enough to vouch for you. You're all released on your good behavior.

Lucy: Oh, yay! You see honey, nothing to it!

Ricky: Nothing to it, eh? All it took to get you out of this mess was the United States Navy!

LUCY MAKES ROOM FOR DANNY

The Ricardos are leaving town and have leased their house to the Williams family. When Ricky learns the trip is postponed, the Ricardos move in with the Mertzes. Lucy wants her house back and makes such a nuisance of herself that the adults end up in a snowball fight, after which they all sue each other in an unforgettable day in court!

Lucy: While Danny is asleep I am going to tiptoe over to the bedroom, take the check and the note and tiptoe out again. Danny will think Kathy has paid us, Kathy will think Danny has paid us and the first thing tomorrow morning out they go for non-payment of rent.

Ethel: Lucy, you can't take that check; that's stealing.

Lucy: Ethel, how can you say that? In the first place the check is made out to us, so it's really our check. In the second place the check isn't signed so it isn't worth anything. So how can you say taking something that belongs to you already, and isn't worth anything anyway, is stealing?

---

[559]

Who throws the first snowball?

BONUS: At whom is it thrown?

[560]

Ricky is going on a trip to _____ for _____ months to _____.

[561]

How much rent do Fred and Ethel pay each month for the guesthouse?
a) $75
b) $100
c) $125
d) $150

Fred calls Danny "banana nose."

The kids save the day in court with their solution—the Ricardos move back home, the Williams move to the guest house, and Fred takes Ethel to Florida for two months (so he can prove he's not a tightwad!).

The Williams family is played by the same actors from the TV hit *The Danny Thomas Show* (filmed and produced at Desilu Studios).

Danny Thomas was born Amos Jacobs on January 6, 1914. He began his career as a candy butcher in a burlesque house and later landed his first professional role on radio. He married Rose Cassaneti and raised three children (including actress Margaret, or Marlo Thomas, as she is better known). Throughout his life he honored St. Jude, the patron saint of the lost, by building hospitals and facilities for sick children.

Lucille Ball and Desi Arnaz appeared in a 1959 episode of *The Danny Thomas Show* entitled "Lucy Upsets the Williams Household." The premise of this episode is that the Ricardos move into the Williams' Manhattan apartment, and Lucy's antics start World War III between the husbands and wives.

Westinghouse sponsored this program and had several long commercials, one featuring Lucille and Desi. The others featured one Mrs. Tom Sparks, the mother of three children and owner of a Westinghouse Laundromat washer. The Sparks home in Cheshire, Connecticut was described as being part of the Westinghouse "total electric" series of new houses heated, cooled, and run only by electricity.

LUCY GOES TO ALASKA

Ricky is going to Nome, Alaska, to appear in a TV special with actor Red Skelton, so the gang decides to go along. Fred and Ricky have bought some Alaskan property, and after Lucy and Red go to see it, they have to fly the plane back themselves when the pilot passes out! Later they sell their land only to find out it was worth millions.

This episode was shot in Lake Arrowhead, California.

In 1867, the U.S. bought Alaska from Russia for $7.2 million. Alaska was made the forty-ninth state on January 3, 1959.

Richard (Red) Skelton was born July 18, 1913, in Vincennes, Indiana, and attended school only through the third grade. He grew up in the circus and in vaudeville, and in 1938 made his first movie for RKO (*Having a Wonderful Time*,

with Lucille Ball and Ginger Rogers). In 1940, Skelton signed a long-term contract with MGM that allowed him to work in TV and radio. When Skelton received the 1952 Emmy for Excellence in Comedy, he said in his acceptance speech, "Ladies and gentlemen, you've given this to the wrong redhead. I don't deserve this. It should go to Lucille Ball."

This episode was sponsored by Viceroy Cigarettes, Ajax, and Chex cereal.

[562]
How much did Fred and Ricky pay for their one hundred acres of Alaskan land?

[563]
When the gang is forced to share Red's suite, they draw straws to see who gets to sleep where. Match the character with his or her sleeping accommodations.

Lucy	bed
Ricky	sleeping bag
Ethel	hammock
Fred	cot

[564]
True or False: Lucy and Red ski out to see the property.

Red: What's that blue stuff out there?

Pilot: Sky?

Red: Yeah? Sure is clear.

Pilot: You act as though you've never seen sky before.

Red: I haven't—I live in Los Angeles.

LUCY WANTS A CAREER

Lucy is tired of being a housewife, so she decides to go out and get herself a job! She lands the job of a Girl Friday on *The Paul Douglas Early Bird Show*. At first she loves it, but then when she only glimpses Ricky in the train station as they pass and, even worse, Little Ricky calls Ethel "mommy," she decides she's better off at home.

[565]
How many young ladies does Lucy have to scare away in order to get her job?

[566]
Finish Lucy's "Housewife's Lament": Being a housewife is a big bore. Cook the _____, do the _____, make the _____, dust the_____."

[567]
True or False: Paul Douglas gives Lucy a three-year contract.

Lucy: Ethel, this is it! Paul Douglas is starting a new early-morning television program, and he's looking for a Girl Friday!

Ethel: Well, how do you fit in there?

Lucy: All a Girl Friday has to do is walk across the stage, pass things to the star, and sit and smile into the camera. And the four things I do best are walk, pass, sit, and smile.

Yale graduate Paul Douglas was born November 4, 1907, and had a variety of careers, including professional football player, radio announcer, sportswriter, and star of stage, film, and TV.

Lucy and Paul advertise a new cereal product called Wakey Flakies.

At the end of this episode, Desi Arnaz announces the premiere of a Desilu Playhouse production based on *The Untouchables* by Elliott Ness, and starring Robert Stack and Keenan Wynn. This two-part "pilot" episode would become the Desilu TV series *The Untouchables*.

Desi Arnaz graduated high school with Sonny Capone, son of gangster Al Capone. *The Untouchables* was based upon the life of Elliott Ness and his agents, who finally arrested the senior Capone in 1931. Sonny Capone sued Desi Arnaz for defamation—unsuccessfully.

Little Ricky is in Cub Scout Pack 714; they used Mr. Ramsey's neckties to learn how to tie knots.

Lucy has cooked 19,710 meals.

Ethel is hired to take care of the Ricardos' house, and Little Ricky, while Lucy works.

The final commercial shows radio and newspaper reporter John Cameron Swayze flying in a helicopter over Desilu Studios to promote the new Westinghouse portable transistor radios.

LUCY'S SUMMER VACATION

Lucy is looking forward to some romance when she and Ricky vacation in a mountain cabin. But when Ida Lupino and Howard Duff arrive at the lodge, the men fish while the girls stew. In desperation, Lucy drills holes in the bottom of the boys' fishing boat, just before Ricky and Howard invite their wives for a moonlit row.

Friend and agent Harry Bailey mistakenly tells both couples they can have the lodge for the week.

Fred and Ethel go to Atlantic City, but decide to change their plans and come up to stay with Ricky and Lucy at the lodge, just as Ida and Howard are about to leave them in peace.

Sponsor Westinghouse introduced its new product during this episode, the hot-dog cooking Dog-O-Matic, which cooked six hotdogs in ninety seconds and sold for under $10.

Born February 4, 1918, in London, England, Ida Lupino studied at the Royal Academy of Dramatic Arts where she made her professional debut at age fourteen in the play *Heartbreak House*. After making several British films, she made her way to Hollywood in the 1930s and married fellow actor Howard Duff in 1951. In 1957, she and Duff teamed to star in the TV comedy *Mr. Adams and Eve*. They also appeared in several films together and created a company, Bridget Productions, named after their daughter.

Duff was born on August 24, 1913, in Bremerton, Washington. He served in the Armed Forces Radio Service during World War II, and made his movie debut in 1947. He appeared in movies such as *Kramer vs. Kramer*, and on many TV series, including *Knots Landing*, *The Golden Girls*, and *Murder, She Wrote*.

[568]
Name the lake where the lodge is located.

BONUS: In what state is the lake located?

[569]
How many holes does Lucy drill before Ida stops her with the news of the moonlight picnic?
a) 2
b) 3
c) 4
d) 5

[570]
When the husbands give on up their card game to go to bed, the wives take over and play _____.

Ida: Howie baby, I thought this evening we'd take a moonlight boat ride.

Howard: Sounds like a good idea.

Ida: You really think so?

Howard (indicates Lucy and Ida): Yeah, you two go right ahead.

Ricky: I hope one of you knows how to row.

MILTON BERLE HIDES OUT AT THE RICARDOS'

[571]
Lucy asks Milton Berle to sign her copy of his book _____.

BONUS: How many times does she say she has read the book?

[572]
What is the name of Milton's agent?
a) Chuck Jones
b) Tim Nelson
c) Dick Phillips
d) George Watson

[573]
Match the characters with the part they played in the PTA show:

Lucy	bartender
Ricky	cattle rustler
Ethel	sheriff
Fred	dance-hall girl
Milton	horse
Little Ricky	native

Lucy (to Ricky and Fred): Mildred just stopped by to discuss some PTA business.

Mildred (Milton in drag): Yes, that's right. And thanks a million for allowing me to use your powder room. My make-up was just terribly messy.

Lucy: Oh no it was not, you look divine, Mildred.

Ethel: You never looked lovelier.

Lucy wants Milton Berle to appear at the PTA benefit. Milton needs a quiet place where he can finish his book. Lucy offers her house to the author and all goes well until nosy Fred tells Ricky a strange man has been coming to the house every day while Ricky is at work. The sparks fly when Ricky runs home in a jealous rage.

Regular extra Elvia Allman, famous for her portrayal of the foreman in Kramer's Kandy Kitchen, appears in this episode as Miss Trent, Berle's secretary.

Ethel and Fred celebrated their twenty-fitth anniversary as far back as 1952, but for some reason they have still been married for only twenty-five years.

Born Milton Berlinger on July 12, 1908, in New York City, "Uncle Miltie" appeared in his own hour-long NBC TV show every Tuesday from 1948 until 1956 (366 shows). Berle grew up performing in vaudeville but did not try comedy until he was eighteen. In 1920, he made his Broadway debut and appeared in many Broadway shows, Hollywood films, and nightclubs. Berle was a published author.

THE RICARDOS GO TO JAPAN

The gang is headed to Japan for Ricky's two-week tour of Tokyo. Lucy's one wish is for a string of real pearls, and when she meets actor Bob Cummings she convinces him to help her acquire some. She steals money from Fred and then is forced to give it—and the pearls—back. In the end, big-hearted Ricky buys her the pearls.

Mrs. McGillicuddy is seen very briefly at the beginning of the episode.

The gang stays at the Hotel Teito in Tokyo.

Ricky eats fried grasshoppers in the geisha house.

Ethel even gets some pearls from penny-pinching Fred.

Watch as Lucy and Ethel take the money from Fred's money belt, causing Lucy to fall backward into the fishpond, and listen as Ricky sings "Tokyo Pete"—in Japanese!

Born Clarence Robert Orville Cummings on June 10, 1910, in Joplin, Missouri, Bob Cummings's first dream was to be an aeronautical engineer. Forced to leave school during the Depression, he drifted into acting and, in 1931, first appeared on Broadway. He left for Hollywood in 1935, and began to get starring roles in films including the classic *Dial M for Murder* in 1955. The same year, he began starring in his own TV series, *The Bob Cummings Show.*

[574]
What did Ethel not have to do to buy her plane ticket to Japan?
a) cash in her Christmas Club
b) sell her war bonds
c) pawn the family silver
d) sell her Green Stamps

[575]
Lucy temporarily shares the pond with _____ the goldfish.

[576]
How much does Lucy's string of pearls cost?

BONUS: Name the Japanese friend who sells them to Ricky.

Ethel: Oh Lucy, what are we gonna do? When he finds out that money's gone he'll kill us!

Lucy: You're right! Wait a minute, what're we worrying about? How's he gonna find out we took it?

Ethel: Well, I'll be the first one he'll suspect!

Lucy: Yeah, but how's he gonna prove it?

Ethel: He'll ask me and I'll confess?

Lucy: Why?

Ethel: Because while he's asking he'll have his hands around my throat!

LUCY MEETS THE MUSTACHE

Ricky can't get a TV job. Lucy seeks to remedy the situation by making friends with acting neighbor Ernie Kovacs. After she manages to offend Ernie in every possible way, Lucy makes one last desperate move and impersonates the actor's chauffeur! But when Ricky joins them for a drive, Lucy's cover is soon blown.

Ricky: I've got to teach that woman a lesson.

Ernie: She's only trying to help you.

Ricky: Yeah, yeah, trying to help me, yeah. She was only trying to help me when she almost made you cut your throat. She was only trying to help me when she gave you a cigar that exploded in your face. If she doesn't stop trying to help me, you're gonna end up in the hospital!

Ernie: Maybe you oughta teach her a lesson.

Ricky: You want to join the faculty?

Ernie: Huh?

Ricky: We'll just have a little fun with her.

Ernie: Okay, professor.

For 2¢ Ricky would move right back to Cuba and become a tobacco farmer.

Watch the scene where Lucy, laden with luggage and golf clubs, drops everything on the hotel stairs.

There is no mention of this being the last show.

Westinghouse advertised its new 1960 center-drawer refrigerator in this episode.

Actor and comedian Ernie Kovacs was born in Trenton, New Jersey, on January 23, 1919. As a young man he worked as a disc jockey before making his way into television. In 1957 he not only made his first Hollywood movie, but he wrote a book, Zoomar, in just thirteen days. He was considered one of America's most creative clowns.

DESI ARNAZ DESCRIBED THE LAST TELEVISION KISS BETWEEN LUCY AND RICKY IN HIS 1976 AUTOBIOGRAPHY, *A BOOK*: "THIS WAS NOT JUST AN ORDINARY KISS FOR A SCENE IN A SHOW. IT WAS A KISS THAT WOULD WRAP UP TWENTY YEARS OF LOVE AND FRIENDSHIP, TRIUMPHS AND FAILURES, ECSTASY AND SEX, JEALOUSY AND REGRETS, HEARTBREAKS AND LAUGHTER ... AND TEARS. THE ONLY THING WE WERE NOT ABLE TO HIDE WAS THE TEARS."

BEHIND THE
SCENES

JESS OPPENHEIMER
1913-1988

~~~~~~

LUCILLE BALL CALLED JESS OPPENHEIMER "the brains" behind *I Love Lucy*, and with good reason. As series creator, producer, and head writer, "Jess was the creative force behind *The Lucy Show*," confirms director Bill Asher. "He was the field general. Jess presided over all the meetings, and ran the whole show. He was very sharp."

Oppenheimer was born in San Francisco in 1913, and attended Stanford University in the 1930s, during radio's "golden age." He was especially drawn to radio comedy, and during his junior year he managed a visit to the KRFC radio studios in San Francisco. He soon found himself spending every spare moment there. He penned a comedy routine and quickly made his broadcasting debut, performing his own material coast to coast on the station's popular comedy-variety program, *Blue Monday Jamboree*.

In 1936, he made the short hop down to Hollywood where, through a combination of skill and impeccable timing, he managed to land a writing job on Fred Astaire's radio program—on his first day in town. When Astaire left the airwaves a year later, Oppenheimer became a gag writer for Jack Benny, then tackled comedy-writing chores for such other variety programs as *The Chase and Sanborn Hour* with Edgar Bergen and Charlie McCarthy, *The Lifebuoy Program* starring Al Jolson, *The Gulf Screen Guild Show*, and *The Rudy Vallee Program*. As a staff writer on those programs, Oppenheimer wrote sketch comedy for many of Hollywood's biggest stars, including Fred Allen, Talullah Bankhead, Jack Benny, Charles Boyer, Fanny Brice, Burns and Allen, James Cagney, Gary Cooper, Joan Crawford, Bing Crosby, Bette Davis, Marlene Dietrich, Clark Gable, Judy Garland, Bob Hope, Carole Lombard, William Powell, Ginger Rogers, Barbara Stanwyck, Jimmy Stewart, and Spencer Tracy.

At the start of World War II, Oppenheimer joined the United States Coast Guard and was promptly posted to the Public Relations Department. The sailor at the next desk was an agent named Ray Stark, who happened to be the son-in-law of the renowned comedienne and musical star, Fanny Brice. Almost immediately, Stark hired Oppenheimer to write for his mother-in-law's popular radio program, *Baby Snooks*. It marked Oppenheimer's introduction to the sitcom form—*Baby Snooks* was a comic examination of the relationship between adults and children. It starred Fanny Brice as a wise-beyond-her-years little girl who constantly drove her daddy crazy. During his six years on the show, Oppenheimer learned the ins and outs of plotting character-driven comedy.

On August 5, 1947, Jess married Estelle Weiss. Together they raised son Gregg and daughter Jo. In 1948, shortly after *Baby Snooks* went off the air, Oppenheimer accepted an assignment from CBS—to write a script for the network's struggling new radio sitcom, *My Favorite Husband*. The show starred Lucille Ball, one of the few stars in Hollywood with whom he had never worked. In the few episodes that had already aired, Lucille Ball's character in the show, Liz Cugat, had been a gay, sophisticated, socialite wife of a bank vice president, quite the opposite of the Snooks character Oppenheimer had been writing. After watching Lucille Ball at rehearsal, Oppenheimer decided to make some changes. He made Lucy's character more like Snooks—less sophisticated, more childlike, scheming, and impulsive—taking Lucy and the show in a new direction, with broad, slapstick comedy. His instincts paid off. Lucy took to her new role like a fish to water, and the show was a huge success. Recognizing a good thing, CBS quickly signed Oppenheimer as the show's head writer, producer, and director, and in no time the series gained a sponsor and a much larger

Jess Oppenheimer (right) on the set.

audience. *My Favorite Husband* also marked the beginning of Oppenheimer's successful collaboration with *I Love Lucy* writers Madelyn Pugh-Davis and Bob Carroll, Jr.

In December, 1950, when CBS agreed to produce a TV pilot starring Lucille Ball and Desi Arnaz, Lucy insisted that Oppenheimer head up the project. With the completed pilot due in just a few weeks, there was just one problem—nobody knew what the series should be about. Everyone asked, "What do you do with a comedienne and a Cuban orchestra leader?" Then Oppenheimer had a million-dollar idea—"Why don't we do a show," he suggested, "about a middle-class working stiff who works very hard at his job as a bandleader, and likes nothing better than to come home at night and relax with his wife, who doesn't like staying home and is dying to get into show business herself?" He decided to call the show *I Love Lucy*.

He remained as producer and head writer of the series for five of its six seasons, writing the pilot and 153 episodes with Madelyn Pugh-Davis and Bob Carroll, Jr. (They were joined in 1955 by writers Bob Schiller and Bob Weiskopf.) He appeared on the show only once, as one of the three TV executives for whom Ricky performed at the Tropicana in Episode #6, "The Audition."

Oppenheimer left *I Love Lucy* in 1956 to take an executive post at NBC, where he produced a series of landmark TV specials, including *The General Motors 50th Anniversary Show, Ford Startime, The Ten Commandments,* and *The 1959 Emmy Awards.* Oppenheimer and Ball were reunited in 1962, when he produced *The Danny Kaye Special,* nominated as "Program of the Year" by the TV Academy, and again in 1964, when he executive-produced the *The Lucille Ball Comedy Hour.* During the 1960s, Oppenheimer created and produced three sitcoms: Angel (starring Annie Fargé and Marshall Thompson), Glynis (starring Glynis Johns), and *The Debbie Reynolds Show.* His other TV credits include *The U.S. Steel Hour, Bob Hope's Chrysler Theatre, a Bob Hope Comedy Special, Get Smart,* and *All in the Family.* He received five Emmy nominations and, two Emmy Awards, a Sylvania Award, and the Writers' Guild of America's Paddy Chayefsky Laurel Award for Television Achievement.

An avid inventor, Oppenheimer held eighteen patents covering a variety of devices, including the in-the-lens teleprompter used by everyone from news anchors to presidents. Upon his passing in 1988, Lucille Ball called Jess Oppenheimer "a true genius." She added, "I owe so much to his creativity and his friendship." His best-selling memoir, *Laughs, Luck . . . and Lucy: How I Came to Create the Most Popular Sitcom of All-Time,* was completed after his death by his son, Gregg.

THE WRITERS

It is now fifty years after the debut of *I Love Lucy*, and most sitcoms are written by teams of dozens of writers, which often change from week to week. *I Love Lucy* is amazing in that it was written by no more than five people at any time, and the five were always the same. Jess Oppenheimer, Madelyn Pugh, and Bob Carroll, Jr. wrote the show together for the first four seasons (1951–55). Partners Bob Schiller and Bob Weiskopf joined them for the fifth season and stayed until the end (1955–60). Creator/producer Jess Oppenheimer was there from the beginning and left in 1956, after the end of the fifth season.

There are so many factors that make a successful television show. Of course, on *I Love Lucy*, the star was Lucy. But without the talent and dedication of the writing staff, *I Love Lucy* would not be the classic that it is today. Lucille Ball and the rest of the cast, although brilliant actors and comedians, did not invent the lines they spoke, the stunts they performed, or the situations which make us all roar with laughter. All of the brilliance that the actors brought to the screen so magnificently was first dreamed up, discussed, attempted, and finally written down, by the writers. Without the writers we would not have words such as "Vitameatavegamin," "zorch," "Maharincess," and "dawncy" as part of our common vocabulary. We would not count Mrs. Trumble, Carolyn Appleby, and Cousin Ernie as our friends.

The writers at work.

Although they never received an Emmy Award for their work, and for the joy that they brought to millions, *I Love Lucy* and *The Lucille Ball-Desi Arnaz Show* would not be the comedies that we love today without Oppenheimer, Pugh, Carroll, Schiller, and Weiskopf. Fans all over the world owe them their greatest praise and thanks for creating and bringing to life Lucy, Ricky, Ethel, and Fred.

What follows is an interview with *I Love Lucy* writers Madelyn Pugh-Davis, Bob Carroll, Jr., Bob Schiller, and Bob Weiskopf, who were all generous enough to contribute their memories and their wisdom in celebration of the fiftieth anniversary of a show that will never go off the air.

Bob Carroll, Jr. and Jess Oppenheimer.

When were you hired to work on *I Love Lucy*?

PUGH-DAVIS AND CARROLL: We wrote the pilot of *I Love Lucy* with Jess Oppenheimer and stayed with the show for six years.

SCHILLER AND WEISKOPF: For the opening of the fifth season—"Lucy Visits Graumans"—where Lucy digs up John Wayne's cement slab with his footprints for a souvenir of their trip to Hollywood. That was show number 128. We worked on all the subsequent episodes until it went off the air—then all the Lucy-Desi Comedy Hours (three years) and the first two years of The Lucy Show.

What were your previous jobs in TV or radio?

PUGH-DAVIS AND CARROLL: Madelyn started at radio station WIRE in Indianapolis. Bob started in the mailroom at CBS West coast. Next we were staff writers for the CBS Pacific radio network, and someone had the idea of putting us together as a team. As staff writers we wrote all sorts of shows—drama, game shows, and a comedy show starring Steve Allen called, *It's a Great Life*. From there we wrote a CBS radio network show, *My Favorite Husband*, starring Lucille Ball, which lasted two and a half years. When that ended, CBS decided Lucy was meant for the new medium of television, and we wrote the pilot for *I Love Lucy*.

SCHILLER: I started in radio in 1946 on *Duffy's Tavern* for four years, off and on.

WEISKOPF: Radio shows with stars such as Bob Hope, Eddie Cantor, and Rudy Vallee.

How did you decide on the premise for each episode?

PUGH-DAVIS AND CARROLL: We met for breakfast, looked at each other and said, "What'll we do this week?" and hoped one of us had a good idea.

SCHILLER AND WEISKOPF: In committee—the other two writers, Pugh and Carroll, and the producer, Jess Oppenheimer, and my partner and I would sit in Jess's office until a story emerged. We would not leave the premises until we had one nailed down. We'd work backwards, by the way, conjuring up a final block comedy scene, and then justifying reaching that scene logically. Not easy that way.

After you dreamed up those amazing stunts (Lucy in the grape vat, chocolate factory, landing on the deck of the SS Constitution) how did you go about planning them?

PUGH-DAVIS AND CARROLL: When we got an idea for a physical routine we sometimes checked with the Special Effects Department to see if what we had in mind was possible. They were wonderfully gifted people, and never said something wouldn't work. We often tried the stunts out on Madelyn to see if a woman could do them. Trying it out also helped us to see if the stunt presented any problems, and if it was as funny as we hoped. Often when we tried things out, we found funnier things to do than if we had just imagined them.

SCHILLER AND WEISKOPF: We'd get an idea for a block comedy scene and then plot our way into it logically. "Would Lucy be funny on stilts?" Sure, but now we'd write a story to get her on the stilts logically.

Were your scripts ever rejected?

PUGH-DAVIS AND CARROLL: No. The first years, the three of us (Oppenheimer, Pugh, and Carroll) wrote thirty-five scripts, and then next year we wrote thirty. In the early days they didn't do reruns. The theory was that if people had seen something once, they wouldn't look at it again. We were writing close to deadline, so if a script was thrown out, it was all we had, so we were off the air.

SCHILLER AND WEISKOPF: Never. And the rewrites were the shortest in our recollection. There was never an "allnighter" and we rarely, if ever, worked on the weekend.

Describe your I Love Lucy workweek.

PUGH-DAVIS AND CARROLL: The schedule varied through the years, but the way we remember it, we had a reading Monday morning (the cast hadn't seen it until then), then the three of us would leave to fix things and add new lines and the cast would start rehearsal. Tuesday, they rehearsed without cameras and we started on the next script. Tuesday afternoon we had a run-through and fine-tuned the show, with a note session after, with cast, directors, and writers. Wednesday the cast had a camera rehearsal and a camera run-through, with a note session after. Thursday the cast came in at noon, had more rehearsal and performed the show with an audience that night. Friday the three of us met (and later with Bob Schiller and Bob Weiskopf) and plotted the new script.

SCHILLER AND WEISKOPF: The five of us would hole up in Jess's office on Monday and toss ideas back and forth until we were happy with the story. Then Madelyn would type it out, scene by scene, and hand it to Bob and me the next day. We'd write the first draft Tuesday, and Thursday morning we'd turn our draft in to Jess, who would make notes and hand it to Bob and Madelyn to make changes. They then would hand that to Jess who did the final "brush." We never had a script thrown out!

What were your favorite episodes? Why?

PUGH-DAVIS: "Job Switching" with the candy assembly line was my favorite. Also, the one where Lucy meets Bill Holden and sets fire to her nose. I guess they are my favorites because no matter how many times I see them, they make me laugh.

CARROLL: My favorite is "Never Do Business with Friends," when the Ricardos sell the Mertzes their old washing machine. I guess because it is such a familiar situation, in that everyone recognizes the time that they sold something to a friend with disastrous results.

SCHILLER: I liked the grape-stomping—not because it was showing off the writing, but because it showed what a brilliant physical comedienne Lucille was. *The Danny Thomas Comedy Hour* show was superb.

WEISKOPF: Grape-stomping stands out in my mind as being a great episode. I also loved "Hollywood Anniversary" when Ricky threw a surprise party for Lucy at the Mocambo. The best hour-long show had to be the one with Danny Thomas.

Your least favorites? Why?

PUGH-DAVIS AND CARROLL: Can't remember one we really didn't like.

SCHILLER: A couple at the end of the last season—the statue, the power lawn mower.

WEISKOPF: Nothing stands out in my mind.

Did you enjoy appearing in the actual productions?

PUGH-DAVIS: I was only in one, "Paris at Last." I was sitting at the table with Bob, but all you can see is my elbow. It made me so nervous I never wanted to do it again.

CARROLL: I loved being an extra. You can see me in "Bon Voyage" at the rail of the ship, "Paris at Last" at the sidewalk cafe, and "Lucy Goes to Monte Carlo" at the roulette table.

Who were some of your favorite guest stars?

PUGH-DAVIS AND CARROLL: We were all very proud of the show with Harpo Marx, when Lucy and Harpo did the "mirror" routine. We also liked the one with meeting Bill Holden in the Brown Derby ("L.A. at Last!"). The Ricardos and Mertzes going to Hollywood gave us great opportunities for guest stars. We really liked Rock Hudson, John Wayne, Charles Boyer, and Van Johnson. All the stars were wonderful to work with—it's hard to choose!

SCHILLER: Bob Hope, Danny Thomas, Ann Sothern.

WEISKOPF: John Wayne, Charles Boyer, Bob Hope, and Danny Thomas were my favorites, but they were all great.

Backstage with Jess Oppenheimer (center).

Describe the relationships between the four stars.

PUGH-DAVIS AND CARROLL: Looking back on some of the shows which we hadn't seen for years, it dawned on us that maybe one of the big appeals of the show to the audience is that you could see that Lucy and Desi were really in love. It was very obvious. And although Vivian Vance and Bill Frawley complained about each other, they worked excellently together. And Lucy adored Vivian. As someone once remarked, Vivian was the greatest second banana in the business.

SCHILLER AND WEISKOPF: No point in belaboring the animosity between Vivian and Bill. And Lucy deferred to Desi. If she didn't think it was funny, and Desi said, "Try it honey, the 'kids' think it is," she'd try it—and give it her all. She trusted his judgment—which was always right on target. He was a wonderful judge and critic of comedy.

In your opinion, what one or two factors lead to the success of I Love Lucy?

PUGH-DAVIS AND CARROLL: We would have to say the remarkable talent of the cast. And then, maybe too, the fact that we dealt with ordinary married problems that were familiar to the audience. Everybody would like to be in love like Lucy and Ricky Ricardo. And everybody would like to have best friends they could count on like the Mertzes to tell their troubles to. Also, unlike some of the shows today, the foursome was never mean to each other. They might get in a fight, but they were sorry and cried and hugged and apologized before the show was over.

SCHILLER: Good, clean, funny comedy done by a superb cast, led by the best comedienne ever!

Madelyn Pugh-Davis and Bob Carroll, Jr. (center) as extras

WEISKOPF: A family show that you could watch with your kids, and everyone laughed and felt good.

Can you describe why I Love Lucy is as popular today as it was in 1951?

PUGH-DAVIS AND CARROLL: Lucille Ball.

SCHILLER AND WEISKOPF: Two words: Lucille Ball. And then three more: Desi, Viv, and Bill. And of course, the writers. A perfect mix.

Did the actors have any input into the scripts?

PUGH-DAVIS AND CARROLL: Not in the writing or the ideas. Of course, they all added things on the set. We wrote all the physical routines out, move by move, but Lucy added incredible touches of her own as rehearsal went along. Later, when Desi was executive producer, he was more active in the script process, and we always used to check with him before we wrote things, to see if they were possible.

SCHILLER AND WEISKOPF: Rarely. But Lucy's physical moves were usually even funnier than we had imagined. She constantly surprised us.

Were any of the cast members ever frightened or nervous about any of the physical stunts?

PUGH-DAVIS AND CARROLL: Lucy was the one who had to do most of the physical stuff, but she never complained. If it was funny, that was all that mattered.

SCHILLER AND WEISKOPF: Lucy was fearless.

Considering it had never been done before on TV, how easy or difficult was it to write the "pregnancy series"?

PUGH-DAVIS AND CARROLL: At the time we wrote those, we had never been married or had children, but it didn't seem too hard to write. We just had to be careful not to use the word "pregnant," which incredibly enough, could not be said on the air in the '50s. We had to use "expecting," or as Desi called it, "spectin."

Was there one moment that you can recall that was the high point of your years on *I Love Lucy*?

PUGH-DAVIS AND CARROLL: Not really. It was a thrill just to sit in the audience every week and hear the audience roaring with laughter.

SCHILLER: An ongoing high point was the love and respect and trust that all four of the regulars had for us writers. A rare thing in most facets of show business.

WEISKOPF: The satisfaction of doing a good show.

Was there a "lowest" moment?

PUGH-DAVIS AND CARROLL: Yes. At two in the morning when the script is due the next day and you realize the last scene doesn't work.

SCHILLER AND WEISKOPF: There was no time for low moments. A script a week written by three writers, then five of us, four when Jess left—that was *I Love Lucy*.

If Lucille and Desi had not been divorced, do you think the show would have continued in the hour-long format?

PUGH-DAVIS AND CARROLL: Maybe. It might have gone a few more years. We only did thirteen hour-long shows, and they were treated as special.

SCHILLER AND WEISKOPF: I don't think so. What other stories would work? What was left? Fatigue eventually trumps pride and joy.

If you could get Lucille, Desi, Viv, and Bill together once more, what would you say to them?

PUGH-DAVIS AND CARROLL: How about doing a series called *I Still Love Lucy*?

SCHILLER: Thank you! You're the greatest!

WEISKOPF: Be nice to each other.

Any final thoughts you might like to add?

PUGH-DAVIS AND CARROLL: Whenever anyone talks about the success of *I Love Lucy* they never seem to give much credit to Desi Arnaz. He was the one who wanted to shoot the show on film in Los Angeles in front of a live audience (which had never been done before) because CBS originally wanted them to do it live (and on kinescope) in New York. And, importantly to us, he was the one who, when Lucy wasn't too sure about something she was supposed to do in a script said, "Honey, the writers said they tried it out, so give it a try and if you don't like it, they'll think of something else." She trusted his judgment and tried it and usually liked it. He had tremendous enthusiasm, and if there was a problem, he would say, "Now, there has to be a way," and figure out how to solve it. He was not only an excellent straight man for Lucy, he was the Cuban glue that often held the show together.

SCHILLER: I only wish we got paid for the never-ending reruns. (We don't!)

WEISKOPF: It was a marvelous experience and I would never trade it.

Madelyn Pugh-Davis

CREATOR:

I Love Lucy (with Bob Carroll, Jr. and Jess Oppenheimer)
The Lucy Show (with Bob Carroll, Jr.)
The Mothers-in-Law (with Bob Carroll, Jr.)

WRITER:

My Favorite Husband
I Love Lucy
The Lucille Ball-Desi Arnaz Show
The Lucy Show
The Mothers-in-Law
Yours, Mine, and Ours
Lucille Ball Special, "Lucy Calls the President"

EXECUTIVE PRODUCER:

Private Benjamin (TV series)
Alice (TV Series)

AWARDS:

"Woman of Achievement"
Los Angeles Times "Woman of the Year"
Kappa Kappa Gamma Outstanding Achievement Award
Two Emmy nominations
Golden Globe Award for Producing (for Alice)
TV Academy's Hall of Fame (for I Love Lucy)
Writers' Guild of America Paddy Chayevsky Laurel Award
Women in Film Award
Indiana Broadcasters Hall of Fame Award

Bob Carroll, Jr.

CREATOR:

I Love Lucy (with Madelyn Pugh and Jess Oppenheimer)
The Lucy Show (with Madelyn Pugh)
The Mothers-in-Law (with Madelyn Pugh)

WRITER:

My Favorite Husband

I Love Lucy
The Lucille Ball-Desi Arnaz Show
The Lucy Show
The Mothers-in-Law
Yours, Mine, and Ours
Lucille Ball Special, "Lucy Calls the President"
Executive Producer:
Private Benjamin (TV series)
Alice (TV Series)

AWARDS:

Sylvania Award
Two Emmy nominations
Golden Globe Award for Producing (for Alice)
TV Academy's Hall of Fame (for I Love Lucy)
Writers' Guild of America Paddy Chayevsky Laurel Award

Bob Schiller

WRITER:

Duffy's Tavern
Abbott and Costello
The Adventures of Ozzie and Harriet
The Mel Blanc Show
Sweeney and March
The Jimmy Durante Show
December Bride
Our Miss Brooks
I Love Lucy
The Lucille Ball-Desi Arnaz Show
Make Room for Daddy
The Bob Cummings Show
That's My Boy
It's Always Jan
My Favorite Husband
The Ann Sothern Show (also creator)
Guestward Ho!
Pete and Gladys
The Lucy Show
The Red Skelton Show
The Good Guys (also producer)
The Phyllis Diller Show
The Carol Burnett Show

The Flip Wilson Show
Maude (also producer)
All in the Family
Archie Bunker's Place
Living in Paradise
The Boys

AWARDS:

Two Emmy Awards
Two Peabody Awards
Golden Globe Award
Writers' Guild of America Paddy Chayevsky Laurel Award

Bob Weiskopf

WRITER:

The Bob Hope Show
The Eddie Cantor Show
The Rudy Vallee Show
The Fred Allen Show
The Chesterfield Supper Club
Our Miss Brooks
I Love Lucy
The Lucille Ball-Desi Arnaz Show
Make Room for Daddy
The Bob Cummings Show
That's My Boy
It's Always Jan
My Favorite Husband
The Ann Sothern Show (also creator)
Guestward Ho!
Pete and Gladys
The Lucy Show
The Red Skelton Show
The Good Guys (also producer)
The Phyllis Diller Show
The Carol Burnett Show
The Flip Wilson Show
Maude (also producer)

AWARDS:

Two Emmy Awards
Two Peabody Awards
Golden Globe Award
Writers' Guild of America Paddy Chayevsky Laurel Award

AN INTERVIEW WITH KEITH THIBODEAUX "LITTLE RICKY" 1956-1960

Keith Thibodeaux (or Richard Keith, as he was called professionally during his *I Love Lucy* years) was born December 1, 1950, in Lafayette, Louisiana. He loved making music from an early age; at two he was performing in public, and at three he was invited to attend the National Drummer's Convention. On March 13, 1956, Keith was signed to a seven-year contract to work on *I Love Lucy*, at a starting salary of $300 per week. He would be on *I Love Lucy* through its final four seasons. In 1962, two years after *I Love Lucy* ended, Keith landed a job as Opie's best buddy, Johnny Paul Jason, on the popular comedy, *The Andy Griffith Show*. He also acted on such popular shows as *Route 66*, *The Shirley Temple Playhouse*, and *Hazel*. During his high school years he was very involved in music, and founded a band called the Sussex Six. In 1969, Keith joined the pop group David and the Giants and signed record deals with United Artists, MGM Records, Capital Records, and others. On October 26, 1976, he married ballet dancer Kathy Denton, and soon rejoined his old group, David and the Giants, which had become a Christian rock band. Today, Keith is the executive director of Ballet Magnificat, a national touring ballet company founded by his wife. He lives in Jackson, Mississippi, with his wife and daughter, Tara Kristen.

Keith is the only surviving regular cast member of *I Love Lucy*. He was the longest running Little Ricky, and the only Little Ricky who spoke on camera.

How did you start performing on television?

I played drums professionally—if you can believe it—at the age of three with the *Horace Heidt Swift Premium Hour*. I toured with that show for about a year until it ended. Horace Heidt had a big ranch in the San Fernando Valley where we lived after completing a tour of the United States and Canada.

Describe your *I Love Lucy* workweek.

The workweek began with a meeting in which we went over the script. The meeting was either in Desi's office or on the set. The meeting included the actors, writers, directors, etc. After all this happened I went home to learn my part. My dad would coach me. I hated it! He had a way of saying a line, which I thought sounded babyish and silly. Not natural. But he thought he had a feel of what Lucy and Desi wanted from me. Then from that point came a regular routine of rehearsals, blocking, light sittings, changes, and finally a dress rehearsal. The night of the final shoot was always exciting and electric. Also, between the times that I was needed, I went to school three hours a day there on the set.

What was your favorite episode(s)? Why?

My favorite episode by far was the Superman show (Episode 166). George Reeves was my hero and he was coming to my birthday party. I actually thought he was Superman. Other than that, Vitameatavegamin was really funny, a classic.

Your least favorite(s)? Why?

I think the move to Connecticut. Lucy and Desi were having more marital difficulties. By this time I was friends with Desi Jr. and Lucie, and I was spending a lot of time at their home. I began to experience some emotional pressure. At one point I was hypnotized in my dressing room by a therapist in order to remember my lines, which I began to forget. I even began to stutter. Lucy gave me a short period of time off and I was sent to a speech therapist.

Who were some of your favorite guest stars?

George Reeves, Maurice Chevalier, Danny Thomas, and Milton Berle.

Describe the relationships between the four stars. Did they enjoy working together?

I think they did. Their relationship was professional. Of course, Lucy and Desi were married, but on the set everyone was professional. I never saw any bickering between Viv and Bill. Lucy had given explicit orders to tone down any crude language when I was around.

In your opinion, what one or two factors lead to the success of *I Love Lucy*?

I think the fact there was this real love and passion between Lucy and Desi, along with great writers mirroring the real lives of the characters. By that, I don't mean we were those characters, but certain aspects of the actors real lives were brought to the show—Lucy's real-life jealousy of Desi's womanizing, Bill and Vivian's problems with one another, my stage fright and drumming abilities.

Can you describe in twenty-five words or less why I Love Lucy *is as popular today as it was in 1951?*

Funny. Charming. Crazy. Loving. Real. American. Latin. Musical. Chemistry. Professional. Family. Talent.

Photo courtesy of Marion and Gary Silber

Was there one moment that you can recall that was the high point of your years on I Love Lucy?

It was the Maurice Chevalier episode. I was very confident, and had fun doing the little dance routine and playing the drums.

Was there a "lowest" moment?

The Ernie Kovacs show. Because it was the last.

Would you have wanted the show to continue after 1960, provided the Arnaz marriage was still intact?

Of course I would have. Lucy and Desi's divorce affected not only the lives of the people on the show, but Lucy and Desi's children as well.

Did you have a favorite among the regular cast members? Describe your personal relationships with them.

Desi was a real guy with real problems, but I saw glimpses of Desi that not many people knew. Once when he found out that an employee's daughter needed an operation desperately and the man didn't have the money, Desi gave him a check for the whole thing. Whenever Desi Jr. and Lucie received a toy or a gift, Desi never left me out if I was at their home. I really looked up to Desi; he was a gracious and polite guy.

Now that you are an adult looking back, what do you think about the magic that you helped to create?

I look back to the show and it seems literally three lifetimes ago for me. Sometimes as I'm watching the show I'm thinking to myself, "Is that really me?" I'm just amazed!

How do fans react when they meet you and learn who you are?

Most people's eyes widen, and when it finally sinks in they want to hug me or touch me, along with getting my autograph. Most of the fans are very polite.

Do you like being associated with *I Love Lucy*?

It's not that bad. In my teen years I literally ran from any association with the show. Now that I'm older I can appreciate the quality of the show.

Compare *I Love Lucy* to some of the shows on TV today.

I really don't watch any of the sitcoms today. I guess that's my best answer to the question.

Any other thoughts?

I just wish that Desi Jr. and I were not mixed up in real life and make believe. I think if I had received credit on the show as myself, it would have cleared up any confusion as to who we are.

THE LEGACY OF LUCY

Fifty years after the premiere of *I Love Lucy* on October 15, 1951, the Ricardos and the Mertzes are as popular as they ever were. Fans of all ages, races, and backgrounds continue watch the antics of Lucy and company, on networks such as Nickelodeon and TV Land. They visit theme parks and exhibits like the ones at Universal Studios, and the Lucy-Desi Museum in Jamestown, New York. They buy and trade merchandise, whether made in the 1950s or manufactured today.

I Love Lucy fans are some of the most loyal in the world. While the show was in production in the 1950s, there were fan clubs made up of mostly young women who would occasionally visit the set and meet with the cast. After the show stopped filming in 1960, the fan clubs continued to gain new membership. Today there are hundreds of fan clubs devoted to the show, and to individual cast members. There are thousands of websites and online chat rooms to which fans can go to visit with others, and swap ideas or memorabilia.

In the 1950s, a host of *I Love Lucy* merchandise was available for purchase. Any fan could find dolls, pajamas, infant layettes, nursery furniture, clothing patterns, conga drums, books and comics for sale in the U.S. After *I Love Lucy* went off the air, the merchandise disappeared as well.

In the late 1980s, right before the death of Lucille Ball, a few products were created, including t-shirts, dolls, and a board game. These were quickly snatched up by eager fans who had had nothing to purchase for many years. In 1995, Desilu, too, LLC and CBS Worldwide, Inc. teamed up with licensing company Unforgettable Enterprises, and began to develop a large and varied list of items. Lucie Arnaz and Desi Arnaz, Jr. were concerned at that time that there were many unlicensed products on the market, some of which were of dubious quality and taste. The family wanted to make sure that everything that was available to *I Love Lucy* fans was top quality and worthy of the show the couple had produced. In the words of Lucie Arnaz, "There is too much 'tutt' out there." Over the past fifteen years, products have been developed and designed with the fans in mind, as they are what keeps the memory of the show—and its actors—alive.

The following pages contain photos of some current merchandise, everyday fans, and even some people who make their livings recreating the magic of *I Love Lucy*. It is to the fans that *I Love Lucy* owes its past success, and its future.

"To this day I still watch *I Love Lucy* in total amazement of how they can make me laugh over and over again with the same scene I've watched for thirty years! The humor is so simple and well-written. It took those talented writers to make it look so natural!"
ROBERTA WALL, an Ethel Mertz of Universal Studios, Hollywood (with Suzanne La Rusch as Lucy)

"One of my favorite things about *I Love Lucy* is its innocence. Instead of violence and sex, there's good clean fun about a Cuban bandleader and his wacky redheaded wife. There is also something so wonderful knowing that the whole country was watching at the same time. A type of unity. Today there has to be a disaster before that happens!"
MELISSA RADLEY, a Lucy Ricardo of Universal Studios, Florida

"I knew the warm fuzzy feeling I got every time I flipped the channel and stopped because *I Love Lucy* was on. When I proposed re-creating the Lucy Ricardo character ten years ago, I'd hoped the masses would also get that same warm fuzzy feeling watching her in 3D . . . I was right!"
SUZANNE LA RUSCH, a Lucy Ricardo of Universal Studios, Hollywood

"I remember growing up in Cuba, being fascinated by *Yo Quiero a Lucy*, and how the whole family sat together to watch the show. Regretfully, it was banned shortly after Castro took over the country. I rediscovered the sitcom when I arrived in the USA. The candor, clean fun, and masterminded show has endured all these years! It is still as fresh as a recently cut beautiful flower. Now I sit again in front of the TV, this time with my grandkids, and they enjoy it as much as I used to—and still do."
ADRIAN ISRAEL FLOWERS, a Ricky Ricardo of Universal Studios, Florida

"William Holden wearing his lunch, an operetta gone wrong, a prenatal rehearsal, 'Slowly I Turn' . . . I laughed yesterday and I'll laugh tomorrow."
DIANE VINCENT, a Lucy Ricardo of Universal Studios, Florida

Tom Watson, right, with writers Bob Carroll, Jr. and Madelyn Pugh-Davis.

"I feel something like 'the fan who came to dinner.' I started out in life as a fan of the original prime-time airings of *I Love Lucy*, loved Lucille Ball's subsequent shows, started a fan club in her honor, and wound up producing an annual fan festival that draws fellow fans from all over the world. In between, I had the honor of working for the lady the last few years of her life.

The scripts for *I Love Lucy* were fabulous because they presented normal everyday situations with which everyone could identify—Lucy Ricardo merely handled them more outlandishly than most of us! Lucille Ball, the actress, not only internalized Lucy's weekly plights (again through hours and hours of rehearsals!), but was able to 'telegraph' her thoughts and emotions to us through her very expressive face and body language. Consequently, we know—and feel—everything that Lucy Ricardo is going through. Thanks to her expressiveness, we participate in the action—virtually taste the Vitameatavegamin, if you will—making the viewing experience all the more wonderful."

TOM WATSON

President, We Love Lucy Fan Club
Producer, "Loving Lucy"
Author, *I Love Lucy: The Classic Moments*

Information about the We Love Lucy Fan Club and the annual "Loving Lucy" Conventions can be found on the internet at www.lucyfan.com. Fans can also write to We Love Lucy at P.O. Box 56234, Sherman Oaks, CA 91413.

"When *I Love Lucy* first aired in 1951, it pioneered the essence of the sitcoms we watch today. Very few programs have matched the comedic innocence enjoyed by people of all ages. Now, fifty years later, we still love Lucy!"
ROBIN RILEY MARTIN, a Lucy Ricardo of Universal Studios, Florida

"The love and friendship between Lucy and Ethel has always been the most inspiring aspect of the *I Love Lucy* show. No matter what happened, they always stayed friends forever."
RHONDA RICHARDS, an Ethel Mertz of Universal Studios, Hollywood
(with Diane Vincent as Lucy)

"They graced the stage with elegance and pride, and entertained the American public up to and beyond our own standards, brought joy to their cast members and made millions smile. . . . Whenever I had the available time or a weekday off from school I always looked forward to watching *I Love Lucy* because it some-how enlightened my day. I always looked forward to discovering the next stunt that Lucy and Ethel might plot against Ricky and Fred, or Ricky and Fred might plot against Lucy and Ethel."
EVA TOUNAS, a young fan of Astoria, New York

Young fans SHEA, JACK, AND GRACE PHINNEY of Wilton, Connecticut, with their dogs, Lucy and Ethel.

I Love Lucy fan JUSTINE DIAZ, of Toms River, New Jersey, stomps grapes at the Ocean County Library's Salute to *I Love Lucy*, February 14, 1999.

JANIE REEVE, PENNY EDWARDS, NELL SMITH, AND MAXINE NANCE loving Lucy in Linville, North Carolina.

Congratulations to all those talented individuals who helped shape and define the most famous sitcom in television history—*I Love Lucy*. Here at the Lucille Ball-Desi Arnaz Center in Lucille's hometown of Jamestown, New York we celebrate that legacy everyday. Beyond *I Love Lucy* and the gift of laughter the show gave to the world, we celebrate the lives of Lucille Ball and Desi Arnaz. We celebrate their ingenuity, perseverance, and the enduring contributions they made to television. Through trying times, their comedy is proof of the healing power of love and laughter.

On behalf of the Lucille Ball-Desi Arnaz Center, we invite you to visit and celebrate with us at our two museums. The Lucy-Desi Museum, originally opened in 1996, is located at a spacious facility at 10 West Third Street and houses the personal effects of the First Couple of Comedy. The Desilu Playhouse Museum, which features recreated *I Love Lucy* sets, opened at 2 West Third Street in 2005. Additionally, we are pleased to offer guests and visitors from around the world access through our website, www.lucy-desi.com. Over the years we have had the pleasure of welcoming thousands of people to Jamestown to join us in celebrating the legacies of Lucille Ball and Desi Arnaz.

On a personal note, as a native of Jamestown, New York, it is an honor for me to serve as a steward of the Lucille Ball-Desi Arnaz Center. For all fans of Lucille Ball, Desi Arnaz, *I Love Lucy*, and comedy overall, the Center strives to be an on-going celebration of the lives of these two extraordinary people. Along with several other area attractions, we feel the Center is a true gem of the Jamestown community, and we are proud to share our treasures with the world.

Since its inception, the Lucille Ball-Desi Arnaz Center has worked diligently to build a solid organization. Now that the foundation has been laid, we are planning for the future! While we will continue to celebrate the legacies of Lucille Ball, Desi Arnaz, and *I Love Lucy*, we are committed to returning to our roots and our founding mission. Thus, as we honor the legacy of the First Couple of Comedy, we also intend to define Jamestown as a premier destination for comedy.

CORIE CURTIS
Executive Director
The Lucille Ball-Desi Arnaz Center, Inc.

I LOVE LUCY PRODUCTS

Brighten up someone's day! Hallmark's newest *I Love Lucy* cards are imbedded with voice and music chips, to make the card giving and receiving experience even more special. You can see all the *I Love Lucy*-themed cards in your local Hallmark store, and at www.hallmark.com.

In 1999, the United States Postal Service issued the first official U.S. postage stamp commemorating the *I Love Lucy* show, as part of their Celebrate the Century stamp program. This newest stamp, unveiled in 2009, is part of their Early TV Memories collection, a salute to classic TV of the 1950s. Stamp design © 2009 U.S. Postal Service.

Good friends are like candy...

Vandor, LLC has been making licensed *I Love Lucy* products since 1996, and currently manufactures a long and varied list of merchandise including cookie jars, shopping bags, lunch boxes, kitchenware, and clocks. View all the licensed *I Love Lucy* merchandise at www.lyon.com.

The official *I Love Lucy* fiftieth anniversary artwork was created by internationally renowned 3-D pop artist Charles Fazzino in 2001. It was produced as a limited edition, and retails for $1,000. You can get your own copy of "For the Love of Lucy" by contacting www.fazzino.com.

Lehi Roller Mills first began manufacturing flour in Utah in 1906. Today you can purchase their cookie, muffin, and pancake mixes for use in your own kitchen. Young and old alike will love their newest tasty treat, Lucy's Old-Fashioned Brownie Mix, which is available in stores and online at www.lehirollermill.com.

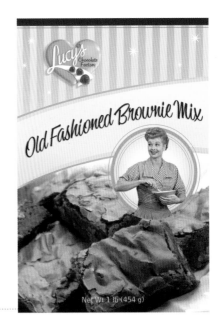

Have fun paying your bills! *I Love Lucy* checks in eight fun designs, have been available since 1998; also available are *I Love Lucy* checkbook covers and address labels. You can check out all the Custom Direct products at www.styleschecks.com.

American Greetings has been designing *I Love Lucy* ornaments as part of their Heirloom Collection since 1998. They also produce *Lucy*-inspired greeting cards. Visit them at www.americangreetings.com and check out all things *Lucy*.

Available since 1991, calendars are some of the most popular and practical *I Love Lucy* items on the market. Each year MeadWestvaco produces several versions of *I Love Lucy* desk and wall calendars for your enjoyment and use. You can visit them at www.mead.com.

One of the first companies to contract with CBS and Desilu, too, LLC to produce *I Love Lucy* merchandise was Talicor, whose popular board game was introduced in 1990. Since then they have added a trivia game, as well as a series jigsaw puzzles, for hours of friendly fun. Check out all their games and toys at www.talicor.com.

The only company licensed to produce chocolate based upon the famous "Job Switching" episode, Rocky Mountain Chocolate Factory sells chocolate bars, candies, and chocolate assortment boxes, including many sugar-free varieties. Visit them in retail stores or at www.rmcf.com.

In 1997, Mattel produced its first *I Love Lucy* doll, as part of its Timeless Treasures Collection. Since then, they have produced at least one doll each year, including special Lucy-Ricky, and Lucy-Ethel sets. Their latest production, from the "Lucy Tells the Truth" episode can be found in stores, and at www.BarbieCollector.com.

In 2008, Mattel debuted *I Love Lucy* "Kelly" dolls! "Kelly" dolls are tiny versions of the larger Mattel "Barbie" dolls. This first set, Lucy and Ethel in their famous "women from Mars" costumes from the "Lucy is Envious" episode, can be found in many retail stores, as well as on-line at www.mattel.com.

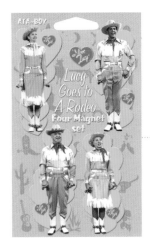

Ata-Boy has been making *I Love Lucy* products since 1992. They make individual magnets, magnet sets, bumper stickers, mouse pads, nightlights, key chains, and buttons. If you would like to see Lucy and the gang all over your house, visit www.ataboy.cameoez.com!

Accutime introduced its first *I Love Lucy* watch in 2005. They currently manufacture several different best-selling designs, including this grape-stomping themed purple timepiece. You can view this, and all their other designs, at accutimewatch.com.

Cathy's Closet, opened in 1992 by owner and manager Cathy Kelley, was the first full-service *I Love Lucy* store. Today, Cathy still sells hundreds of licensed *I Love Lucy* items. You can find her at www.lucystore.com.

All U Activewear has been designing and manufacturing *I Love Lucy* t-shirts and sweatshirts since 1996. They currently have a large collection of *I Love Lucy* hoodies, "snuggie" wraps, and hats, to compliment their line of best-selling t-shirts. You can learn more about them at www.allu.com.

GUEST STARS AND EXTRAS

During the six seasons of *I Love Lucy* (1951–57) and the three seasons of *The Lucille Ball-Desi Arnaz Show* (1957–60), Desilu employed many actors. Some of them were friends of Lucille and Desi, some were Hollywood celebrities. Some appeared in only one episode, others, such as Lou Nicoletti, Hazel Pierce, and Bennett Green, appeared in dozens. Some, such as Frank Nelson and Mary Jane Croft, had recurring roles; while others, like Elvia Allman, are best known for one role, although they appeared in many episodes as other characters. Many of the names chosen for characters, such as Charlie Pomerantz, Marion Strong, and Dan Jenkins, were names of friends or associates of the actors or the writers. Here is a list of the "extras" and guest stars who graced the screen of *I Love Lucy*.

HARRY ACKERMAN (TV executive, Episode 6)

EDIE ADAMS (as herself, Comedy Hour 13)

CLAUDE AKINS (as himself, Episode 161)

JACK ALBERTSON (dispatcher, Episode 140)

FRED ALDRICH (regular extra)

BETTY ALLEN (resident of Kildoonan, Episode 144)

SUE ALLEN (member of Pied Pipers, Episode 137)

ELVIA ALLMAN (regular extra; forewoman of Kramer's Kandy Kitchen, Episode 39)

HARRY ANTRIM (Mr. Feldman, Episode 137)

PILAR ARCOS (Señora Hoyos, Episode 105)

EVE ARDEN (as herself, Episode 114)

DESI ARNAZ, IV (boy in crowd, Episode 179)

PHIL ARNOLD (Harry Henderson, Episode 49; man in hotel, Episode 62)

GERTRUDE ASTOR (flapper, Episode 44)

ELEANOR AUDLEY (Eleanor Spaulding, Episode 167; contest judge, Episode 178)

HY AVERBACK (Charlie Appleby, Episode 71; Charlie Pomerantz, Episode 118)

IRVING BACON (Bert Willoughby, Episode 26; Will Potter, Ethel's father, Episode 113)

PARLEY BAER (Walter Reilly, Episode 126; Mr. Perry, Episode 170)

TALLULAH BANKHEAD (as herself, Comedy Hour 2)

JOAN BANKS (Eleanor Harris, Episode 83)

ROSA BARBATO (vineyard worker, Episode 150)

VIRGINIA BARBOUR (assistant in club act, Episode 105; woman on ship, Episode 141)

LITA BARON (Renita Perez, Episode 28)

HARRY BARTELL (regular extra)

FLORENCE BATES (Mrs. Pettibone, Episode 25)

LEON BELASCO (art store clerk, Episode 55)

BEA BENADERET (Miss Lewis, Episode 15)

MARJORIE BENNETT (Mrs. Van Fossen, Episode 156)

MILTON BERLE (as himself, Comedy Hour 11)

AUDREY BETZ (woman on bus, Episode 127)

ROBERT BICE (moving man, Episode 169)

LAURIE BLAINE (young flautist, Episode 156)

MADGE BLAKE (Mrs. Mulford, Episode 85; potential tenant Martha, Episode 166)

OLIVER BLAKE (shop owner Zeb Allen, Episode 76)

JOHN BLEIFER (waiter, Episode 147)

GLORIA BLONDELL (Grace Foster, Episode 36)

FORTUNIO BONANOVA (Spanish professor, Episode 105)

GAIL BONNEY (Mrs. Hudson, Episode 14)

MARILYN BORDEN (Teensy, Episode 112)

ROSALYN BORDEN (Weensy, Episode 112)

CHARLES BOYER (as himself and Maurice DuBois, Episode 146)

HAZEL "SUNNY" BOYNE (regular extra)

RUTH BRADY (Grace Munson, Episode 177)

BART (BRADLEY) BRAVERMAN (Giuseppe, Episode 149)

VIRGINIA BRISSAC (Mrs. Hammond, Episode 97)

PETER BROCCO (Dominic Orsatti, Episode 158; contest judge, Episode 178)

DONALD BRODIE (ticket agent, Episode 131)

SHEILA BROMLEY (Helen Erickson Kaiser, Episode 138)

HILARY BROOKE (Angela Randall, Episode 143)

JOHN BROWN (Mr. Murdoch, Episode 23)

ROBERT BRUBAKER (orderly, Episode 136)

ARTHUR BRYAN (Mr. Chambers, Episode 44)

JAMES BURKE (Mr. Watson, Episode 92; delivery man, Comedy Hour 4)

DICK BYRON (resident of Kildoonan, Episode 144)

ALBERTO CALDERONE (Alberto, Episode 76; diner patron, Episode 92)

KATHRYN CARD (regular extra; recurring as Mrs. McGillicuddy)

MONA CARLSON (actor's wife as herself, Episode 117)

BOB CARROLL, JR. (Episodes 140, 145, 152)

ANGELA CARTWRIGHT (guest star as Linda Williams, Comedy Hour 7)

SUE CASEY (girl Friday, Comedy Hour 9)

CHALO CHACON (bullfighter, Comedy Hour 6)

CHICK CHANDLER (Billy Hackett, Episode 113)

JACK CHEFE (waiter, Episode 146)

HARRY CHESHIRE (Sam Johnson, Episode 84)

MAURICE CHEVALIER (as himself, Comedy Hour 6)

KEN CHRISTY (Ken, the detective, Episode 84; dock agent, Episode 140)

EDUARDO CIANNELLI (Mr. Martinelli, Episode 158)

GORDON CLARK (gambler, Episode 152)

IRON EYES CODY (Eskimo, Comedy Hour 8)

TRISTRAM COFFIN (recurring as Harry Munson)

RITA CONDÉ (Maria Ortega, Episode 28)

OONA CONNERS (showgirl in movie, Episode 116)

HANS CONRIED (Dan Jenkins, Episode 43; Percy Livermore, Episode 53)

ELLEN CORBY (Miss Hannah, Episode 155)

SALLY CORNER (fur shop customer, Episode 49)

FRANCO CORSARO (Vittorio Philippi, Episode 150)

ALAN COSTELLO (Alfredo, Comedy Hour 6)

LEE COTCH (member of Pied Pipers, Episode 137)

LORRAINE CRAWFORD (girl Friday, Comedy Hour 9)

JOSEPH CREHAN (detective, Episode 132)

RICHARD CRENNA (Arthur Morton, Episode 20)

MARY JANE CROFT (regular extra; recurring as Betty Ramsey)

BOB CUMMINGS (as himself, Comedy Hour 12)

HENRY DAR BOGGIA (Italian border guard, Episode 151)

ALLEN DAVIES (member of Pied Pipers, Episode 137)

RICHARD DEACON (Winslow the butler, Comedy Hour 2)

JAOQUIN DEL RIO (prison trustee, Comedy Hour 1)

AMAPOLA DEL VANDO (Ricardo relative, Episode 162)

JIMMY DEMARET (golf pro as himself, Episode 96)

VERNON DENT (Santa Claus in the original "bonus" scene, Episode 9)

ALMOST ALL THE CELEBRITY GUEST STARS ON *I LOVE LUCY* WERE MEN.

BEPPY DEVRIES (Mrs. DeVries, Episode 98)

ANGELO DIDIO (cigar roller, Episode 162)

LARRY DOBKIN (regular extra)

JAMES DOBSON (Pete the delivery boy, Episode 103)

DOLORES DONLAN (starlet, Episode 115)

LESTER DORR (subway passenger, Episode 164)

PAUL DOUGLAS (as himself, Comedy Hour 9)

JODY DREW (Miss Ballentine, Episode 119)

PAUL DUBOV (Jerry the agent, Episode 37; Crandall, Comedy Hour 13)

HOWARD DUFF (as himself, Comedy Hour 10)

RALPH DUMKE (potential tenant Herbert, Episode 166)

BARBARA EDEN (Diana Jordan, Episode 177)

SAM EDWARDS (bellboy, Episode 142)

JOHN ELDREDGE (box seat ticket holder, Episode 174)

DICK ELLIOTT (tourist Henry, Episode 89; baseball fan, Episode 164)

ROSS ELLIOTT (regular extra; recurring as Ross Elliott)

BOBBY ELLIS (office assistant, Episode 32)

JUNEY ELLIS (housekeeper, Episode 127)

JOHN EMERY (Harold the tramp, Episode 5; Mr. Stewart, Episode 165)

MARY EMERY A.K.A MARIA CAVAZOS (Ricky's mother, Mrs. Ricardo, Episodes 105, 162)

WILLIAM ERWIN (bum in subway, Episode 164)

NICK ESCALANTE (diner patron, Episode 92)

JOAQUIN ESCARUGA (deliveryman, Episode 29)

DOUGLAS EVANS (Doug the beauty salon manager, Episode 93)

STANLEY FARRAR (Bennett Green, Episode 86; ferry worker, Episode 139)

WILLIAM FAWCETT (prospector, Comedy Hour 3; man, Comedy Hour 10)

JESSLYN FAX (subway passenger, Episode 164)

FRITZ FELD (tour guide, Episode 145)

VERNA FELTON (Mrs. Simpson, Episode 45; Mrs. Porter, Episode 58)

RAY FERRELL (recurring as Bruce Ramsey)

EVELYN FINLEY (train passenger, Episode 132)

LILA FINN (train passenger, Episode 132)

JAMES FLAVIN (immigration officer, Episode 158)

JUNE FORAY (bark of Fred the dog, Episode 165)

TENNESSEE ERNIE FORD (as himself, Episodes 94, 95, 112)

ALDO FORMICA (pizza chef, Episode 158)

ROBERT FORREST (Sidney Kaiser, Episode 138)

BYRON FOULGER (Friend of the Friendless, Episode 60)

ROBERT FOULK (police officer, Episode 164)

ABEL FRANCO (Ricardo relative, Episode 162)

JOHN FRANK (Bonus Bucks newspaper man, Episode 87)

MILTON FROME (Sam Carter, Episode 99)

NACHO GALINDO (cigar store owner, Episode 162)

JOHN GALLAUDET (agent Johnny Clark, Episodes 134, 135)

JAMES JOHN GANZER (newborn Little Ricky, Episode 56)

DON GARNER (delivery boy, Episodes 87, 92)

BOB GARVIN (man in closet, Episode 40)

HAL GERARD (tourist, Episode 128)

FRANK GERSTLE (actor in Indian routine, Episode 59; helicopter pilot, Episode 140)

ALAN GILBERT (theatergoer, Episode 174)

LARRY GLEASON (young accordionist, Episode 156)

PAT GOLDIN (bicycle messenger, Episode 140)

GALE GORDON (Mr. Littlefield, Episodes 33, 35, judge, Comedy Hour 7)

SANDRA GOULD (Nancy Johnson, Episode 84; woman in subway, Episode 164)

BETTY GRABLE (as herself, Comedy Hour 4)

CAMERON GRANT (Santa Claus, 1956 Christmas special)

HARVEY GRANT (Kenneth Hamilton, Episode 141)

GARY GRAY (delivery man, Episode 169)

BENNETT GREEN (regular extra)

SAUL GROSS (train passenger, Episode 132)

JOHN GUSTAFSON (resident of Kildoonan, Episode 144)

FLORENCE HALOP (woman on phone, Episode 43)

WILLIAM HAMEL (regular extra)

RUSTY HAMER (Rusty Williams, Comedy Hour 7)

ROBERT HAMLIN (resident of Kildoonan, Episode 144)

JOHN L. HART (regular extra)

PAUL HARVEY (Times Art Critic, Mr. Harvey, Episode 55)

JERRY HAUSNER (regular extra; recurring as Ricky's agent, Jerry)

JUNE HAVER (as herself, Comedy Hour 3)

JAMES HAYWARD (boat captain, Episode 160)

SAM HEARN (Dr. Peterson, Episode 138; audience member, Comedy Hour 9)

FRANCES NEAL HEFLIN (actor's wife as herself, Episode 117)

JOHN HENSON (theatergoer, Episode 174)

GIL HERMAN (assassin, Episode 31)

MAURY HILL (Tom Williams, Episode 81)

RAMSEY HILL (French gendarme, Episode 145)

HOWARD HOFFMAN (Dr. Barnett, Episode 136)

MARY ALAN HOKENSON (woman from House and Garden, Episode 171)

BRENDA MARSHALL HOLDEN (actor's wife as herself, Episode 117)

WILLIAM HOLDEN (as himself, Episode 114)

BOB HOPE (as himself, Episode 154)

HEDDA HOPPER (gossip columnist as herself, Episode 118, Comedy Hour 1)

EDWARD EVERETT HORTON (Mr. Ritter, Episode 15)

OLIN HOWLIN (cafe/motel owner George Skinner, Episode 111)

RUDOLFO HOYOS, JR. (Señor Hoyos, Episode 105; Ricardo relative, Episode 162)

HAL HUDSON (TV executive, Episode 6)

ROCK HUDSON (as himself, Episode 123)

GLADYS HURLBUT (theatergoer who loses purse, Episode 174)

ALVIN HURWITZ (Acme Employment Agency manager Mr. Snodgrass, Episode 39)

JOHN HYND (resident of Kildoonan, Episode 144)

FRANK JACQUET (laundry worker, Episode 87)

HARRY JAMES (as himself, Comedy Hour 4)

VIVI JANISS (club member, Episode 57; Lou Ann Hall, Episode 81)

JILL JARMYN (starlet as herself, Episode 161)

ROBERT JELLISON (regular extra; recurring as Bobby the Beverly Palms Hotel bellboy)

ALLEN JENKINS (regular extra)

SUSAN JOHNSON (theatergoer, Episode 174)

VAN JOHNSON (as himself, Episode 125)

DICK KALLMAN (bellboy, Comedy Hour 13)

BYRON KANE (Morris Williams, Episode 85; subway passenger, Episode 164)

STEVEN KAY (Stevie Appleby, Episode 166)

MARY ELLEN KAYE (newlywed Mrs. Taylor, Episode 168)

RICHARD KEAN (voice in play, Episode 106)

JOSEPH KEARNS (Dr. Tom Robinson, Episode 27, theater manager, Episode 174)

LARRY KEATING (Mr. Watson, Comedy Hour 11)

RAY KELLOGG (regular extra)

PHYLLIS KENNEDY (Elsie the maid, Comedy Hour 2)

HUBIE KERNS (train passenger, Episode 132)

RICHARD KING (busboy, Comedy Hour 3)

WALTER KINGSFORD (Sir Clive Richardson, Episode 143)

JESS KIRKPATRICK (ticket clerk, Episode 169; show director, Comedy Hour 8)

HELEN KLEEB (Miss Klein, Episode 126)

ERNIE KOVACS (as himself, Comedy Hour 13)

LOU KRUGMAN (regular extra)

HENRY KULKY (baseball trainer, Episode 154)

NANCY KULP (hotel maid, Episode 142)

FERNANDO LAMAS (as himself, Comedy Hour 5)

ELSA LANCASTER (Mrs. Grundy, Episode 159)

CHARLES LANE (regular extra)

JOI LANSING (as herself, Episode 161; girl Friday, Comedy Hour 9)

MARY LANSING (voice in play, Episode 106)

MILDRED LAW (stewardess, Episode 153)

CHARLOTTE LAWRENCE (club member, Episode 57; Ricardo neighbor, Episode 133)

ROY LAZARUS (theatergoer, Episode 174)

NORMAN LEAVITT (regular extra)

EDDIE LEBARON (club emcee, Episode 162)

MAY LEE (extra, Comedy Hour 12)

PETER LEEDS (reporter, Episode 31; Mr. Krausfeld, Episode 164)

SHELDON LEONARD (salesman Harry Martin, Episode 45)

MARTIN LEWIS (photographer Jim White, Episode 8)

MARGIE LISZT (regular extra)

JOHN LITEL (Harvey Cromwell, Episode 101)

DOROTHY LLOYD (Mercedes Minch, Episode 72)

BARBARA LOGAN (stewardess, Episode 162)

SAVERIO LO MEDICO (bellboy, Episode 150)

SHORTY LONG (theatergoer, Episode 174)

HAZEL LONGDEN (jockey's wife as herself, Episode 164)

JOHNNY LONGDEN (jockey as himself, Episode 164)

ADELE LONGMIRE (nurse, Episode 56)

DON LOPER (as himself, Episode 117)

MARJORIE LORD (Kathy Williams, Comedy Hour 7)

DAYTON LUMMIS (regular extra)

ART LUND (theatergoer, Episode 174)

IDA LUPINO (as herself, Comedy Hour 10)

HERBERT LYTTON (man on deck, Episode 141)

FRED MACMURRAY (as himself, Comedy Hour 3)

SHEILA MACRAE (actor's wife as herself, Episode 117)

MAGGIE MAGENNIS (starlet, Episode 115)

HAL MARCH (Hal March, Episode 16; Eddie Grant, Episode 62)

MAURICE MARSAC (headwaiter Maurice, Episode 35; Parisian waiter, Episode 145)

MYRA MARSH (club member, Episode 17, 38)

JEANNE BIEGGER MARTIN (actor's wife as herself, Episode 117)

STROTHER MARTIN (diner waiter, Episode 159)

HARPO MARX (as himself, Episode 124)

MONTY MASTERS (TV director, Episode 134)

EVE WHITNEY MAXWELL (Eve Whitney, Episode 81)

EVA JUNE MAYER (mother of Mayer twins as Ricardo neighbor, Episode 133)

JOSEPH DAVID MAYER (toddler Little Ricky, 1953–56)

MICHAEL LEO MAYER (toddler Little Ricky, 1953–56)

KATHLEEN MAZALO (Teresa, Episode 149)

SAM MCDANIEL (Sam the porter, Episode 132)

BILLY MCLEAN (hotel bellboy, Episode 160)

HOWARD MCNEAR (Mr. Crawford, Episode 156)

EVE MCVEAGH (Roberta the hairdresser, Episode 93)

TYLER MCVEY (regular extra)

EDITH MEISER (Phoebe Littlefield, Episodes 33, 35)

SID MELTON (bellboy, Comedy Hour 8, Shorty, Comedy Hour 11)

SHEPARD MENKEN (regular extra; Jean Valjean Raymond, Episode 12)

LOUIS MERRILL (Dr. Rabwin, Episode 54)

SUSIE MEYER (girl in crowd, Episode 179)

TORBEN MEYER (Swiss Oom-pa bandleader, Episode 148)

TONY MICHAELS (Charlie, episode 3; laundry worker, Episode 87)

LEE MILLAR (regular extra)

JOE MILLER (diner patron, Episode 92)

AMANDA MILLIGAN (candy dipper, Episode 39)

FRANK MITCHELL (tumbling act, Comedy Hour 11)

SHIRLEY MITCHELL (regular extra; recurring as Marion Strong)

GERALD MOHR (Dr. Molin/Chuck Stewart, Episode 46)

LILLIAN MOLIERI (young señorita, Episode 78; Ricardo relative, Episode 162)

ERNESTO MOLINARI (grape vineyard manager, Episode 150)

RALPH MONTGOMERY (police officer, Episode 56)

IDA MOORE (Mrs. Knickerbocker, Episode 47)

PAT MORAN (Buffo the Clown, Episode 6)

PATSY MORAN (laundry worker, Episode 87)

KENNY MORGAN (real-life husband of Lucille's cousin as press agent Kenny, Episode 8)

ALBERTO MORIN (Carlos Ortega, Episode 28, Robert DuBois, Episode 73)

CHARLIE MURRAY (man in closet, Episode 40)

JOHN MYLONG (French gendarme, Episode 145; casino manager, Episode 152)

FRANK NELSON (regular extra; recurring as Freddy Fillmore and Ralph Ramsey)

PATTI NESTOR (circus act dancer, Episode 142)

WILLIAM NEWELL (hotel desk clerk, Comedy Hour 8)

LOUIS "NICK" NICOLETTI (regular extra)

BEN NIEMS (police officer, Episode 128)

BUDDY NOBLE (young bass player, Episode 156)

DANI SUE NOLAN (secretary, Episode 114)

ROBERT NORMAN (young trumpet player, Episode 156)

JAY NOVELLO (Mr. Merriweather, Episode 7, Mr. Beecher, Episode 97, and gondolier Mario, Episode 158)

BETTY NOYES (resident of Kildoonan, Episode 144)

PHIL OBER (Vivian Vance's husband as Arnold, Episode 5; Dore Schary, Episode 119)

DOYE O'DELL (announcer, Episode 135)

GEORGE O'HANLON (Charlie Appleby, Episode 166)

SAMMY OGG (Jimmy Hudson, Episode 14)

MORONI OLSEN (judge, Episode 42)

JESS OPPENHEIMER (audience member, Episode 6)

LARRY ORENSTEIN (Mayor Ferguson, Episode 144)

DORIS PACKER (box seat ticket-holder, Episode 174; Miss Massey, Comedy Hour 9)

VINCENT PADULA (regular extra)

MABEL PAIGE (Mrs. Hansen, Episode 68)

NESTER PAIVA (Cuban jailer, Comedy Hour 1)

MANUEL PARIS (Ricardo relative, Episode 162)

EMORY PARNELL (police officer, Episode 68)

MILTON PARSONS (Mr. Thurlow, Episode 34)

ELIZABETH PATTERSON (regular extra, recurring as Mrs. Trumble)

GEGE PEARSON (tourist, Episode 128)

BARBARA PEPPER (early Hollywood friend of Lucille, regular extra)

PEPITO PEREZ (Pepito the Clown, pilot, Episode 52)

GIL PERKINS (train passenger, Episode 132)

RUTH PERROTT (regular extra)

BARNEY PHILLIPS (Mr. Jamison, Episode 137)

  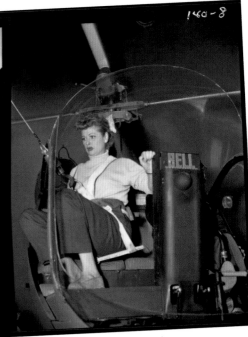

HAZEL PIERCE (Lucille Ball's stand-in and regular extra, recurring as Grace Munson)

WALTER PIETILA (tumbling act, Comedy Hour 11)

GEORGE PIRRONE (golfing caddy, Episode 96)

PAUL POWER (regular extra)

MADELYN PUGH (café patron, Episode 145)

FRANCIS RAVEL (French border guard, Episode 151)

ALAN RAY (regular extra)

PEGGY REA (regular extra)

GEORGE REEVES (Superman, Episode 166)

RICHARD REEVES (regular extra)

ELLIOTT REID (TV show host Edward Warren, Episode 134)

GENE REYNOLDS (newlywed Mr. Taylor, Episode 168)

JACK RICE (Macy's salesman, Episode 155)

ADDISON RICHARDS (American Consul, Comedy Hour 6)

CAROL RICHARDS (Juanita, Episode 59)

MARCO RIZO (Desi's lifelong friend, pianist, as himself on recurring basis)

EARL ROBBIE (young ukulele player, Episode 156)

CESAR ROMERO (Carlos Garcia, Comedy Hour 1)

FELIX ROMANO (Italian border guard, Episode 151)

HAYDEN RORKE (Tom O'Brien, Episode 21)

ROY ROWAN (radio announcer, Episode 32; train passenger, Episode 132)

BENNY RUBIN (bus driver, Episode 127)

DAVID SABER (young baseball fan, Episode 154)

HUGH SANDERS (hotel clerk, Comedy Hour 8)

RALPH SANFORD (baseball stadium security guard, Episode 154)

FRANK SCANNELL (burlesque comic, Episode 19)

NATALIE SCHAFER (Phoebe Emerson, Episode 81)

ROY SCHALLERT (Ricardo neighbor, Episode 133)

CANDY ROGERS SCHOENBERGER (Suzy Brown, Episode 163)

CHUCK SCHROUDER (resident of Kildoonan, Episode 144)

BETTY SCOTT (circus act dancer, Episode 142)

ROLFE SEDAN (Parisian chef, Episode 145)

SARAH SELBY (Dorothy Cook, Episode 99)

MAXINE SEMON (regular extra)

ROBERT SHAFTO (British gentleman on street, Episode 142)

FLORENCE ANN SHAWN (young woman on subway platform, Episode 164)

FRED SHERMAN (drunken customer, Episode 92)

RANSOM SHERMAN (Friend of the Friendless, Episode 60)

IVA SHEPARD (Beverly Palms Hotel maid, Episode 115; nurse, Episode 136)

TERU SHIMADA (extra, Comedy Hour 12)

MARIO SILETTI (Professor Falconi, Episode 72; Italian farmer, Episode 151)

HELEN SILVER (dancer Rosemary, Episode 11)

RICHARD LEE SIMMONS (infant Little Ricky, 1953 season)

RONALD LEE SIMMONS (infant Little Ricky, 1953 season)

DORIS SINGLETON (regular extra; recurring as Lillian/Carolyn Appleby)

RED SKELTON (as himself, Comedy Hour 8)

IDA SMERALDO (hotel guest on phone, Episode 149)

HERMAN SNYDER (Harry, Comedy Hour 11)

SONDI SODASI (extra, Comedy Hour 12)

OLAN SOULÉ (Dr. Gettleman, Episode 136)

ANN SOTHERN (Susie MacNamara, Comedy Hour 1)

AARON SPELLING (Country Boy, Episode 112)

CHARLIE STEVENS (Alaskan native, Comedy Hour 8)

K. T. STEVENS (Mrs. O'Brien, Episode 21)

DAVID STOLLERY (Timmy Hudson, Episode 14)

CLARENCE STRAIGHT (police officer, Episode 128)

AMZIE STRICKLAND (sales assistant, Episode 117)

FRANK SULLY (delivery man, Episode 29)

CLINTON SUNDBERG (screen test director, Episode 104)

PHILIP SYLVESTRI (man in closet, Episode 40)

DUB TAYLOR (Rattlesnake Jones, Episode 135)

PHIL TEAD (man on subway platform, Episode 164)

MAX TERHUNE (Sir Hume, Episode 85)

KEITH THIBODEAUX (older Little Ricky, 1956–60)

DANNY THOMAS (Danny Williams, Comedy Hour 7)

LARRI THOMAS (girl Friday, Comedy Hour 9)

BEVERLY THOMPSON (starlet, Episode 115)

MAURY THOMPSON (Desilu employee; stage hand, Episode 17; script clerk, Episode 30)

SHIRLEE TIGGE (starlet, Episode 115)

TERESA TIRELLI (grape stomper in vat with Lucy, Episode 150)

GEORGE TREVINO (Uncle Alberto Ricardo, Episode 162; judge, Comedy Hour 1)

MARYLIN JOHNSON TUCKER (actor's wife as herself, Episode 117)

ROSA TURICH (Carlota Romero, Episode 78)

LURENE TUTTLE (club president, Episode 47)

RUDY VALLEE (as himself, Comedy Hour 1)

DIANA VAN FOSSEN (young violinist, Episode 156)

NORMA VARDEN (Mrs. Benson, Episode 61)

CHARLES VICTOR (man hiding in closet, Episode 40)

HERB VIGRAN (regular extra)

JACQUES VILLON (croupier, Episode 152)

RALPH VOLKE (masseur, Episode 129)

VEOLA VONN (mistress of ceremonies, Episode 37)

JANET WALDO (Peggy Dawson, Episode 20)

ANN ELLEN WALKER (resident of Kildoonan, Episode 144)

ARTHUR WALSH ("King Kat" Walsh as himself, Episode 77)

TREVOR WARD (stable groom, Episode 143; arresting officer, Episode 145)

JODY WARNER (theater usher, Episode 174)

RICK WARRICK (desk clerk, Comedy Hour 3)

PIERRE WATKIN (Mr. Dorrance, Episode 90; Mr. Robinson, Comedy Hour 9)

JOHN WAYNE (as himself, Episode 129)

BEN WELDON (thief, Episode 10)

ORSON WELLES (director as himself, Episode 155)

JUNE WHITLEY (club member, Episodes 57, 64)

MARY WICKES (longtime Lucy-Desi friend as Madame Lemond, Episode 19)

RICHARD WIDMARK (as himself, Episode 127)

FRANK WILCOX (Joe Spaulding, Episode 167)

CORNEL WILDE (as himself, Episode 122)

KAY WILEY (regular extra)

HELEN WILLIAMS (flapper, Episode 44)

ROBERT WILLIAMS (bailiff, Episode 42)

ALICE WILLS (Madame X, Episode 75)

CHARLES WINNINGER (Barney Kurtz, Episode 102)

PAULA WINSLOW (woman on deck, Episode 141)

DOROTHEA WOLBERT (Mrs. Wolbert of the Ladies Overseas Aid charity, Episode 137)

LINDA WONG (extra, Comedy Hour 12)

JEFFREY WOODRUFF (young trombonist, Episode 156)

STEPHEN WOOTTON (Barney's grandson, Episode 102)

WILL WRIGHT (locksmith Mr. Walters, Episode 37; Bent Fork sheriff, Episode 112)

CLARK YOKUM (member of Pied Pipers, Episode 137)

NORMA ZIMMER (resident of Kildoonan, Episode 144)

THE SONGS

The fact that Desi Arnaz was a musician added depth to *I Love Lucy*. The writers wove many songs into the *I Love Lucy* plots. Signature Latin songs such as "Babalu" and "Cielito Lindo" were used regularly. Old-time vaudeville favorites such as "The Charleston" and "By the Light of the Silvery Moon" can be heard in episodes in which Fred and Ethel were hired to work at Ricky's club. Original songs such as "I Am the Queen of the Gypsies" and "A McGillicuddy is Here" were written for the show and used in episodes such as "The Operetta" and "Lucy Goes to Scotland." Here is a list of all the music that can be heard in *I Love Lucy* episodes.

AH, SWEET MYSTERY OF LIFE (Episode 103)

ANNIVERSARY WALTZ (Episode 121)

APACHE (Episode 73)

AUF WIEDERSEH'N, MY DEAR (Episode 13)

BABALU (pilot, Episodes 6, 20, 31, 53, 65, 162)

BAYAMO, THE (Comedy Hour 4)

BIG "D" (Episode 174)

BIM BAM BOOM (Episode 105)

BIRMINGHAM JAIL (Episodes 112, 135)

BY THE BEAUTIFUL SEA (Episode 102)

BY THE LIGHT OF THE SILVERY MOON
    (Episode 52)

BY THE WATERS OF MINNETONKA
    (Episode 59)

CALIFORNIA, HERE I COME (Episode 110)

CANTA GUITARRA (Episode 104)

CAROLINA IN THE MORNING (Episodes 44, 52)

CIELITO LINDO (pilot, Episodes 29, 45, 47, 88,
    141, Comedy Hours 1, 10)

CHARLESTON, THE (Episode 44)

CHEEK TO CHEEK (Episode 51)

CHOPSTICKS (Episode 113)

CUBAN CABBY (pilot, Episode 47)

CUBAN PETE (Episode 118)

CUBAN PETE-SALLY SWEET (Episode 4)

DEAR OLD DONEGAL (Episode 120)

DON'T CRY (Episode 174)

DOWN ARGENTINE WAY (Episode 36)

DOWN BY THE OLD MILL STREAM
    (Episode 135)

DRAGON WALTZ, THE (Episode 144)

EL CUMBANCHERO (Episodes 11, 18)

EMBRACEABLE YOU (Episode 117)

FIVE FOOT TWO, EYES OF BLUE
    (Episodes 44, 156)

FOREVER DARLING (Episode 137)

FRERE JACQUES (Episode 73)

FRIENDS OF THE FRIENDLESS (Episode 60)

FRIENDSHIP (Episode 69)

GLOW WORM, THE (Episode 40)

GOODNIGHT LADIES (Episode 52)

GRANADA (pilot, Episodes 50, 76)

GREEN EYES (Episode 118)

GUADALAJARA (Episode 2)

HABAÑERA (Episode 103)

HAPPY BIRTHDAY TO YOU (Episodes 60, 149)

HAWAIIAN WAR CHANT, A (Episode 88)

HERE COMES THE BRIDE (Episode 36, 38)

HOME ON THE RANGE (Episode 135)

HONEY (Episode 88)

HOW ABOUT YOU? (Episode 125)

HOW DEEP IS THE OCEAN (Episode 88)

HOW DRY I AM (Episode 6)

HUMORESQUE (Episode 120)

I AM THE GOOD PRINCE LANCELOT (Episode 38)

I AM THE QUEEN OF THE GYPSIES (Episode 38)

I FOUND A PEACH ON THE BEACH (Episode 102)

I GET IDEAS (Episodes 31, 130)

I GET THE BLUES WHEN IT RAINS (Episode 88)

I'LL SEE YOU IN C-U-B-A (Episodes 23, 107)

I LOVE LUCY (Episode 60)

I LOVE YOU TRULY (Episode 26)

I'M AFRAID TO GO HOME IN THE DARK (Episode 111)

I'M AN OLD COWHAND (Episode 86)

I'M BREAKING MY BACK (Episode 14)

I'M IN LOVE WITH THE DRAGON'S DINNER (Episode 144)

I'M PUTTING ALL MY EGGS IN ONE BASKET (Episode 88)

IN A LITTLE SPANISH TOWN (Episode 103)

IN ACAPULCO (Episode 71)

IN SANTIAGO, CHILE (Episode 37)

I WANT A GIRL JUST LIKE THE GIRL THAT MARRIED DEAR OLD DAD (Episodes 18, 102)

JEZEBEL (Episode 11)

JINGLE BELLS (1956 Christmas special)

KING KAMEHAMEHA (Episode 88)

LA CUCARACHA (Episodes 88, 148, Comedy Hour 6)

LADY IN RED, THE (Episodes 28, 50)

LADY OF SPAIN (Episode 65)

LA RAPSA (Episode 18)

LA VIE EN ROSE (Episode 121)

LET ME GO LOVER (Episode 120)

CHANGO, AN AFRICAN GOD OF WAR, IS THE SUBJECT OF "BABALU."

LET'S HAVE ANOTHER CUP O' COFFEE (Episode 88)

LILY (Episode 38)

LILY OF THE VALLEY (Episodes 38, 74, 135)

LOUISE (Episode 73, Comedy Hour 6)

LOVELIEST NIGHT OF THE YEAR, THE (Episode 65)

LUCKY GUY, A (Episode 162)

MADEMOISELLE FROM ARMENTIERES (Episode 138)

MAMA INEZ (Episode 29)

MAMA YO QUIERO (Episode 3)

MAN SMART, WOMAN SMARTER (Episode 173)

MARTHA (Episode 19)

MCGILLICUDDY IS HERE, A (Episode 144)

MELANCHOLY BABY (Comedy Hour 5)

MEXICAN HAT DANCE, THE (Episode 18)

MIMI (Comedy Hour, Episode 6)

MISSISSIPPI MUD (Episode 44)

MOCKINGBIRD (Episode 135)

MY BONNIE LIES OVER THE OCEAN (Episode 5)

MY HERO (Episode 113)

NOBODY LOVES THE UMP (Episode 154)

NOTRE DAME VICTORY SONG (Episode 53)

OH BY JINGO (Episode 102)

OLD CHISHOLM TRAIL, THE (Episode 135)

OLD FOLKS AT HOME (Episode 120)

OLD MACDONALD HAD A FARM (Episode 112)

ON THE BOARDWALK IN ATLANTIC CITY (Episode 102)

OUR SHIP IS COMING IN (Comedy Hour 1)

PASS THAT PEACEPIPE (Episode 59)

POOR EVERYBODY ELSE (Comedy Hour 8)

PRETTY GIRL IS LIKE A MELODY, A (Episode 116)

RAGTIME COWBOY JOE (Episode 14)

SWEET AND LOVELY (Episode 44)

SWEET SUE (Episodes 18, 101, 173)

SWISS YODEL (Episode 148)

TAKE ME OUT TO THE BALLGAME (Episode 124)

TANGO (Episode 172)

TEXAS PETE (Episode 135)

THANKS FOR THE MEMORY (Episode 154)

THAT MEANS I LOVE YOU (Comedy Hour 1)

THAT'S ALL (Comedy Hour 13)

THEM THERE DAYS (Comedy Hour 11)

THERE'S A BRAND NEW BABY AT OUR HOUSE*
(Episode 45)

THERE'S NO BUSINESS LIKE SHOW BUSINESS
(Episode 77)

THEY GO WILD OVER ME (Episode 102)

TIPPY-TIPPY-TOE (Episode 53)

'TIS NAY A BRA BRICHT NICHT (Episode 144)

TOKYO PETE (Comedy Hour 12)

TURKEY IN THE STRAW (Episode 94)

TWELFTH STREET RAG (Episode 91)

TWO HEADS ARE NAY BETTER THAN ONE
(Episode 144)

VALENTINE (Episode 73, Comedy Hour 6)

VARSITY DRAG, THE (Episodes 44, 77)

VAYA CON DIOS (Episodes 69, 86)

VESTI LA GIUBBA (Episode 83)

VOODOO (Episode 56)

WABASH CANNON BALL (Episodes 94, 95)

WE ARE THE TROOPS OF THE KING (Episode 38)

WE'LL BUILD A BUNGALOW (Episode 13)

WE'RE HAVING A BABY (Episode 50,
1956 Christmas special)

WE'RE THE PLEASANT PEASANT GIRLS (Episode 38)

WHEN IRISH EYES ARE SMILING (Episode 122)

WHEN THE RED, RED ROBIN COMES BOB, BOB
BOBBIN' ALONG (Episode 69)

WHEN THE SAINTS COME MARCHING IN (Episode 16)

WHEN YOU'RE SMILING (Episode 107)

WHILE STROLLING THROUGH THE PARK ONE DAY
(Episode 25)

WHO? (Episode 46)

Y'ALL COME (Episode 95)

YANKEE DOODLE DANDY (Comedy Hour 6)

*written in 1951 for Lucie Desirée Arnaz, by her father and Eddie Maxwell

TRIVIA ANSWERS

Bonus answers are starred.

[1] c

[2] Ann, Mary, Helen, Cynthia, Alice, and Theodore

[3] In his hip because he had to take so many bows at the club

[4] Copa Cabana, Steak House

[5] b *because Lucy told him it was part of the American marriage ceremony

[6] Ginny Jones

[7] If you play games with your husband, be sure not to beat him

[8] false, she sets it on fire

[9] d

[10] a *to get married

[11] true

[12] horse

[13] d

[14] Harold, the bum, and Arnold, who is pretending to be Lucy's first husband

[15] 39¢

[16] the brakes locked

[17] false, he gets home after 3AM

[18] b

[19] Lucy, 3; Ricky, 5; Ethel, 7; Mr. Merriweather, 1

[20] $10 *that a woman would come to visit and bring Lucy money

[21] Nick Bascapoulis

[22] c

[23] Kenny *played by Kenny Morgan, the husband of Lucille Ball's cousin

[24] feet

[25] Florida *4:30

[26] false, they brought them milk

[27] a

[28] a dress, a pair of shoes, and a hat

[29] d

[30] the drain in the kitchen sink *August 6, 1948

[31] in Ricky's coat pocket

[32] b

[33] false, it says Mr. Ricardo *a star

[34] c

[35] kisses her hand

[36] five

[37] How to Sing *by F. Alsetto

[38] 85¢

[39] a

[40] toilet plunger

[41] d

[42] true

[43] c

[44] 31, 25 of which are in the apartment *6 are missing

[45] false, the lock is rusted shut

[46] a zorchectomy

[47] a dance team and a show girl

[48] a

[49] d

[50] a sandwich

[51] false, it was called *Pearl One, Drop Two*, or *Much Ado About Knitting*

[52] a

[53] forever

[54] Sweet Sue

[55] Lido

[56] b *Slowly I Turn

[57] to dance a solo

[58] "that little monster from next door"

[59] d

[60] "H"

[61] c

[62] Lucy, living room; Ricky, bedroom; Ethel, kitchen; Fred, hallway

[63] Sergeant Morton *the 32nd Precinct

[64] roast beef, gravy, mashed potatoes, string beans *on the piano bench

[65] c

[66] weasel

[67] like a little boy who drank chocolate milk

[68] true

[69] b

[70] false *honeydew melon and strawberries, Eggs Benedict, and hot chocolate

[71] awake

[72] a

[73] c

[74] Lucy, $50; Ricky, $30; Ethel, $20; Fred, $10

[75] $23.75

[76] Xavier Cugat *in the woods at the proposal site

[77] d

[78] true

[79] tortillas, flap cakes, hot jacks

[80] Lucy the Lip and Baby Face Ethel

[81] a

[82] scrub women

[83] b

[84] false, his name was Tom Robinson

[85] 75¢

[86] d

[87] Johnson's Meat Company *700 pounds

[88] b

[89] Your Saturday Night Variety

[90] Ethel

[91] true *Kenny Morgan

[92] The Shah of Persia

[93] c

[94] b

[95] get all three questions wrong

[96] Showmanship Award for Best Quiz Master

[97] stuffed pork chops, baked potatoes with cheese and butter, asparagus tips with Hollandaise sauce *5 pounds

[98] 7:30PM

[99] kisses

[100] she catches toast in it

[101] a

[102] false, he wears a toupee

[103] cheesecake

295

[104] c *Mary

[105] Xavier Valdez and His Orchestra

[106] Joseff Jewelry Company

[107] "Sam"

[108] b

[109] "Babalic" (Babalu)

[110] a, b, and d

[111] false, it was 1919

[112] $246 *$0

[113] Lucy, Camille; Ricky, Prince Lancelot; Ethel, Lily; Fred, Squire Quinn

[114] 18

[115] coffee, juice, eggs, fried potatoes *The New York Herald-Tribune

[116] c

[117] four

[118] a

[119] true

[120] Lake Chautauqua *a rainbow sardine

[121] Home Sweet Home

[122] Mrs. Sanders

[123] a *on his head

[124] the red and blue wires

[125] d

[126] Señor Know-it-All

[127] b *Hazel

[128] false, his first offer is $100

[129] slack

[130] orange juice, coffee, toast with butter, bacon, and poached eggs

[131] b *red, white, blue, pink, and burnt orange

[132] Ricky's new boss, Mr. Chambers, who loves the new show

[133] d

[134] Bulldozer

[135] true

[136] a

[137] "treatment"

[138] F

[139] false

[140] Lillian, secretary; Marion, vice president; Ethel, president; Grace, treasurer *Lillian

[141] a cut glass punch bowl and twenty cups

[142] Fred *Fred sent flowers to Lucy from Ricky, but mistakenly signed the card Fred

[143] he translates the English to Spanish

[144] the box full of flowers

[145] Lucy, roast beef; Ricky, sirloin steak; Ethel, lamb chops; Fred, pork chops

[146] Jubilee *Henry

[147] three

[148] his Yankee cap, a bat, a glove, and a baseball signed by Joe DiMaggio

[149] b *work on a sugar plantation

[150] Godmother, Godfather

[151] d

[152] bathing the baby *2 am

[153] a rattle, a bonnet, and plastic pants

[154] The Merry Mertzes

[155] George Watson

[156] false, it's McGillicuddy and Mertz

[157] a, c, and d

[158] a papaya juice milkshake and a dill pickle

[159] football, pair of boxing gloves, Havana U 1974 t-shirt

[160] East 68th Street Athletic and Recreation Society *boar, deer, tiger

[161] a fried egg sandwich

[162] true

[163] Mr. Harvey *$500

[164] c

[165] Ethel and Fred

[166] Dr. Joe Harris *room 354

[167] Mr. Stanley

[168] false, he calls Fred

[169] Fred *Ricky

[170] the mailman, grocery boy, cop on the beat, manicurist, bridge ladies

[171] South Pacific (the musical)

[172] peanut butter on dry bread *roast beef, jelly, salad, milk

[173] b

[174] false, it was Ethel who did it and then smeared it all over the kitchen

[175] scream, hit them on the head with vases and knock them out

[176] true

[177] Blood-Curdling Indian Tales *Lucy wants him to learn American history

[178] an invitation to the opening of Joe's Delicatessen

[179] his watch, he needs to get it fixed

[180] c

[181] sugar *the bathroom

[182] c

[183] false, Lucy does

[184] in the lobby of the Sherry Plaza

[185] Room 925

[186] b

[187] true

[188] butter, steak knife, salt

[189] Little Orphan Annie *a chrysanthemum

[190] d

[191] the new tax laws

[192] a dozen *trout

[193] "LIFE Visits an Orchestra Leader At Home"

[194] false, she practiced six hours a day for three days

[195] a

[196] Queen Elizabeth II

[197] c

[198] Pickpocket Pearl and Sticky Fingers Sal

[199] true

[200] $1.50 *Joe

[201] give it to the Smithsonian Institute

[202] c

[203] "The check is good." "El cheque esta bueno."

[204] $50,000

[205] ham

[206] Lou Ann, plays piano; Jane, bird calls; Carolyn, impersonates Lionel Barrymore; Rosalind, recites the poem "Trees"

[207] The Claw and Cackle Club

[208] c

[209] the steam room at the YMCA

[210] false, while her nails dry

[211] d

[212] he waved bye-bye *13 months

[213] "invented babies"

[214] "eating too much Chinese food"

[215] Ethel gabs, Carolyn cheats, and Marion cackles

[216] Jim and Dorothy *Lucy told them Ricky sprained his ankle

[217] b

[218] "closed on Sundays"

[219] Louise

[220] zero an hour *double for overtime

[221] a bottle of beer and a salami sandwich

[222] a

[223] new locks for all the doors in the apartment building

[224] d

[225] "Merry Christmas to the boss from the boys, 1952"

[226] b

[227] Allen's Used Clothing Emporium

[228] Universidad de la Habana

[229] Parker Prepares Production for Pittsburgh Premiere

[230] c *vanilla

[231] false, he wants them for the alumni scene

[232] Queen of Spades

[233] a

[234] 1,299 weeks

[235] b

[236] 146 tablespoons *$7.21

[237] Aunt who's, Old what, salad which?

[238] d

[239] Spanish omelet *oatmeal

[240] going to see the fights, poker games, and a hunting trip

[241] Ethel got a 30 and Lucy got a 32

[242] false, she models for a living

[243] "well-preserved"

[244] c *a Stone Martin fur stole

[245] Rogers and Hammerstein

[246] raw potatoes and burned roast

[247] a

[248] "Trust"

[249] shrimp cocktail, crepes Suzette, and steak

[250] 10 shares *$1,200

[251] Babalu

[252] b

[253] Jeri's Hat Shop, Mrs. Mulford

[254] d

[255] turns on the radio, files her nails, eats crackers, cracks walnuts, pulls the sheets off his bed while he is in it, nails his slippers to the floor, gives him a dribble glass full of tomato juice, slams door (pick three)

[256] strawberry

[257] c

[258] true

[259] c

[260] Speedy Laundry

[261] $3.85

[262] a new house and clothing

[263] false, he is losing money

[264] a

[265] Cynthia Harcourt

[266] b

[267] Wichita (Kansas)

[268] d

[269] she just got married

[270] Real Gone With the Wind *Sugar Cane Mutiny

[271] c

[272] Lucy, saxophone; Carolyn, drums; Neeva, violin; Marie, trumpet; Jane, trombone

[273] true

[274] Indianapolis

[275] a hamburger with Tabasco sauce and mashed bananas between two tortillas

[276] $1,200 *$3,000

[277] Roberta *Doug

[278] c

[279] 10PM

[280] luckel

[281] false, he sold it for $27

[282] d *his grandfather gave them to him when he was ten

[283] a

[284] Milliken's Chicken Mash Hour *Ernest Ford and his Four Hot Chicken Pickers

[285] true

[286] basketball

[287] c

[288] Denmark

[289] $300

[290] c

[291] pets, children

[292] 10 days

[293] true

[294] Mrs. DeVries

[295] b

[296] he has a recording session the next day

[297] false, they send a telegram saying they are getting married

[298] $473

[299] b

[300] Canadian Allied Petroleum *$1,000

[301] Harvey Cromwell *Cromwell, Thatcher, and Waterbury

[302] garlic sandwich

[303] c

[304] Laugh 'Til It Hurts With Mertz and Kurtz

[305] b *Bronx, NY

[306] Pennsylvania Station

[307] Ben Benjamin

[308] d

[309] false, he plays the trumpet

[310] conga drum

[311] a

[312] $3,000,000

[313] Professor Bonanova

[314] c

[315] false, she scorches it with her iron

[316] b

[317] a box of chocolates *Happy Birthday, Happy Anniversary, Happy Mother's Day, Merry Christmas, and I'm Sorry Dear, Can't We Please Be Friends Again?

[318] *Over the Teacups*

[319] d

[320] Pekinese

[321] Ricky Ricardo Fan Club Number One

[322] Al Hergasheimer

[323] c *$300

[324] one month

[325] d

[326] Holland Tunnel, East Orange, New Jersey

[327] 180 HP

[328] Ethel, Ozark Mountains and Carlsbad Caverns; Ricky, New Orleans and the Rockies; Fred, Cincinnati and Niagara Falls; Everybody, The Grand Canyon

[329] Mickey Richardson

[330] she wrote the story of her family and wants it to be made into a movie

[331] a stale sandwich and a grape *the grape

[332] Chicago

[333] b

[334] c

[335] 15 mph, 30 mph

[336] false, he fined them $50

[337] a

[338] true

[339] Forgot Her

[340] Julius Caesar

[341] c *a suit of armor

[342] she dunks it in a cup of coffee

[343] she made the bed and took his boutonniere from the waste basket

[344] "snores like a buzz saw"

[345] d

[346] 3 chocolate malts, 2 hot fudge sundaes, a pineapple soda, and a banana split

[347] b

[348] her name, Lucy Ricardo

[349] orange grove

[350] c

[351] false, she wears a 12

[352] Mickey Mikado

[353] a

[354] false, she waits in the hotel lobby

[355] d *Mother forgets to put stamps on them

[356] $7.50

[357] true

[358] 24 *20

[359] Fernando, Toro

[360] b

[361] d

[362] ring

[363] The Mocambo

[364] At the Farmer's Market *her orange

[365] ventriloquism

[366] true

[367] Lucy, stirs coffee; Ricky, drums fingers; Ethel, chews loudly; Fred, jingles keys

[368] Dore Schary's

[369] Good Humor

[370] c

[371] "Take Me Out to the Ballgame"

[372] Groucho and Chico

[373] Hazel

[374] true

[375] a

[376] b

[377] Walter Reilly

[378] breaks all the hotel bric-a-brack

[379] d

[380] false

[381] she hides under a bearskin rug *Cap, the dog

[382] c

[383] Trigger's

[384] sleeping

[385] frousy, dishwater *Mr. and Mrs. Irving Massey of New Jersey

[386] a

[387] false, his name is George

[388] waves

[389] b

[390] true

[391] Ralph Berger

[392] c *pool cue tips

[393] dumping rubbish

[394] b

[395] 107B

[396] Estes

[397] Sky View Cab

[398] coat closet

[399] c

[400] Associated Artists, Johnny Clark

[401] Ed Warren

[402] true

[403] Rattlesnake

[404] a

[405] false, he pays them $25

[406] "poopitus"

[407] Dr. Spock

[408] b

[409] d *"going through husband's pants"

[410] 20

[411] Fred

[412] c

[413] "droopy drawers" *Kaiser

[414] Fred Bigelow

[415] Lucy, French; Ricky, English; Ethel, Italian; Fred, German

[416] 50 *he is the same man who took Lucy and Ricky's wedding photos

[417] true

[418] My Sin perfume

[419] a

[420] false, she can sail on the SS *Independence*

[421] Kenneth Hamilton *shuffleboard

[422] b

[423] ". . . vaccinated for that."

[424] c

[425] The London Palladium

[426] false, he gives her ten British pounds

[427] Sir Clive Richardson *Berkshire Manor

[428] d

[429] in a hedge

[430] d

[431] Enchilada

[432] Fuddy, McGillicuddy

[433] 9,000 francs

[434] Pierre Charpentier

[435] a

[436] c

[437] false, she peeled an orange

[438] "blowtorch."

[439] bologna, in a book; lettuce, under a lamp skirt; mustard, in an atomizer; milk, in a vase

[440] "as fat as a pig."

[441] b

[442] Locarno, Lucerne *Ricky made the reservations for the gang and Fred made the reservations for the band

[443] d

[444] a cheese sandwich

[445] $118

[446] new shoes *it wasn't really his birthday

[447] mountain goats

[448] b

[449] Yankee Stadium

[450] typical American tourist, Ethel

[451] a

[452] true

[453] in her knapsack, on the French side of the border

[454] c

[455] false, he hides it under the mattress

[456] Yvette

[457] Chester *Carolyn

[458] ". . . a lot of fun."

[459] true

[460] d

[461] hotdog vendor

[462] false, she wears number 19

[463] b *skin-diving equipment

[464] *The Caine Mutiny Court Marshall*

[465] Herman Schlupp

[466] Lucy, put ice cubes in oven; Ricky, forgot to put on pants; Ethel, couldn't eat breakfast; Fred, got dressed and then took a shower

[467] the ukelele *Earl Robie

[468] false, he comes over to fix the porch railing

[469] a

[470] Schrimer's

[471] true

[472] $60 *$10

[473] b

[474] Martinelli's

[475] Evelyn Holmby *Kentucky

[476] d

[477] buttered grass

[478] $68, $72 *$150

[479] c

[480] false, Lucy wins because she catches Ricky on the end of her pole and Ricky has a fish in his shirt

[481] lemonade

[482] a

[483] Little Ricky

[484] c

[485] $15 *Corona Grande

[486] ". . . alright with me."

[487] Hippity Hoppity, hollow tree

[488] b *because he will give them free orange juice to hand out during the show

[489] true

[490] the sandman tells him

[491] $5.00 *50 cents

[492] bike, drum, set of trains

[493] c

[494] Bleecker Street

[495] beekeeper

[496] turtles, Tommy and Jimmy; birds, Alice and Phil; frog, Hopalong; fish, Mildred and Charles

[497] Billy Palmer and his mom Lillian *Fred

[498] "grouch"

[499] d

[500] clown, magician, puppet

[501] Ethel's sterling silver flatware

[502] a

[503] $500 *$550 for damages

[504] Eleanor and Joe

[505] 56

[506] change lamp shade, cut off sofa legs, paint table black

[507] false, the savings equal $145,500

[508] b

[509] he carries Lucy over the threshold *he carries his dog, Fred, over the threshold

[510] $2, $6.16

[511] $500 *$3,272.65

[512] Chinese modern

[513] true

[514] *House and Garden *Chicken Breeder's Gazette*

[515] c

[516] Mrs. Trumble's sister

[517] 6 *200

[518] d

[519] false, it was five dozen

[520] Roosevelt

[521] Lucy, cuica; Ethel, sinciro; Fred, ganarrya; Little Ricky, bongos

[522] chicken and rice with fried
bananas

[523] a

[524] Imperial

[525] eight

[526] Hired Hands, Poultry Growers,
Babysitter's

[527] Albuquerque, NM *Ethel Potter
and Betty Foster

[528] true

[529] b

[530] hamburger

[531] ". . . felt wet cement."

[532] 9, 13, 8 *Ricky

[533] false, she looked like Grace Kelly

[534] c

[535] pink *yellow

[536] Boston Post

[537] true

[538] $30

[539] d

[540] the head, one boot, and the gun

[541] a

[542] $10 *the ship's cruise director

[543] false, she sees *100 Men and a Girl*

[544] d

[545] true

[546] Foghorn

[547] c

[548] $100 *his wife, June

[549] false, it cost $45

[550] Whirling Jet *$1000

[551] $300, Fred Mertz

[552] true

[553] "Jingle Bells" *Christmas Eve

[554] Ferdinand

[555] Ricky followed by Ethel, Fred,
and finally Lucy

[556] b

[557] true

[558] Alfredo

[559] Lucy *Fred

[560] Hollywood, 2, make a movie

[561] a

[562] $1,000

[563] Lucy, hammock; Ricky, cot;
Ethel, bed; Fred, sleeping bag

[564] false, they drove out in a Jeep

[565] four

[566] meals, dishes, beds, house

[567] true

[568] Lake Wachasockapoo *Vermont

[569] c

[570] Old Maid

[571] Earthquake *4

[572] d

[573] Lucy, native; Ricky, horse; Ethel,
dancehall girl; Fred, bartender;
Milton, cattle rustler; Little
Ricky, sheriff

[574] b

[575] Sam

[576] $100 *Mr. Osako

[577] a

[578] false, Crandall

[579] 10:05pm

AUTHOR'S NOTES

I Love Lucy was originally filmed to have a commercial introduction, a commercial in the middle, and one at the end. When it went to syndication, the commercials were placed at different intervals, and the shows were shortened by several minutes. Scenes deemed less important were cut from *I Love Lucy* episodes so the show would fit the new commercial format.

Because of my job, I was fortunate to have all the original *I Love Lucy* materials at my disposal for the writing of this book. I watched all the original episodes, in their entirety (including most original commercials). If there is something the reader does not recognize, it is probably because the material is no longer shown on television. When it first aired on Nick-at-Nite, *I Love Lucy* was shown in all its original glory. CBS has made complete episodes available in their *I Love Lucy* DVD collection.

I was also fortunate to have the original scripts from which I could check spellings and other facts. I have tried to be as accurate as possible with all the information presented in this book.

You may notice that the episodes are listed in numerical order, but not air-date order. This is because sometimes the episodes were not aired in the order they were shot. I decided to celebrate the episodes in numerical order to make it easier for fans to hunt down their favorites.